The Family, the Market or the State?

International Studies in Population

VOLUME 10

The International Union for the Scientific Study of Population (IUSSP)

The IUSSP is an international association of researchers, teachers, policy makers and others from diverse disciplines set up to advance the field of demography and promote scientific exchange. It also seeks to foster relations between persons engaged in the study of demography and population trends in all countries of the world and to disseminate knowledge about their determinants and consequences. The members of the IUSSP scientific group responsible for this book were chosen for their scientific expertise. This book was reviewed by a group other than the authors. While the IUSSP endeavours to assure the accuracy and objectivity of its scientific work, the conclusions and interpretations in IUSSP publications are those of the authors.

International Studies in Population (ISIP) is the outcome of an agreement concluded by the IUSSP and Springer in 2004. The joint series covers the broad range of work carried out by IUSSP and includes material presented at seminars organized by the IUSSP. The scientific directions of the IUSSP are set by the IUSSP Council elected by the membership and composed of:

For further volumes:
http://www.springer.com/series/6944

Gustavo De Santis
Editor

The Family, the Market or the State?

Intergenerational Support Under Pressure in Ageing Societies

Springer

Editor
Gustavo De Santis
Department of Statistics
University of Florence
Firenze, Italy

ISBN 978-94-007-4338-0 ISBN 978-94-007-4339-7 (eBook)
DOI 10.1007/978-94-007-4339-7
Springer Dordrecht Heidelberg New York London

Library of Congress Control Number: 2012941610

Printed on acid-free paper

Springer is part of Springer Science+Business Media (www.springer.com)

Preface

In 2009, a committee of the International Union for the Scientific Study of Populations was created with the task of studying the 'Impacts of Population Ageing' (http://www.iussp.org/Activities/ipa-index.php). Its members (Gustavo De Santis, Jorge Bravo, Jocelyn Finlay, Alexia Fürnkranz-Prskawetz, Kohei Wada) engaged in various activities, one of which was the organisation of an International Seminar, 'The family, the market or the state? Intergenerational economic support in an ageing society' (Geneva, Switzerland, 23–24 June 2010), jointly with AIDELF, the International Association of French-Speaking Demographers. More precisely, AIDELF convened its 16th international conference (Relations intergénérationnelles: enjeux démographiques, Université de Genève, 21–24 juin 2010; see http://www.aidelf.org/), a few sessions of which were conceived in such a way that they could be considered both as a part of the AIDELF conference and also as an autonomous IUSSP seminar. This very innovative solution required a few technical and linguistic adjustments (for instance, with slides prepared in French but presented in English, or vice versa), but it worked out extremely well and will hopefully pave the way for a new format in the future joint organisation of conferences and seminars of two or more entities. I would therefore like to take this opportunity to thank all the parties involved for their very constructive help: AIDELF, IUSSP, and, especially, the scientific and local organising committee of the conference. Special praise should also go to the presenters: not only did they fully cooperate in this rather unconventional situation, but they also constructively commented and criticised all the papers of the seminar, thus contributing to enhancing their quality. And, finally, a sincere thank you to the two anonymous referees for their invaluable contribution to all the chapters of this book.

What distinguished the (IUSSP) seminar from the rest of the (AIDELF) conference was the focus of the former on the problem of intergenerational support and on its difficulties in a phase of rapid change in the population age structure. Adapting social arrangements is rarely an easy process: the process is multifaceted, takes place both at macro- and micro-levels, and may have winners and losers, for instance, by generation, gender, social class, etc. It can work well in a country and poorly in another, and it may evolve smoothly up to a certain date and collapse afterwards.

All of this was very clearly elucidated in the 13 papers presented at the seminar, 9 of which are collected in this volume. They do not cover all the possible themes or countries, of course, but each of them tackles the issue from a different perspective, which constitutes, in my opinion, the specific value of this collection: it gives a sense of how complex the ageing issue is. Several of these papers present empirical data for a specific country or set of countries, typically rich and old or, as in the case of the Republic of Korea, not yet old but ageing rapidly. From each of these papers, we learn a lot about the specific country or region under study, but, perhaps as importantly, we are also led to consider that the same problems are already present elsewhere or will emerge shortly and will demand solutions.

Ageing is a pervasive phenomenon: it may arrive sooner or later, more or less rapidly, at different stages of development, in different social and political contexts. But, all in all, similarities prevail over differences: the relative weight of the age classes changes; horizontal ties (e.g. siblings) become rarer, while vertical ties (e.g. with parents and grandparents) last longer; health needs increase; public and private arrangements for retirement must be adapted; etc.

And all of these elements are presented and discussed in this book – very frequently with elements of surprise with respect to the conventional wisdom. For instance, we learn that, even with ageing, pension problems can be solved; that the mounting pressure on public finances will likely not grow beyond control; and that even the baby boom generations (now close to retirement and whose pensions are generally considered to be most at risk) are much richer than any preceding generations, so that worries about their future standards of living should not be exaggerated. Taking care of the aged is a time-consuming activity, but families and kin (together with neighbours and volunteers) have done their part up to now – and will likely continue do to so in the future. And living with elderly relatives may have a few advantages: they are healthier than ever in the past, they can take care of the youngest generation, and, when they are economically well off, they can give more than they receive in current transfers and prospective future bequests.

In short, ageing, like any other process in modern society, is a complex phenomenon, with pros and cons, with risks and opportunities. The question is not whether it will happen (which is certain), or when (which is shortly), but what consequences it will have. And these consequences depend basically on us: on the arrangements that societies have and will set up and on how quickly and effectively these arrangements will adapt to the changes that await us.

This collection of essays will hopefully give its readers some (more) clues as to what to expect for the future and how to channel the course of history in the best possible direction.

Gustavo De Santis

Contents

Introduction

Is the world population really ageing? Is the developed world older than the developing one? Apparently, these are two senseless questions: whatever indicator one uses, the tendency is clearly upwards, and the classical division between rich and poor countries is just. . . as it should be. The median age, for instance, currently close to 29 years for the world as a whole, is on the rise and could reach 38 years by 2050 (Fig. 1). Besides, the more developed countries have been in the recent past, are currently, and will continue to be in the foreseeable future, older than their less developed counterparts, even though, from 2040 on, the differences will start to shrink.

Plotting the proportion of elderly people (for instance, those aged 65 and over) conveys the same message: The world population is old and, by all historical standards, is ageing further (possibly, at an accelerated pace), and, in this respect, the rich countries are definitely worse off (Fig. 2).

But these measures, and the many more that could be produced along the same lines, all assume that the correct way of assessing how old a person is is to measure the distance from her birth. Implicitly, we are thus asserting that physical strength and intellectual lucidity sort of wear out with age, little by little, and that this depletion is always the same, so that we can safely compare persons of the same age, in different places and times.

What if this assumption were unwarranted? Being 60 years old may not mean the same today as, say, 50 years ago, or 100 years from now: if we are healthier, stronger, better educated, more productive, etc., then Figs. 1 and 2 (and all the others of the same kind) make little sense, because they are basically comparing the incomparable.

To criticise existing indicators is easy, but to find satisfactory alternatives is not. Attempts to measure the average 'value' of individuals at various ages in different places and times (e.g. their health, education, productivity) are not fully convincing, as yet. But education is increasing rapidly (K.C. et al. 2010) and so is health

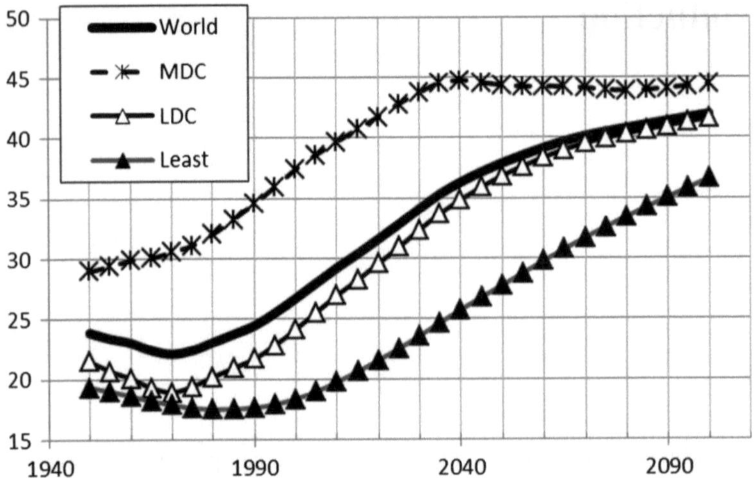

Fig. 1 Median age, 1950–2100. World and macro-regions. Notes: *MDC* more developed countries, *LDC* less developed countries, *Least* least developed countries, by UN definition (Source: UN 2011 (http://www.un.org/esa/population/unpop.htm))

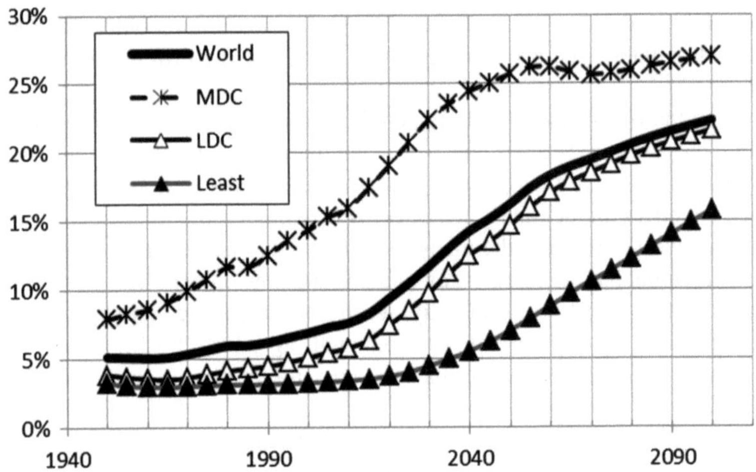

Fig. 2 Share of the population aged 65 and over, 1950–2050. World and macro-regions. Notes: *MDC* more developed countries, *LDC* less developed countries, *Least* least developed countries, by UN definition (Source: UN 2011 (http://www.un.org/esa/population/unpop.htm))

(Cambois et al. 2006),[1] in part precisely because of the increase in education (K.C. and Lentzner 2010). As for productivity, the debate is still open (Prskawetz et al. 2005), but the age when its decline begins to be important has not been clearly identified, as yet, and it is its global increase over time that has thus far dominated

[1]See also the data, for instance, here: http://www.euphix.org/object_document/o5180n27073.html

the scene (Maddison 2005). All in all, it seems reasonable to suspect that the threshold for old age, wherever one decides to set it at first, should not remain constant over time and, therefore, need not be the same in different epochs or countries, characterised by different levels of socio-economic development.

An ingenious and simple alternative criterion for making more sensible comparisons of ageing across countries and periods is to consider how far, on average, a person is from her death (Caselli and Egidi 1992). In order to do so, one needs to calculate the remaining life expectancy at each age. There is the non-trivial question of what life table one should use to that end (Guillot and Kim 2011), but in order to keep things simple, let us use the current cross-sectional life table, and let us further simplify the matter by conventionally assuming that a person is old when she is <15 years away from her death, on average. The first consequence is that the threshold for old age varies with life expectancy at birth: indeed, with UN data, it ranges from a low of 47 years (least developed countries in 1950–1955) to a high of 88 (more developed countries, in 2095–2100).[2]

Of course, this has a strong impact on our measure of ageing, the proportion of people past this threshold age (i.e. relatively close to death), and contributes to the rather astonishing conclusion that, in the past 60 years, the world as a whole has become younger, not older. Ageing will start only in 10 years or so, and even then, it will proceed at a moderate pace. By 2050, the world population will be slightly younger than it was in 1950, and the least developed countries will even be markedly younger than a century earlier and remain so until at least 2100. The more developed countries will be older, yes, but the process is slow, not linear: from 8% in 1960 to 17% in 2060 and then down again to about 16%, which appears to be the end point of the process.

The indications that come from Fig. 3 should not be taken at face value, of course, but what they suggest is that ageing, more than a predicament (MacKellar 2000), is largely a social construction, whose relevance and future effects will depend on us: on the conventional threshold ages that we define; on the fertility level that will eventually prevail, which should not be much below replacement level; on the health conditions that we will secure for the elderly in the future; on the strength of the social and relational networks that we will set up and be able to maintain during our lifetime, etc.

Indeed, it is perhaps this last preoccupation that has been evoked more and more often in the recent work of social scientists: what kind of life will await our elderly in the future – ourselves, in most cases? At least in the developed countries, the economic resources of the old should suffice, all in all, but the lack of kin, of a solid family structure, of children living nearby – this could constitute a major personal and social problem, especially in the final phases of one's life, when physical and cognitive limitations of various kinds are more likely to emerge.

---

[2] I estimated the period life table for each region and period with Brass' logit, forcing the life expectancy of my model life table to coincide with that published by the UN (both sexes combined). Using alternative criteria for old age (e.g. '<10 years away from ones death, on average') changes levels, but not region ranking or time trends (not shown here).

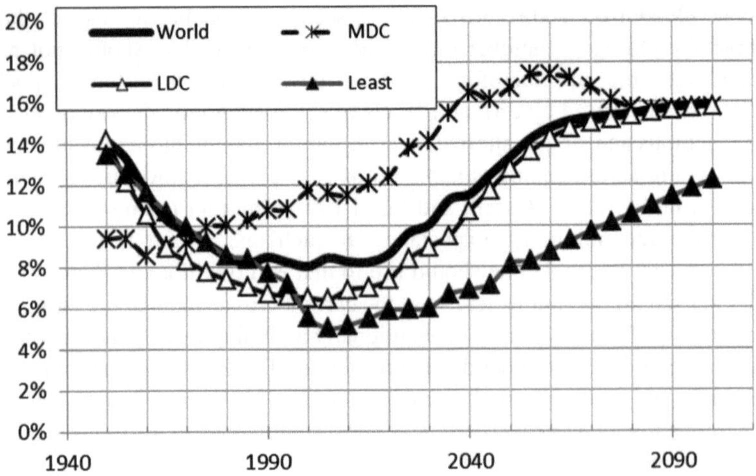

Fig. 3 Share of the population past the (moving) threshold of old age β, such that the remaining life expectancy (e_β) is <15, 1950–2100. World and macro-regions. Notes: *MDC* more developed countries, *LDC* less developed countries, *least* least developed countries, by UN definition (Source: Own elaborations on UN (2011) data (http://www.un.org/esa/population/unpop.htm))

And all the projections for the future, typically based on micro-simulations, suggest that after a relatively golden period of about 20 or 30 years (with fewer widows, because of improved survival conditions in the past century, and fewer childless elderly, because of the baby boom of the 1960s), things will rapidly start to deteriorate: childlessness will become an issue, aggravated by geographical mobility (with children possibly living far away from their parents), and the changes in family formation and dissolution (with more divorces and short-lived cohabitations) will reduce the solid, life-long relationships that the preceding generations could take for granted (see, e.g. Kaneko 2007; Gaymu et al. 2008; Keilman and Christiansen 2010).

All this is extensively discussed in the nine chapters of this volume, which are organised in three parts. The first three chapters tackle macro-economic issues: how can governments make ends meet if, in times of ageing, especially if measured in the conventional way, outlays tend to increase and revenues tend to diminish? In all the three chapters, the answer is basically the same: in a way, yes, things will be slightly worse in the next 30 or 40 years, because fiscal pressure will increase (especially due to pensions and health expenditure) and the normal age at retirement will have to be increased. But with a proper balance of these two levers (higher pension contributions and higher age at retirement), with some immigration (to attenuate the effects of low fertility in the recent past), and with a moderate increase in labour participation and productivity (in line with recent trends), the outlook is not as dire as it is sometimes presented.

Besides, and here comes the second set of chapters, in real terms, standards of living are much higher today than they have ever been in the past (Maddison 2005), and this holds also for the cohorts who are about to retire in the next few years.

Interestingly, they belong to the baby boom generations, but, contrary to the predictions of the so-called Easterlin (1987) hypothesis, their large numbers did not harm them in any significant way.

Accumulation of resources and welfare systems can do much to preserve a decent standard of living for the elderly. When both these mechanisms fail, the family intervenes, much as it did in the past, and, not surprisingly, this holds in particular where family ties are still strong, as, for instance, in Japan or in the Republic of Korea. But what is less frequently considered is that the connection works in both directions: adult children (sons, especially) support their needy elderly parents, but rich elderly parents (or parents in law) may transfer resources downwards to the next generation and, occasionally, make their adult descendants better off. This is largely in line with the results of the most recent literature on intergenerational transfers (Lee and Mason 2011).

Exchanges between generations are not limited to transfers of money, however, and this is the topic of the third and final part of this volume. There is an issue of personal care for the elderly who suffer from long-term impairments, and the connected worries about the availability and willingness of kin and relatives to step in and give a hand. There is a question of contacts, both personal and at a distance (e.g. by telephone): are the elderly abandoned to themselves or are they still relevant social actors, involved in the flow of emotions, exchanges, conversation, and the like, that contribute to fill one's life with meaning? Last, but not least, there is the time that (adult) parents devote not only to the preceding (old) but also to the next generation (the young). Time is a limited resource, and striking the best balance between work for the market, homework, care for others (old and young), and leisure is not as easy as it may appear at first. Rearing children, for instance, is a time-consuming activity, especially for mothers, at least in Italy – and this may be one of the causes of Italy's very low fertility of the past 30 years, which, in turn, has exacerbated ageing. Relieving adult parents (and notably mothers) of part of this workload may be costly. It may require, for instance, an increased supply of kindergartens. And one may once again wonder, also in this respect, what the best balance is, between the family, the market, and the state.

As is almost invariably the case with scientific writings, the papers collected in this book raise more questions than they can answer. But asking the right questions, in the proper way and at the appropriate time, is already a remarkable achievement in itself, especially when some of them have a special policy impact: how to take care of the needs of the old in the rapidly changing context of Korea, how best to provide personal assistance and care to the mounting needs of the elderly in Canada, etc. The papers collected here are scientific, not policy papers – but, for once, papers that policy-oriented readers will find stimulating and pertinent. At least, this was our intention and is our hope.

Gustavo De Santis

References

Cambois, E., Clavel, A., & Robine, J. M. (2006). L'espérance de vie sans incapacité continue d'augmenter. *Solidarité Santé, 2*, 7–22.

Caselli, G., & Egidi, V. (1992). New frontiers in survival: The length and quality of life. In: *Proceedings of the conference on human resources in Europe at the dawn of the 21st century*, Luxembourg, November 27–29, 1991 (pp. 95–120). Luxembourg: EUROSTAT and the Government of Luxembourg.

Easterlin, R. A. (1987). *Birth and fortune. The impact of numbers on personal welfare*. Chicago: University of Chicago Press.

Gaymu, J., Festy, P., Poulain, M., & Beets, G. (eds.). (2008). *Future elderly living conditions in Europe* (Les cahiers de l'INED, no. 162). Paris: INED.

Guillot, M., & Kim, H. S. (2011). On the correspondence between CAL and lagged cohort life expectancy. *Demographic Research, 24*, 611–632.

Kaneko, R. (2007). Population prospects of the lowest fertility with the longest life: The new official population projections for Japan and their life course approaches. In: *Work session on demographic projections*, Bucharest, October 10–12, 2007 (pp. 177–194). Luxembourg: EUROSTAT Methodology and working papers, Office for Official Publications of the European Communities.

K.C, S., & Lentzner, H. (2010). Time effect of education on adult mortality and disability: A global perspective. In *Vienna yearbook of population research* (Vol. 8, pp. 201–235). Vienna: Publisher of the Austrian Academy of Sciences.

K.C, S., Barakat, B., Goujon, A., Skirbekk, V., Sanderson, W. C., & Lutz, W. (2010). Projection of populations by level of educational attainment, age, and sex for 120 countries for 2005–2050. *Demographic Research, 22*(15), 383–472. http://www.demographic-research.org/volumes/vol22/15/

Keilman, N., & Christiansen, S. (2010). Norwegian elderly less likely to live alone in the future. *European Journal of Population, 26*(1), 47–72.

Lee, R. D., & Mason, A. (2011). *Population aging and the generational economy. A global perspective*. Cheltenham/Northampton: Elgar.

MacKellar, F. L. (2000). The predicament of population aging. *Population and Development Review, 26*(2), 365–397.

Maddison, A. (2005). Measuring and interpreting world economic performance 1500–2001. *Review of Income and Wealth, 51*(1), 1–35.

Prskawetz, A., Skirbekk, V., & Lindh, T. (2005). Will population ageing decrease productivity? In *Vienna yearbook of population research* (Vol. 3, pp. 1–15). Vienna: Publisher of the Austrian Academy of Sciences.

Part I
Demographic Changes and Transfer Systems, Between Equity and Sustainability

Introduction to Part I

Demographic Changes and Transfer Systems Between Equity and Sustainability

Modifications in population structures are one of the most powerful driving forces behind most types of social change and especially those that can be measured with a monetary metric, as, for instance, pensions or, more generally, social expenditure. Every quantitative phenomenon Q can be imagined to derive from the product of two forces: the number of people involved, P, and the individual 'propensity' to cause (or, more neutrally, give origin to) that specific phenomenon, q. The basic relation $Q = Pq$ can then be broken down by population subgroups: age x is the first candidate, and the equation then becomes $Q = \Sigma P_x q_x$. Detailing by both age and gender g, one gets $Q = \Sigma_x \Sigma_g P_{xg} q_{xg}$. With other dimensions still (e.g. marital status, health, income, education, regions of residence), the formula becomes longer but maintains the same structure. For the sake of simplicity, let us just refer to the simplest case $Q = \Sigma P_x q_x$.

From this starting point, the conceptually simplest step forward is to imagine that individual propensities q_x will not vary: demographic forecasts, which are generally considered reliable (or at least 'relatively reliable', in comparison with other social sciences: economics, politics, etc.), indicate by how much the structure will change (the population of the future, P'), and the consequences on the phenomenon under study Q' emerge as $Q' = \sum P'_x q_x$. In practice, with regard to the topic of this part, in times of ageing, this process translates into forecasts of higher pension transfers, fewer tax revenues, more intensive use of health-care services, and the like.

But it is also possible to imagine that individual propensities will somehow evolve in the future (and thus become q'_x): because of normative changes (for instance, about the minimum retirement age), because the supply of certain goods and services is limited (think of health assistance, for example), because some other variables are also known to exert an influence (education, secularisation, individualism,...), or for some other reason. And it is this interplay of future population P' and future age-specific behaviours q' (retirement, contributions, taxes, demand for health,...) that shapes macro-outcomes and that constitutes the common element of the three chapters of this part.

Gustavo De Santis (Chap. 1) tackles a theoretical problem: can a pension system be designed in such a way as to be isolated from twists in the age structure of the population (demographic bonuses and maluses, which are here formally defined) and from periods of economic turmoil (e.g. growth or recession, inflation, unemployment, changes in labour productivity, and the like)? Can it stimulate employment at later ages, instead of discouraging it, as most, if not all, pay-as-you-go pension systems do? The answer to almost all of these questions is yes, if the pension system is designed in a certain way and thereby falls in the category that he labels *AIPS* – Almost Ideal Pension Systems. What is perhaps even more surprising is that this still leaves several degrees of freedom for country-specific preferences: an *AIPS* can work with low or high contribution rates, with early or late retirement, with full actuarial equity or with some (even a lot of) redistribution towards the poor, etc. But, of course, several of these objectives are mutually incompatible, and the trade-off between contrasting options must be explicitly chosen – parametrically, in *AIPS*. Besides, and this is why the proposal leads to something which is 'almost', but not 'completely' ideal, the system can be isolated from economic shocks, but not from the distortions in the population age structure caused by fertility swings (and, to a much lesser extent, migration flows): these distortions will affect the equilibrium contribution rate, the fluctuations of which will impact on the standard of living of the adult population and, from there, on the standard of living of the entire population.

Fernando Gil-Alonso (Chap. 2) is confronted with the same problem, the viability of the pension system, but he studies it by looking at the likely future path of certain (31) developed countries, under various possible scenarios (e.g. with and without immigration, with and without fertility recovery). Using 2008 as a benchmark, Gil-Alonso wonders what can be done, up to 2050, in order to keep the pension burden under control or, better still, unchanged at its starting (2008) value. Not surprisingly, his analysis shows that the coming wave of population ageing is such that no single measure proves sufficient in itself. However, a combination of immigration, higher age at retirement, greater participation in the labour market (especially on the part of women and mature workers), and lower pension benefits will likely produce an acceptable result. The developed countries are not (yet) going bankrupt because of ageing, but in order to survive, they will be forced to accept changes, even relevant ones, in various domains.

Luc Godbout et al. (Chap. 3), finally, analyse a specific case, the state balance of Quebec over the next 50 years, but consider the interplay of several outlays (especially pensions and health expenditures) and revenues (taxes and pension contributions). The question is whether the current set of rules is viable in the long run and can remain unchanged in the future. Not surprisingly, the answer is negative: the ageing of the population will create imbalances, even large ones in certain scenarios. However, under what currently seem to be the most reasonable assumptions, the worsening of the financial situation should prove manageable, all in all, and require only relatively modest and gradual adjustments. Among the several alternatives considered, one is particularly noteworthy: do health expenses depend (primarily) on age or do they depend on how far each individual is from death? An increasing body of literature, consistent with the improvements in health conditions that have generally accompanied the lengthening of the human life span, suggests that most health expenses are incurred in the final stages of one's life. This assumption leads to substantial saving in future public health expenses. True, as the authors note, in part this is a tempo effect: expenses are postponed, but sooner or later, they will have to be sustained. Seen from another perspective, however, this does represent a saving. The assumption, here, is basically that the health outlay for each of us is more or less given and is spent in part at birth and at very young ages and in part, the more relevant part, in the last 2 years of life. But if we live longer, and costs are fixed, the costs per year lived diminish.

Chapter 1
The Demographic Phases and the Almost Ideal Pension System (*AIPS*)

Gustavo De Santis

1.1 Introduction

The reputation of *PAYG* (pay-as-you-go) pension systems is bad, everywhere. In part, this depends on objective reasons: everywhere, *PAYG* systems have proved unviable in the long run, at least in their original formulation, and this has forced continuous downward adjustments (OECD 2011). In part, it also depends on changes in the prevailing ideas (Kohli and Arza 2011), probably linked to greater individualism (the same that has brought about the second demographic transition (Billari et al. 2004)), by which whatever is 'free market', or 'private enterprise', is, almost by definition, preferable to public intervention – and this despite clear theoretical indications to the contrary due to the specific nature of pension systems, notably very long-term commitment, inter-temporal preferences (which affect the choice of the discount rate; De Santis 2006), moral hazard, adverse selection, and free riding (Hansson 2010: 43–44).

In all cases, *PAYG* pension systems are now almost universally considered an inferior form of providing for economic security in old age. They can be reluctantly accepted only in specific, but unfortunately frequent, cases: when the need arises to set up a safety net for the poor old (this is the main role of the first pillar, where the three-pillar system is in force) and, as is the case in Italy and in most other European countries, where a large *PAYG* pension system, inherited from the past, is already operating and cannot be easily dismantled. But private, funded solutions are definitely better.

My purpose here is to counter this view and to show that there is a class of *PAYG* pension systems (which I label 'almost ideal pension systems' or *AIPS*) that is theoretically sound and immune from (almost) all the criticisms that are customarily addressed to this type of arrangement. Their most distinctive common trait is

G. De Santis (✉)
Department of Statistics, University of Florence, Viale Morgagni, 59, 50134 Florence, Italy
e-mail: desantis@ds.unifi.it

G. De Santis (ed.), *The Family, the Market or the State?: Intergenerational Support Under Pressure in Ageing Societies*, International Studies in Population 10,
DOI 10.1007/978-94-007-4339-7_1, © Springer Science+Business Media Dordrecht 2012

that they consistently rely on the notion that 'everything is relative' – and especially so their key dependent variables, which are pegged to the proper exogenous ones through fixed parameters, to be decided by national governments. By construction, all the relevant variables adapt automatically to changing circumstances (exogenous variables in the system) – even to the unforeseen ones, e.g. rising unemployment or longer life spans and bursts of inflation or greater female or immigrant participation in the labour market. Flexibility in the variables, but invariability in the basic, relative choices (=parameters), generates a number of, in my opinion, desirable consequences: for instance, financial invulnerability, under all possible circumstances; independence from political contingencies; maintenance of the preferred balance between actuarial equity and 'social justice' (i.e. redistribution towards the poor); stimulus to extend one's working life at least up to, if not beyond, the threshold age that society itself considers standard for retirement; and so forth.

The logic of *AIPS* is simple, and so is each single piece of the puzzle that I will try to compose in the next few pages. But the pieces are numerous: putting them all together in the right order and understanding the deep connections between them is rather complex. Besides, the proposed system partly differs, in its conception and priorities, from the usual approach to the pension issue as presented, e.g. in Takayama (2003, 2005), Immergut et al. (2007), OECD (2011), and, as far as I know, everywhere else. I am not claiming that all the ingredients of 'my recipe' are new: actually, most of them I borrowed, sometimes with adjustments, from others already proposed in the literature. It is the way in which I combine them that produces what I believe is an original dish – possibly with a strange taste, at least at first. To go into all of the details of this approach would require more space than I can take here. I will therefore just try to highlight its essential characteristics and its general philosophy.

1.2 An Unconventional Presentation

Let me proceed in an unconventional way: I will adopt the point of view of a policymaker who, even though he/she does not fully understand the logic of my system, is forced to accept it but who is free to choose its parameters (second column of Table 1.A.1, in the Appendix). Fortunately, as we will see shortly, this can be done by trial and error, examining the consequences in simulations, until a satisfactory balance between the pros and cons of each choice is reached. Admittedly, the notion of 'satisfactory' is subjective, but the mechanism that I will present below should make it clear that, while certain choices *must* be made at certain points (including non-intervention), actual choices may differ. They will affect the outcome, obviously (e.g. younger or older standard retirement age, higher or lower pension benefits), and they will also reflect the currently prevailing policy and ideological orientations (e.g. greater or smaller role for public pension provisions, greater emphasis on actuarial equity or redistribution towards the poor), but they all share what I believe should be the essential characteristics of these schemes: financial viability extends forever into the future and in all possible scenarios; the underlying logic is simple; the economic and demographic risks of the future are 'fairly' distributed among all the participants, including future generations; and all the relevant policy decisions must be explicitly taken from the start, in the form of parameters. The numerical example that I introduce refers to Italy: either at the most recent possible date (2008–2011, depending on the variable at hand) or, when using the UN (2011) demographic projections, with reference to the period 2010–2100. This may not adequately reflect the demo-economic situation of other developed countries, but it should nonetheless give an idea of the order of magnitude of the relevant variables and of their possible evolution over time.

This way of proceeding presents, in my opinion, two main advantages: first, it is original (besides, more conventional presentations can be found elsewhere: see, e.g. De Santis 1995, 1997, 2003, 2006), and, second, it forces the reader to put things in what I deem to be the only correct order, because asking the right questions at the right time is essential in this field. The underlying logic of the whole construction is thus unveiled little by little. My hope is that it will emerge clearly at the end of these pages.

1.3 Choices and Constraints

Policy choice #1: What share of life should a 'typical' citizen pass in his/her young, adult, and old years?

The basic idea, here, is that one should be provided for by his/her parents when he/she is young, provide for himself/herself in adulthood (and also provide for old age, through transfers and savings), and be entitled to a pension in old age. Although it is tempting to extend one's dependent (young and old) years as much as possible, this has a cost: the more the unproductive period extends, the more transfer needs increase.

Let us assume that our imaginary policymaker fixes these 'target' shares at $\tilde{Y} = 25\%$, $\tilde{A} = 50\%$, and $\tilde{O} = 25\%$, where Y, A, and O stand for young, adult, and old, respectively, and the tilde denotes target values, which do not necessarily coincide with the actual ones.[1] In short, with these choices, we aim at spending half of our life as adults (i.e. at least in principle, as employed and economically

[1] Actual values oscillate around their corresponding target ones, which constitute their long-term average (see De Santis 2006, 2012). Oscillations are slow, however, and there may be several years of imbalance in one sense (i.e. with $A > \tilde{A}$, for instance) before another (long) period of imbalance in the opposite sense ensues ($A < \tilde{A}$). All the symbols and their meaning are listed in the Appendix. All target values are given as examples: actual choices may differ from those adopted here, leaving the properties of the proposed system unaffected.

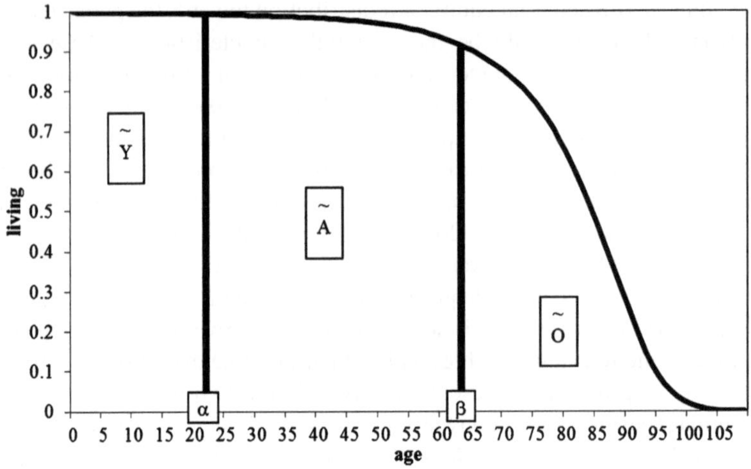

Fig. 1.1 The stationary population for Italy in 2008 (both sexes combined) (Source: Own elaborations on data taken from ISTAT (Italian National Statistical Institute – http://demo.istat.it/) and from the Human Mortality Database (http://www.mortality.org/). Note: $e_0 = 81.36$. α and β are such that $\tilde{Y} = \tilde{O} = 25\%$ (α = 20.43 and β = 62.18))

independent persons) and splitting the remainder evenly between youth and old age. The question now is as follows: what does this choice imply in terms of the threshold ages that separate the young from the adults (α) and the adults from the old (β)? This depends on an exogenous variable: survival.

- Exogenous variable #1: Survival conditions

Let us summarise the survival conditions of our community with the age structure of the stationary population associated with the current life table (Fig. 1.1).

In theoretical circumstances, i.e. with population homogeneity and time invariability, a life table is precisely the instrument that tells us how many years of our life we spend in each phase, on average, regardless of the number of phases that we define. The series of L_x (person years) gives the number of years spent at each age, and letting $T_0 = \Sigma L_x$ stand for the sum of all the fractions of years lived by the population (=total person years), the ratio L_x/T_0 gives the proportion of person years spent at that age. If we select, for instance, $\alpha = 18$ and $\beta = 63$, we get our target values $\tilde{Y} = \frac{L_0+L_1+...+L_{17}}{T_0} = \frac{T_{0-17}}{T_0}$ (youth), $\tilde{A} = \frac{T_{18-62}}{T_0}$ (adulthood), and $\tilde{O} = \frac{T_{63-\omega}}{T_0}$ (old age). With the Italian life table of 2008, for instance, this leads to $\tilde{Y} = 22.03\%$, $\tilde{A} = 53.90\%$, and $\tilde{O} = 24.08\%$ (Fig. 1.1).

In our case, the problem is reversed: we have three target values (cf. Choice #1) $\tilde{Y} = 25\%, \tilde{A} = 50\%$, and $\tilde{O} = 25\%$, and we look for the threshold ages α and β that, in that specific life table, produce exactly the desired result: these happen to be $\alpha = 20.43$ and $\beta = 62.18$.

Consequence No. 1: Threshold ages (in Italy in 2007) must be $\alpha = 20.4$ (separating youth from adulthood) and $\beta = 62.2$ ('normal retirement age', if we want to call it so, although retirement is never compulsory in this system, as we will see shortly).

Note that we are implicitly assuming population homogeneity. There are a few difficulties to overcome when there is instead heterogeneity: for instance, differences between males and females (cf. Choice #2) or variability over time. The latter means that each cohort has its own life table, and, since a population is always made up of different cohorts, it becomes by definition impossible to find a life table that fits perfectly all the groups (cohorts). Besides, all the cohort histories of mortality at any given point in time are, by definition, truncated: we do not know what the future holds, and the history of forecasts tells us that even the best scholars have normally missed the mark, sometimes by far.

This set of problems (heterogeneity and lack of information) influences the choice of how many mortality subgroups one should consider. In my opinion, the best choice is to have only one, i.e. to ignore heterogeneity. This is questionable, of course, and we will come back to it (see Choice #2). But let us now concentrate on a technical question: if we do decide to ignore heterogeneity, we must select an 'average' life table that will provide the best possible synthesis between those who will eventually die at younger ages (presumably, the cohorts who are currently old) and those who are likely to live longer (the young).[2] My proposition, here, is to select the current, cross-sectional life table (or the average of the past, say, 3–5 most recent cross-sectional life tables, in order to minimise random variations).

Why this choice? There are several reasons. In the first place, cross-sectional life tables are calculated accurately and in a timely fashion by technical (non-political) entities: National Statistical Institutes. Second, under the assumption that things will continue to evolve in the future more or less as they did in the past (see Fig. 1.2), the latest cross-sectional life table lies roughly midway between the two extremes defined above: the old with a relatively less, and the young with a relatively more, favourable life table. Note also that with the exception of very special periods (e.g. war, natural catastrophes), life tables tend to evolve smoothly over time: in Italy (and in most other rich countries), this increase has been of about 3 months per year, in the past 50 years, with limited variation. Finally, whatever bias one may introduce with this choice, it will be promptly corrected: next year,

[2] For an indication of how much life expectancy has increased over time, see Shkolnikov et al. (2011). Their paper also highlights (a) by how much the younger generations have outlived older ones (population heterogeneity in each given year) and (b) how unpredictably life expectancy has evolved (normally increased) everywhere in the world in the past 140 years at least (impossibility to forecast the future in any reliable way).

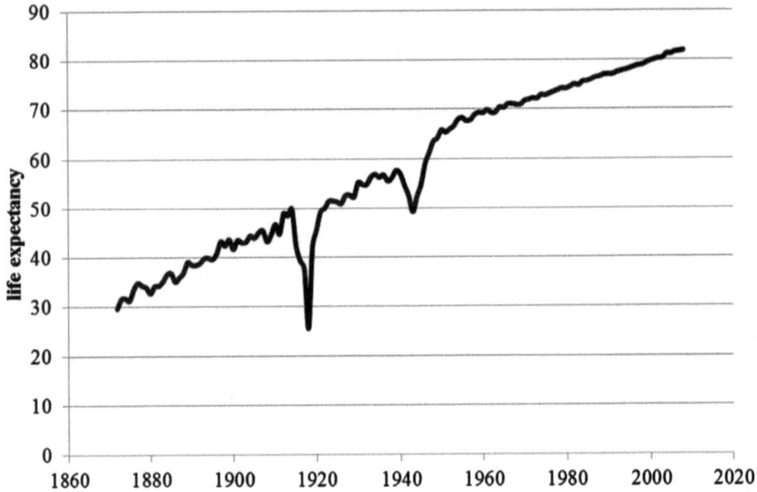

Fig. 1.2 Cross-sectional life expectancy at birth in Italy (both sexes, 1871–2008) (Source: Own elaborations on data of the Human Mortality Database (http://www.mortality.org/))

when a new cross-sectional life table is produced by the National Statistical Institute, a new standard of reference will be adopted.[3]

Consequence No. 2: The threshold ages α and β must evolve over time, in order to guarantee the invariability of the target values $\tilde{Y}, \tilde{A}$, and $\tilde{O}$ (fractions of life spent in young, adult, and old years) as survival conditions change.

Readers will note that the logic proposed here differs from tradition, in at least two respects. First, in the traditional approach, the starting point is threshold ages themselves (e.g. $\alpha = 20$ and $\beta = 65$), and the next step is the decision on whether and by how much either (or both or neither) of them should adjust when conditions change. Second, the age structure that is normally used for these decisions on threshold ages (levels and variations) is the age structure of the actual population P and not that of the reference (stationary) population $\tilde{P}$. Both topics are addressed below.

- Exogenous variable #2: Population age structure

The *actual*, current age structure of the Italian population is shown in Fig. 1.3, along with the age structure of the *stationary* population defined above

[3] More refined indicators of the current level of mortality could be used to obtain basically the same result (see, e.g. Guillot and Kim 2011). I am not contending that period mortality tables are technically better than their alternatives, merely that some measure of the current level of mortality must be used to define the reference age structure and that this measure should be simple (the general public needs to understand what it is) and readily available.

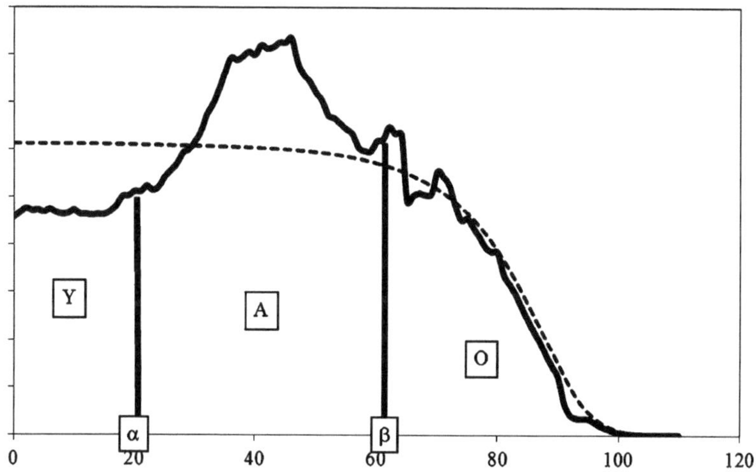

Fig. 1.3 Age structure of the actual (2011) and of the stationary (2008) population (Italy, both sexes) (Source: Own elaborations on ISTAT (http://demo.istat.it/) and HMD data (http://www.mortality.org/))

(or *reference* age structure). Given the threshold ages chosen before ($\alpha = 20.4$ and $\beta = 62.2$), this produces the actual proportions of young, adult, and old, which are, respectively, in the case of Italy (2011),[4] $Y = 19.32\%$, $A = 56.79\%$, and $O = 23.89\%$. Not surprisingly, these percentages do not coincide with the targets indicated before ($\tilde{Y} = 25\%, \tilde{A} = 50\%, \tilde{O} = 25\%$): as mentioned in footnote 1, these targets are indeed the expected values of their corresponding variables (which should be written as Y_t, $A_{t,}$, and O_t, respectively, but, for the sake of simplicity, I will drop the subscript *t*, here). Unfortunately, year-to-year variability may be relevant: simulations show that there is an oscillatory movement, with long intervals (of several years, occasionally up to almost 100) and, in some circumstances, high waves, let us say up to ±8 percentage points off the target, or even more, in some extreme cases (see, e.g. De Santis 2012). This means that with a target of $\tilde{O} = 25\%$, for instance, actual values *A* will normally range between 17% and 33% – although, obviously, they will generally be (much) closer to 25% than to these extremes (see also Table 1.1).

Both the actual and the reference age structure are exogenous variables, and both have an impact on the pension system, but, in this system, they have a different role, and the reference age structure is the only one that (together with the policy decision on target shares $\tilde{Y}$, $\tilde{A}$, and $\tilde{O}$) determines our threshold ages α and β. This makes things easier because the reference age structure is much smoother than

[4] The life table is that of 2008; the population is the de jure one, as of 1.1.2011. The dates do not coincide because life tables are always produced with some delay (although rough estimations for more recent years are frequently available, also in Italy). I am deliberately using the most recent, even if not coinciding, information for both variables, in order to reproduce the actual situation of a policymaker who needs to use whatever data are at hand.

the actual one and depends only on current (observed) survival conditions, not on fertility or migration and not on past or possible future mortality levels. The other advantage is that we can be more consistent: we link the length of the period that each individual is expected to spend at work (and, conversely, is expected to spend in retirement) exclusively to his/her average length of life – except that we ignore individual lengths of life and rely instead on average values.[5] Other choices are possible, of course, but they appear to be weaker, both theoretically and empirically (in simulations, not shown here).

There are basically four alternatives:

(a) Threshold ages do not vary at all. This is what the pension law used to assert in several countries, until recently, and frequently still asserts in a few more (OECD 2011). But things have changed so deeply, and, in particular, life expectancy has increased so much that this promise could not be kept in the past and, most likely, will not be kept in the future.
(b) Threshold ages are adjusted on an ad hoc basis when the need arises.[6] This has thus far been the standard practice of almost all governments, whose guiding principle is, more or less, 'If possible, do not touch anything that concerns pensions. When absolutely unavoidable, make the smallest possible change and hope that it will last for at least some years (when a new government will be in charge)'. This type of adjustment, which is typically guided by emergency, is normally based, among other things, on the actual and projected age structure of that specific country and has a very weak theoretical basis.[7]
(c) The retirement age evolves with e_0, in such a way that the difference $(e_0 - \beta)$ remains constant. This idea has the advantage of simplicity, and, in the long run, it proves beneficial to the pension system, because it is easy to show that when life expectancy increases, the reference value $\tilde{A}$ (share of adults in the population) increases too, but it implies that every year of life earned is a year spent at work. Unfortunately, this runs counter to the historical trend: all populations in

[5] This approach guarantees the ideal of proportionality Lee and Goldstein (2003) discuss. None of the objections they themselves raise against this idea apply here: e.g. biological constraints are far from the range of oscillation of α and β, and changing capital/labour ratio is irrelevant because this is not a funded system. The third objection ('institutional constraints, e.g. on schooling and retirement', p. 183) is precisely what this proposal tries to overcome.

[6] More precisely, not threshold ages in general (α and β) but only age at retirement (β). To the best of my knowledge, no one has ever discussed the other threshold age (α), probably because nobody has ever considered the importance of the adult average wage (W and N, gross and net, respectively: see further in the text).

[7] There are exceptions, of course, and the Swedish pension reform is probably one of these (Kruse 2010). My contention is that my proposal works in the same spirit, although with a different rationale, but is even better: for instance, in my case, pension payments adjust automatically to the variations in the salary mass (not the average wage); there is no need to 'guess' the likely future rate of growth of the economy; the risk of all type of variations is fairly split between workers and pensioners; and the balance between actuarial equity and redistribution towards the poor is explicit (in a parameter Q that ranges between 0 and 1; see further in the text).

the world, whenever possible, have drastically reduced their working schedule, both daily/weekly and with respect to age at retirement (Livi Bacci and Tapinos 1999; Lee and Goldstein 2003; Lee and Mason 2011).

(d) The retirement age β evolves with e_0, in such a way that e_β (life expectancy at retirement) remains constant (Caselli and Egidi 1992). This option is the one that comes closer to mine, both theoretically and empirically. But while Caselli and Egidi's idea implicitly considers only those who reach age β, my approach includes the survival profile of the entire population and is, therefore, more complete.[8]

Whatever the choice on threshold ages, we are interested in the resulting old-age ratio $o = O/A$, for which, too, there is a target value $\tilde{o} = \frac{\tilde{O}}{\tilde{A}}$. In this example, $\tilde{o} = \frac{\tilde{O}}{\tilde{A}} = \frac{0.25}{0.50} = 0.5$. Because of the rather large oscillations in the actual age structure, the actual values of this ratio can vary considerably, by up to ±20 percentage points (i.e. $30\% < o < 70\%$ – for a simulation, see again De Santis 2012).[9] This variability, of course, impacts negatively on the pension system, as we will see shortly.

- Exogenous variable #3: Employment rate ($e = E/A$)

Another important exogenous variable is the number of those who are employed E, which, relative to the number of the adults A,[10] gives the employment rate $e = E/A$. The employment rate is normally defined as the ratio $E/P_{15\text{–}64}$, but here, for reasons of consistency, we will instead consider the ratio E/A, where A are those whom the society itself considers adults, i.e. aged between α and β years. In Italy, the 'standard' employment rate in 2008 ($E/P_{15\text{–}64}$) was 58.7%, but, with our age brackets (20.6–62.1), it climbs up to $e = E/A = 68.5\%$. Note that the employed can be of any age, not necessarily between α and β, although, of course, a substantial age consistency is expected between E and A. If the bulk of the employed population does not fall in the α–β age bracket, the definition of the threshold ages is inadequate (but an *AIPS* works well even in this case). In Italy, for instance, about 86% of the employed in 2008 were aged between 20.6 and 62.1.

- Exogenous variable #4: Gross wage *per employed (G) and per adult* (W)

The gross wage (per employed per year) in Italy was about 47,700 euros, in 2010.[11] However, for reasons that will become clear later, we are more interested in the gross wage per adult, which is that amount multiplied by the employment rate e. Our variable of interest is, therefore, lower: $W = (Ge =)$ 32,700 euros, per year.

---

[8] For instance, it is theoretically possible to imagine variations in survival that have a sizeable impact on the pension balance but leave e_β unaffected and vice versa.

[9] Or more, but then only in extreme cases. Once again, o will normally be closer to its average (here, 50%) than to these extremes.

[10] So as not to add another symbol, A stands here for the total number of adults, although in this paper, it is more often used to indicate their proportion in the population (adults/population).

[11] See http://www.istat.it/it/files/2011/03/testointegrale200902033.pdf for the estimation in year 2000, which I reevaluated to year 2010, with index number provided by ISTAT itself.

Note that W is more informative than G about the state of the labour market because it incorporates two dimensions: how much the employed earn (G) and also how likely it is for an adult to be employed (e). Variations in labour productivity (as measured by G) and in the employment rate (e) immediately reverberate into W.

Now that we have introduced these exogenous variables, let us get back to policy choices.

Policy choice #2: Shall we differentiate between population subgroups? For instance, women live longer than men, and the difference in life expectancy at birth is currently about 5 years. Should we take this difference (or others) into account? If yes, how?

This is a very thorny issue. Let us start from the more general question: should we consider differences in life expectancy within the population? If yes, which ones? This is a policy choice, and everyone is entitled to his/her opinion, but we should bear in mind that the whole system works much better if we ignore these differences. This is not merely a matter of simplicity, although keeping things simple, in terms of both calculus and rationale, has merits of its own. It is also a matter of creating a feeling of participation and social cohesion: a system that differentiates between population subgroups is less likely to be perceived as a 'common good' (Kohli and Arza 2011), less likely to resist the eroding action of lobbies of all kinds, and less likely to survive unchanged in times of strain. And defining rules that may last for very long (ideally, forever) is an essential ingredient of every well-designed intergenerational transfer system.

Another important point is that individual differences exist in virtually every respect, e.g. blood pressure, smoking habits, occupation, education, family of origin, and place of residence (particularly important in an epoch of mounting localism). Each of them affects mortality, but it is virtually impossible to measure precisely the impact of each of these factors on the average length of life of each of us, and the population subgroups that may be formed are innumerable: once one starts to differentiate, it becomes difficult to stop.

In all cases, a sharp distinction should be drawn between ascribed and acquired (and potentially changing) characteristics. Personal characteristics that may vary over time, and especially those that depend on personal choices (e.g. type of occupation, smoking habits, education, place of residence), should not be used to differentiate between participants in the transfer system. Given the current structure of mortality, living less means basically spending proportionally less time in old age. Therefore, those who live less have fewer transfer needs: they could perhaps retire earlier, or pay lower contributions, or receive higher pensions benefits (for a shorter time), or combine these options. But how should we treat those persons that have changed these characteristics during their life or that could change them subsequently after retirement? And what should we do with those about whom we have too little information to infer something about their presumable length of life? Should we implicitly encourage those who more or less voluntarily shorten their life (e.g. drug addicts) by allowing them to retire earlier?

Arrangements of this kind are generally introduced with an (implicit or explicit) idea of compensation, which, in my opinion, confounds matters considerably: as we will see shortly, in the system that I am proposing, redistribution towards the poor can be introduced, but in an explicit way (see further in the text) and not implicitly, as early retirement does (frequently together with several other ad hoc arrangements). Besides, transferring problems to the pension system, instead of facing them, is a very convenient way of passing the costs on to the next generation. Take dangerous or wearing occupations, for instance: one option is to offer earlier retirement as a compensation (that future cohorts, not us, will pay). But other solutions are possible: to improve working conditions, impose rotation and offer an alternative occupation after t years of that job, or encourage private solutions of the type discussed in Sect. 1.7 (i.e. consent to early, but privately paid, retirement) or something of this kind. In all cases, it is worth stressing that this is a problem of the labour market (by definition, we are talking about people who are younger than our conventional threshold age β), which should therefore be solved within the labour market – not transferred to the pension system.

Gender, however, is a different matter. It is not subject to choice, is easy to detect, does not change over time (except in very rare cases), and is known to be systematically associated with marked differences in life expectancy. There are therefore good arguments, at least in principle, to create two separate systems, one for men and one for women – with women retiring later than men, or receiving lower pension benefits, or paying higher contributions, or combining these possibilities. Those who oppose this idea generally do so for reasons that, once again, fall outside the logic discussed here, namely that the pension system should compensate women for the hurdles they encounter in their professional life, especially because of gender discrimination, motherhood, and, more generally, greater family responsibility (see, e.g. Chap. 8 by Bordone, Chap. 7 by Keefe et al., and Chap. 9 by Tanturri, in this volume). Let me skip a detailed discussion about this here: I will just say that in this case too, as before, the general principle applies that corrections should be made where they are needed, i.e. where biases and discriminations appear (in the labour market) and not elsewhere (in the pension system). Besides, a pension system is *one* instrument used to achieve *one* objective (protecting old age from economic hardship): a policymaker with two objectives in mind (that, plus gender re-equilibration) needs at least two separate instruments to pursue both of them.

In my opinion, the only valid, but very strong, reason why a unique pension system is preferable to several, group-specific ones, even when there are easily detectable population subgroups with different mortality, is a policy one: treating everyone in the same way creates a feeling of membership and communality that is essential for a pension system to work smoothly. This, in all cases, is the assumption on which we will work here: only one pension system operates, and its rules are the same for everybody.[12]

Policy choice #3: On average, how high should pension benefits be in comparison to adult wages (net of contributions)? Answer: π *(relative pension)*

[12] We will also disregard operational costs, which are, however, typically low for public, universal, and mandatory pension systems: about 4% of the total revenues (although recently on the rise, at least in Italy: see, e.g. ISTAT 2010a).

Let us define the contribution rate c as the share of the gross wage that goes to contributions for the pension system. Let us call them contributions, not taxes, because, as we will see shortly, there are individual benefits associated with these payments. The net wage *per adult* (not per employed) is therefore $N = W(1 - c)$. Note that 'net' here means net of contributions, but not net of taxes, which will later have to be paid. This net wage N (not W) is the quantity that should be compared to pension benefits P: pensioners do not pay contributions, but both pension benefits P and net wages N will later have to pay taxes (not considered here).

Now, let us define the ratio $\pi = P/N$ (average pension benefit on average net wage *per adult*). One may think of this as a sort of 'replacement rate', which is not unjustified, except that my definition differs from that recently provided by the OECD,[13] which in turn differs from other, previously more common, meanings attributed to this term.[14] Therefore, I will simply name it relative pension.

Policy choice #3 is precisely about this relative pension π: how high do we want it to be? Strictly speaking, we should distinguish between two types of 'average pension benefit', exactly as we did with 'average wages'. Imagine that there are three pensioners and four old people (one of which is not entitled to a pension), and imagine that the three pension benefits amount to 300 euros overall (they might be, for instance, 80, 100, and 120, respectively). The average pension benefit per pensioner is (300/3=) 100, but the average pension benefit per old is (300/4=) 75. Which one do we refer to? Actually, we need to refer to the average pension benefit of the old, but, in order to keep things simple, we will also imagine that all the old are entitled to at least a small pension benefit, so that the number of pensioners coincides with the number of the old, and there is but one average pension to consider.

Let us assume that our policymaker arbitrarily decides that $\pi = 60\%$, i.e. that the average pension be 60% of the average net labour earnings per adult.[15]

[13] According to OECD (http://stats.oecd.org/glossary/detail.asp?ID=5293), 'Replacement rate = The ratio of an individual's (or a given population's) (average) pension in a given time period and the (average) income in a given time period'. Please note that 'net' and 'gross' are not mentioned in this definition (last updated in 2005).

[14] The OECD itself, for instance, in another section defines the 'Old-age pension replacement rate' as 'a measure of how effectively a pension system provides income during retirement to replace earnings which were the main source of income prior to retirement' (http://stats.oecd.org/glossary/detail.asp?ID=7328). This interpretation is actually more frequent, especially in those countries (like Italy and France, for instance) where, up to a few years ago, pension benefits were somehow linked to the wages earned in the last t years of employment. For reasons discussed elsewhere (e.g. De Santis 2006), I find this notion highly misleading.

[15] The idea of a proportionality between pension benefits P and net wages $G(1 - c)$ (net labour earnings of the *employed*) is not new: it can be found, for instance, in Lee (1980), Musgrave (1981), Hagemann and Nicoletti (1990), Gonnot et al. (1995), and others. Its shortcoming is that it is by definition insensitive to variation in the employment rate $e = E/A$ (E = employed; A = adults). Some countries have implicit or explicit mechanisms that take unemployment into account, but nobody, to the best of my knowledge, ever referred to N, the average earnings of the *adults*, as a measure of the capacity of the country to sustain a given pension load. Note, that since $N = W(1 - c) = Ge(1 - c)$, N depends on three variables: gross wages G, employment rate e, and contribution rate c. Note, also, the importance of defining sensibly the threshold ages α and β: the adults A (aged between α and $\beta - 1$) are those that are expected to work. Therefore, by definition, a low employment rate e (=E/A) signals high unemployment, or low labour market participation rates, and both phenomena lower N (net wage per adult), which in turn, through the fixed policy parameter π (relative pension), lowers the average pension benefit P.

Consequence No. 3: The current contribution rate must be $c = 20.1\%$

This derives from the balancing equation $EGc = OP$, where EGc are the revenues of the pension system (the employed E, times their average gross earnings G, times the contribution rate c) and OP are its outlays (the old O, times their average pension P). Since $P = \pi N$, $N = W(1 - c)$ and $W = Ge = GE/A$, with a few passages (see the Appendix), one obtains

$$c = \frac{O\pi}{A + O\pi} = \frac{o\pi}{1 + o\pi} \qquad (1.1)$$

where $o = O/A$. For Italy, given the policy choices and the exogenous variables listed above, the contribution rate is therefore $c = 20.1\%$.

Consequence No. 4: The target contribution rate is $\tilde{c} = 23.1\%$

In order to see this, it suffices to modify slightly Eq. 1.1 and use target instead of actual demographic shares, so as to obtain

$$\tilde{c} = \frac{\tilde{O}\pi}{\tilde{A} + \tilde{O}\pi} = \frac{\tilde{o}\pi}{1 + \tilde{o}\pi} \qquad (1.2)$$

which leads to $\tilde{c} = 23.1\%$. This has no practical implications, but it serves as a warning and a reminder: the current age structure is favourable (see Fig. 1.3), with more adults $\left(A > \tilde{A}\right)$ and fewer old $\left(O > \tilde{O}\right)$ than in the reference case. This is why the current equilibrium contribution rate ($c = 20.1\%$) is lower than its reference value ($\tilde{c} = 23.1\%$).[16]

[16] To the best of my knowledge, the idea of a reference contribution rate has no antecedent in the literature. In former versions of this proposal (e.g. De Santis 2006), I went so far as to suggest that the actual contribution rate c be kept constant at its *reference* value $\tilde{c}$(Eq. 1.2), instead of using the varying c of Eq. 1.1. The use of a varying c guarantees that revenues equal payments each year: worries of sustainability (as those voiced, among many others, by Gil Alonso and by Godbout et al., in this volume) simply disappear in this case. Instead, using a fixed $\tilde{c}$ (which incidentally is the standard practice in all the pensions systems that I know), periods of excess revenues alternate with periods of excess payments for the national pension system. The advantage is that the contribution rate remains constant over time: if favourable and unfavourable periods do indeed compensate in the long run, the inter-temporal balance between revenues and payments will tend to zero. This is almost true (not shown here; it depends also on the rate of interest paid and earned on assets and liabilities), but since these periods may be very long, up to 100 years, and the corresponding imbalances very large, the deficits or the surpluses that are thus generated may grow out of control. All in all, it seems safer to impose a variable contribution rate c, so that revenues match expenses in any given year. Intermediate solutions, with the actual contribution rate that falls somewhere between $\tilde{c}$(Eq. 1.2) and c (Eq. 1.1), may be considered, too.

Let me open a short parenthesis here. The comparison between the actual, c, and the reference contribution rate, $\tilde{c}$, can be interpreted as a measure of the demographic 'window of opportunity' – a notion often loosely referred to in the literature but, to the best of my knowledge, never precisely measured.[17] Since $\tilde{c}$ is the long-term average for c (not shown here), c will oscillate around $\tilde{c}$, and a convenient way of evaluating the demographic phase of a population is to see by how much c falls short of $\tilde{c}$ (demographic bonus) or exceeds it (demographic malus). Notice that each demographic phase (bonus or malus) depends in part on objective variables (the current vs. the reference age structure) and in part on policy choices, i.e. on the parameter π in Eq. 1.1 (but also on the parameter χ in the more comprehensive version of Eq. 1.6) and on the choice of the threshold ages α and β.

Let us now get back to the mainstream of our pension discourse.

Consequence No. 5: On average, the yearly net wage per adult is (currently) $N = 26.1$ (thousand Euros).

Since the net wage (net of pension contributions) is $N = W(1 - c)$, with $W = 32.7$ (thousand Euros) and $c = 20.1\%$, one obtains $N = W(1 - c) = 26.1$ (thousand Euros per adult per year).

Consequence No. 6: On average, the yearly average pension benefit must be $P = 15.7$ (thousand Euros).

Since the average pension benefit is a fixed ratio π of N, and since $\pi = 60\%$ (policy choice #3), with $N = 26.1$ (thousand Euros – Consequence No. 5), $P = \pi N = 15.7$ (thousand Euros per old per year).

1.4 Variability in Pension Benefits? Actuarial Equity (Bismarck) vs. Redistribution (Beveridge)

Choice #4: Should all pension benefits be the same? If not, how do we take past contributions into account and still make sure that the average pension benefit is exactly the P value that we defined before (see Consequence No. 6)?

---

[17] Lee and Mason (2011), for instance, consistently define it as 'an increase in the support ratio' (that is in the ratio of the effective number of producers to the effective number of consumers): see, e.g. pp. 13, 173, 479. The same holds for Mason and Lee (2006: 11) who say, 'A demographic dividend or demographic window arises because the working age populations are growing more rapidly than the number of consumers', and for every other reference to the notion of 'demographic bonus' (another possible term) that I have ever read.

Let K_i represent the current value of all the contributions paid by pensioner i in the course of his/her working life, and let K represent the average of these current values, for all current pensioners. There are, of course, a few difficulties in translating past payments into present-day monetary values, but there are also ways to circumvent these obstacles, which I would rather not discuss here (for the details, see e.g. De Santis 2003): let us simply *assume* that a satisfactory solution has been found. The ratio K_i/K gives the 'standing' of pensioner i with respect to the average pensioner of that year. If we introduce the proportion

$$\frac{P_i}{P} = \frac{K_i}{K} \tag{1.3}$$

we can reconcile two apparently opposing goals: individual pension benefits will reflect past contributions (or, better, their transformation into a current value K_i), and their average will be exactly P, the only value that matches pension benefits with current contributions.

Equation 1.3 implies that the decision has been taken to fully link individual pension benefits to past contributions, i.e. to opt for an actuarially equitable solution, under the constraint that the transfer system does not run into debts or accumulate surpluses. This is what we would today label a 'Bismarckian' arrangement[18]: the more you contributed in the past, the higher your pension benefit is today. This may sound appealing to many (including myself, actually), but it also has a few negative implications: those who paid few or no contributions in the past are not necessarily to blame (think, e.g. of housewives or people living in economically depressed areas or with poor health), and, yet, they will be left with little or even nothing to live on in their old years.

At the other extreme, we can easily define the 'Beveridgean' case, when all pension benefits are the same and equal to the general average.

$$P_i = P \tag{1.4}$$

In this case, too, the general equilibrium will be preserved (contributions match transfers) but with a different logic: every old person receives an identical pension benefit, regardless of how much he/she contributed out of his/her labour earnings.

Equations 1.3 and 1.4 are not a dichotomous alternative: rather, they are the corner solutions of a continuum that depends on a policy parameter Q (Q for equity). In order to see this, let us write

$$P_i = \underbrace{P(1-Q)}_{P_{(Beveridge)}} + \underbrace{P\frac{K_i}{K}Q}_{P_{(Bismarck)}} \quad [0 \leq Q \leq 1] \tag{1.5}$$

[18] For a discussion on the use of this terminology (Bismarckian vs. Beveridgean), see Cigno and Werding (2007) and Lefèbvre (2007).

where the parameter Q (another policy choice) reflects the preferred degree of actuarial equity of the community. If $Q = 1$, Eq. 1.5 simplifies to (1.3): the system becomes actuarially equitable (Bismarckian) and does not redistribute anything to the poor. At the other extreme, if $Q = 0$, Eq. 1.5 simplifies to (1.4), and the system becomes totally redistributive (Beveridgean). The main disadvantage of the latter choice is that contributions become a pure tax on labour (with no direct advantage for the taxpayer), which negatively affects the legal labour market and induces individuals and firms to evade payments, even more than they already do, especially in Italy (see, among others, Cigno and Werding 2007).

Let us now imagine that our policymaker opts for $Q = 0.75$. What does this mean? In order to see this more clearly, let us consider two cases: Mr. White (collar), whose past contributions, as expressed by K_w, are 200 (thousand Euros) and Mr. Blue (collar), whose cumulated contributions only amount to $K_b = 100$ (thousand Euros). Let us assume that these are the only two pensioners of our system: how much will each of them get in pension benefits (with our rules and in our simplified world)?

In our case, because of previous choices and constraints, the average pension benefit is $P = 15.7$, a part of which ($1 - Q$, i.e. 25% in this case) is going to be in common between both pensioners. Note, incidentally, that this part may also be interpreted as the minimum pension benefit granted by the system: $P_{(Beveridge)} = 15.7 \cdot 0.25 = 3.92$.

On top of this, there is also another part, specific for each pensioner. In order to calculate it, let us first determine the average value of K (current value of past contributions), which is 150 in this simplified case, with only two pensioners. This gives two ratios: $K_w/K = 1.33$ for Mr. White and $K_b/K = 0.67$ for Mr. Blue. In monetary terms, we get $P_{w(Bismark)} = QP\frac{K_w}{K} = 0.75 \cdot 15.7 \cdot 1.33 = 15.67$ for Mr. White and $P_{b(Bismarck)} = QP\frac{K_b}{K} = 0.75 \cdot 15.7 \cdot 0.67 = 7.83$ for Mr. Blue (half as much as Mr. White, because he contributed half as much during his working life).

Altogether, our pension benefits become, respectively,

(Mr. White) $P_w = P_{(Beveridge)} + P_{w(Bismarck)} = 3.92 + 15.67 = 19.58$

(Mr. Blue) $P_b = P_{(Beveridge)} + P_{b(Bismarck)} = 3.92 + 7.83 = 11.75$

In short, P_w is higher than P_b but less than twice as much, although White's contributions are twice as high as Blue's. This happens because a parameter $Q < 1$ indicates that the pension system operates also a redistribution from the rich (White) to the poor (Blue), and the more so, the lower Q. Whatever value is chosen for Q, the average pension P will be precisely at the previously defined, or target, value P (=15.7, in this case).

1.5 What Will the Future Hold?

Nobody knows what the future has in store for us. But one of the main advantages of the proposed system is that whatever happens, *nothing* needs to be done, in any case, because everything adjusts automatically. An important implication is that the system does not need forecasts: the only relevant variables are those that can be observed. This is long to prove analytically, but it can be seen both intuitively and illustratively in a simulation.

1.5.1 Qualitative Considerations

What could possibly happen with an impact on our pension system? Let us schematically consider two types of variations: economic and demographic.

All the variations in the economic sphere are immediately neutralised by the constant π (=P/N) ratio, i.e. by pegging the average pension benefit P to N, the net wage of the adults – and let me emphasise *adults*, not just *employed*. For instance, if inflation makes wages G (and therefore also W and N) nominally higher, pensions P, too, will immediately increase in the same proportion. The same applies if productivity increases or if the employment rate e (=E/A) improves (e.g. because more women enter the labour market): in both cases, W (=Ge) will be higher and, given c (contribution rate), so will be N and P because π remains constant (policy choice #3).

Let us now consider immigration, a phenomenon that lies somewhere between economics and demography. Immigration will likely bring about several consequences. The first is that there will probably be both more adults A and more employed E, with a priori undetermined consequences on the employment rate e (=E/A). Normally, however, the balance will be favourable, and the employment rate will increase. The effect on G (labour earnings of the employed) is impossible to calculate a priori. Typically, immigrants' wages are lower than natives', which tends to depress G. It is possible, however, that because of the presence of immigrants, the natives' labour productivity increases: for instance, because cheap domestic help keeps more women in full-time, instead of part-time, work. In this case, G will increase. Most likely, however, the impact on G will be minor, while the effect on e will be positive and sizeable, so that, all in all, the most likely economic effect of immigration will be an increase in (Ge=) W. Besides, more adults A reduce the old-age ratio o (=O/A), which in turn reduces the contribution rate c (cf. Eq. 1.1). All this has a positive effect on N (net adult wage) and also on the average pension benefit P, via the constant π.

As P varies, all the individual pensions P_i will shift proportionally, thus preserving the balance between actuarial equity and redistribution that society itself has chosen, through the (constant) parameter Q (cf. Eq. 1.5).

As for other possible demographic variations, let us consider those linked to a variation in survival. Lower mortality normally brings about an increase in O, the share of the old in the population, and in $\tilde{O}$ (the share of the old in the *reference* population). But not here: the latter effect is immediately and totally neutralised by the parallel movement in our threshold ages α and β, both of which, because of policy choice #1, evolve with e_0 (life expectancy) in such a way as to keep $\tilde{Y}, \tilde{A}$, and

$\tilde{O}$ constant at the desired level.[19] Therefore, ageing 'from above' (as it is sometimes improperly, but colourfully, labelled) is simply impossible in this system.

Ageing 'from below' (the ageing that derives from low fertility, with few children who later become few adults) is instead possible. When this starts to happen, c, the actual contribution rate, increases (cf. Eq. 1.1). Everything else equal, this reduces the average net wage N, which, in turn, reduces the average pension P, via the constant parameter π. Everybody is somewhat poorer: this is regretful, of course, but the good news is that the burden of ageing is equally shared among all the participants in the system, old and adults, alike. The relative economic positions remain unaffected, because the average pensioner still gets a fraction π of the average adult's net wage N, and the distribution of pension incomes remains exactly the same because, given P, P_i only depends on K_i/K and Q, which are not affected by ageing.

In short, no future event, either in the economic or the demographic sphere, can possibly disrupt an *AIPS* system or require corrective interventions. This does not imply that we need not worry about the future: even with *AIPS*, some paths (e.g. with ageing, inflation, unemployment) are definitely worse than others. I am simply contending that it is possible to set up a transfer system that is immune from economic and demographic variations: if things improve (or get worse), they will do so, on average, for everybody, in the same proportion. Of course, this has a price: the standard retirement age β is not fixed but evolves with e_0; the contribution rate c varies with the age structure (around a predetermined reference value $\tilde{c}$); and pension benefits are a fixed proportion π of the average net earnings of the adults, which means that their monetary value cannot be known in advance: it varies from year to year but in such a way that relative positions do not change.

1.5.2 Simulations

Simulations may be misleading: there are infinite possible scenarios with infinite possible time horizons, and the doubt always remains that an alternative specification would have yielded a qualitatively different result and possibly brought to light some weaknesses of the system.

So as to reduce the suspicion that the scenarios prepared 'ad hoc' better serve my cause, I will refer to Italy and use the demographic forecasts of the United Nations (2011), which extend to 2100. The basic demographic changes foreseen in the medium variant of the UN are synthetically shown in Table 1.1.

I will also imagine a gradual increase in the labour market participation of the Italian population, of women in particular, such that in year 2050, Italy as a whole will have the same age-specific labour-force participation rates that northern Italy

[19] Of course, if the threshold ages α and β are not adjusted upwards, this benefit is lost, and there will be an increase in both c (the actual contribution rate) and $\tilde{c}$ (the reference contribution rate).

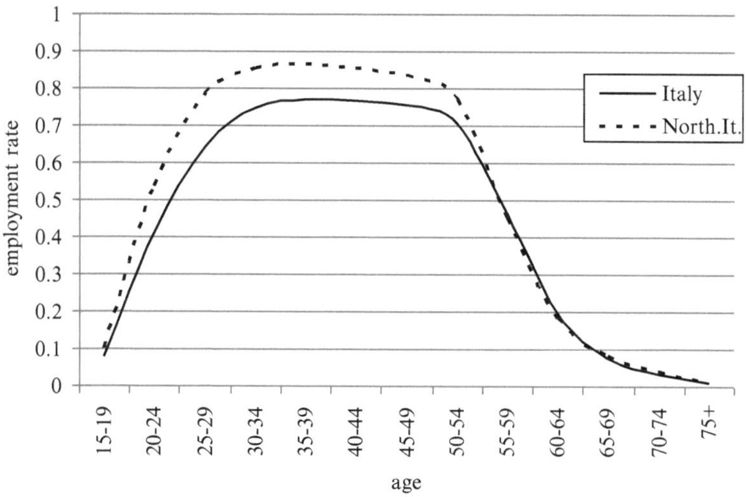

Fig. 1.4 Age-specific employment rates of Italy and northern Italy in 2008 (both sexes) (Source: ISTAT 2010b)

has today (Fig. 1.4). From 2050 to 2100, I will assume that almost nothing changes any more, except for some minor increase in activity rates at ages 55–64, driven by the gradual increase in the threshold age β that I am assuming will follow the assumed increase in e_0.

In this simulation, the gross average nominal wage of the employed (G) increases geometrically by 2% per year, which we can imagine to be equally divided between a real and a nominal part (i.e. productivity gains and inflation, respectively).

The main assumptions and the main results of this simple simulation are summarised in Table 1.1. Apparently, everything changes, but closer inspection reveals that the basics are only little affected, if at all. In short:

(a) The pension system is always in equilibrium: contributions match pension payments in every year (only shown for selected years in Table 1.1 – lines 15–17).
(b) Age at retirement β must increase from 62.2 to 65.0 to 68.3 (line 4) because life expectancy e_0, too, increases from 81.4 to 85.7 to 90.6 (line 2). On average, and similarly to other simulations, the increase in β is of about 8 months for every extra year of life expectancy. Similarly, the other threshold, α, increases from 20.4 to 21.5 to 22.7 (line 3), i.e. by about 3 months for every extra year gained in e_0.
(c) These changes in α and β, along with those in e_0, leave the reference proportions young, adult, and old unaffected ($\tilde{Y} = \tilde{O} = 25\%; \tilde{A} = 50\%$; not shown in Table 1.1).
(d) On the contrary, and despite the variations in α and β, the actual Italian population ages, at least until 2050: Y rises slightly (from 19.4% to 20.4% – line 5), A declines substantially (from 56.8% to 46.9% – line 6), and O increases very markedly (from 23.8% to 32.7% – line 7). After 2050, the shares of all the three age groups (young, adults, and old) converge towards their reference value (Fig. 1.5).

Table 1.1 Basic demo-economic characteristics of Italy and its pension system, according to this proposal, in 2010, 2050, and 2100 (UN medium variant)

		2010	2050	2100	Notes	Source
(1)	Population (million)	60.551	59.158	55.619		UN(2011)
(2)	Life expectancy	81.4	85.7	90.6		UN(2011)
(3)	Age α (beginning of adulthood)	20.4	21.5	22.7	(a)	Author's calculations
(4)	Age β (beginning of old age)	62.2	65.0	68.3	(a)	Author's calculations
(5)	Young (%)	19.4	20.4	24.2		UN(2011)
(6)	Adult (%)	56.8	46.9	49.9		UN(2011)
(7)	Old (%)	23.8	32.7	25.9		UN(2011)
(8)	Employment rate (E/A) (%)	68.5	72.8	70.0		ISTAT and Author's assumptions
(9)	Gross labour earning per employed	47.7	105.3	283.5	(b)	ISTAT and Author's assumptions
(10)	Gross labour earning per adult	32.7	76.6	198.4	(b)	See text
(11)	Contribution rate (%)	20.1	29.5	23.8		See text
(12)	Net labour earning per adult	26.1	54.0	151.3	(b)	See text
(13)	Pension benefit	15.7	32.4	90.8	(b)	See text
(14)	Ratio pension/labour earning per adult	0.6	0.6	0.6	(c)	
(15)	Total contributions	226.1	627.3	1307.9	(d)	See text
(16)	Total pensions	226.1	627.3	1307.9	(d)	See text
(17)	Balance	0	0	0	(d)	

Source: UN (2011) and author's assumptions and elaborations (see text)
Notes: (*a*) consistent with $\tilde{Y} = \tilde{O} = 25\%$ and the life table of 2008 (here in the column headed 2010), (*b*) average per year, in thousand Euros, (*c*) author's assumption (policy choice), and (*d*) in billion Euros

(e) The equilibrium contribution rate climbs up rapidly, from 20.1% to 29.5% in 2050 (line 11), but after that it declines to 23.8. Readers may remember that we had set a target contribution rate $\tilde{c} = 23.1\%$, but we had also warned that the actual contribution rate would oscillate around this target value and that oscillations could be strong. This is the price to pay for the deformation in the age structure: Italy now has more adults than it 'should' ($A = 56.8\%$ against $\tilde{A} = 50\%$), but it will go through a period when they will be scarce ($A = 46.9\%$), while, at the same time, the old will be over-represented (in 2050, $O = 32.7\%$ against $\tilde{O} = 25\%$).

(f) By assumption, the average gross wage per employed (G) increases by 2% per year; up to 2050, the average gross wage per adult (W) increases slightly more, at 2.1% per year, because the employment rate evolves favourably (from $e = 68\%$ to $e = 73\%$, 40 years from now[20]). Instead, because of the increase in the contribution rate, c, net wages N and pensions P increase more slowly, by

[20] But then down to 70% in year 2100, for structural reasons: age-specific employment rates are practically constant (actually very slightly increasing) after 2050.

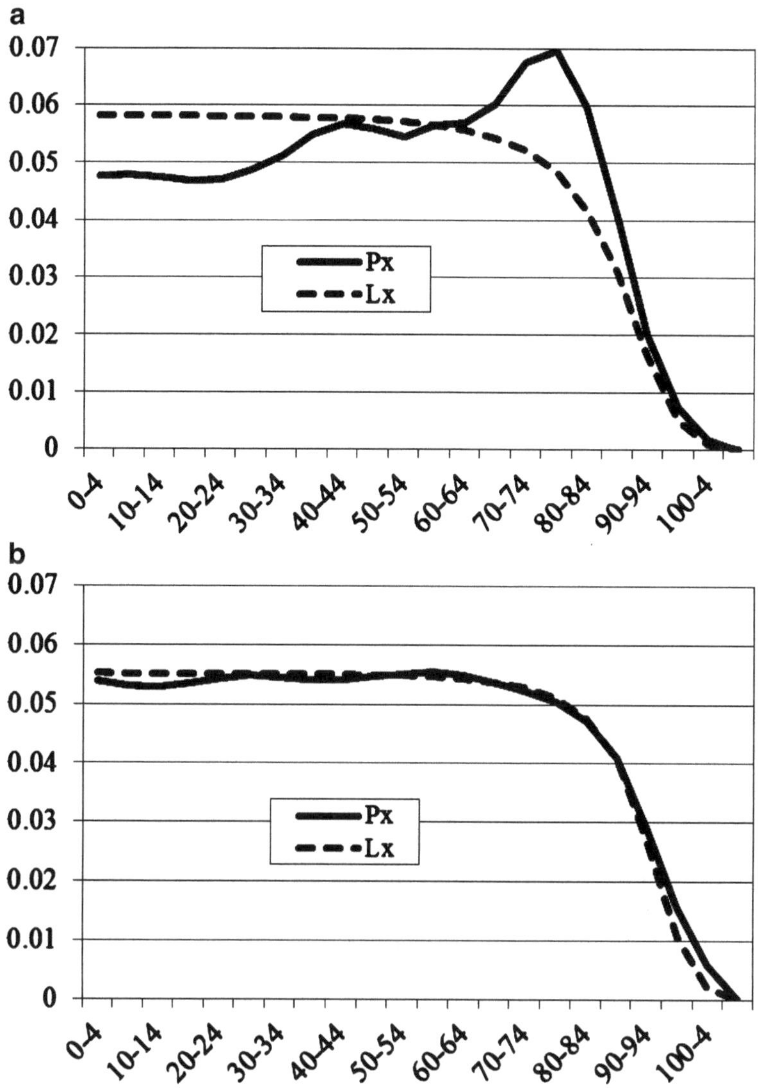

Fig. 1.5 Actual (P_x) and stationary (L_x) population in Italy, both sexes (UN forecast). (**a**) 2050. (**b**) 2100 (Source: Own elaborations on UN 2011 data)

about 1.8% per year. This depends exclusively on the passage from the current 'bonus' to the coming 'malus' of the demographic window – i.e. the fact that the old-age ratio ($o = O/A$), currently at 42%, will increase up to 70% in year 2050, before declining again in the second half of the century.

(g) Relative positions do not vary. The average pensioner still receives $\pi = 60\%$ of the average adult, at the beginning, at the end, and (not shown here) in every other year of the period under consideration. Finally, note also that relative positions remain unaffected among the old: given past individual contributions (K_i) and the equity parameter Q, the relative standing of each pensioner will not change (not shown here).

1.6 Discussion

There are a number of details that I have skipped here: let me just briefly mention (not prove) a few of them. The first is that *AIPS* are immune from all the criticisms customarily addressed to *PAYG* pension systems: basically, advantages for the present at the expense of future generations or for some subgroups at the expense of others. The system is the same for everybody and is constructed in such a way as to be able to go on forever, unchanged, under all possible circumstances. Of course, a legislative modification is always possible (if future collective preferences about pension systems change), but it is never necessary, nor, indeed, advisable.

The system is as actuarially equitable (and as redistributive) as it explicitly declares to be, via the policy parameter Q. If $Q = 1$ (no redistribution towards the poor), the average amount that each person receives back in pension benefits tends to coincide, in real terms, with the average amount paid in contributions and this for every population subgroup (e.g. rich and poor). I said 'tends to coincide', not 'coincides exactly': why? There are several reasons. One is that it is not totally clear what discount rate one should use. The various monetary aggregates we considered before, for instance, all move at slightly different speeds.

Another reason relates to the fact that we do not all die at the same age: those who live longer receive more in pension benefits than those who die early. What is worrying is that these differences in survival are typically correlated with social class and earnings, and if the rich die later, they disproportionately benefit from the existence of a collective pension system, of *every* pension system, not just this one.

In part, this is unavoidable, and any attempt at correction would probably be harmful (cf. the discussion about policy choice #2, on the use of different standards for different population subgroups). In part, however, this effect can be limited by also including in the system a (small) transfer towards the young. Imagine that we define the ratio $\chi = C/N$ (child benefit/net average adult wage), exactly as we defined the ratio $\pi = P/N$ (average pension benefit/net average adult wage).

With a few passages, one finds that the contribution rate c now becomes

$$c = \frac{O\pi + Y\chi}{A + O\pi + Y\chi} \tag{1.6}$$

while everything else adjusts immediately. What basically happens is that part of the money taken from the adults now goes to the young and only part to the old. Let us imagine, for the sake of simplicity, that we only have two groups: the poor and the rich. If the poor live less but have more children, their disadvantage in the transfers towards the old is (partly) compensated by their advantage in the transfers towards the young (De Santis 1997). This still does not guarantee perfect actuarial equity, but, at least, it points in the right direction.

Including moderate transfers towards the young would also have other ancillary advantages, including a stimulus to fertility. Pension systems tend to depress fertility because they weaken one of the reasons for having children: economic support in old age. There are therefore good reasons for accompanying the introduction of pension systems with a few counterbalancing measures.[21] Finally, another advantage of the inclusion of (moderate) child benefits in the pension system is that it attenuates the fluctuations in the contribution rate c (De Santis 1997). The reason why this happens is that, typically, when populations age, O (the share of the old) increases while Y (the share of the young) decreases, and this tends to stabilise c in Eq. 1.6. But, of course, all these advantages come at a cost: including (some) child benefits in the transfer system means that either the contribution rate will be higher or pension benefits lower, or both. Striking the 'right' balance between these pros and cons is, of course, a matter of societal preferences (policy choice #3a, if you want).

One of the great advantages of the proposed system is that, once it is in operation, it never needs ad hoc adjustments, or policy interventions, or periodic revisions by 'experts', or forecasts, or anything of this kind: all the necessary variations in the key variables produce automatically and become a simple by-product of the current activity of national statistical institutes (e.g. the life table) and of the pension system itself (number of officially employed persons, individual and average wage, etc.).

Among these automatic variations, I would particularly like to stress those in the two threshold ages (α and β) that must follow the improvements in the average length of life, if the collective decision is to maintain life shares (not threshold ages) constant. If we live longer, we should also be prepared to work longer, so as to maintain the preferred $\tilde{A}$ ratio, i.e. the proportion of life that we spend at work, on average.[22] The advantage of automatic adjustments is that they are very gradual and almost painless because the year-to-year changes they bring about are minor and because they do not involve difficult discussions in the Parliament, with the contrasts, strikes, delays, and, eventually but inevitably, the discontinuities that they cause, such as ad hoc decisions to raise the retirement age, slow phasing in, and disparities between cohorts. Let me also stress that these adjustments (in α and β)

[21] In the same vein, see also Cigno and Werding (2007), although they complicate matters in that they also try to include a qualitative element (having 'good', i.e. productive, children is preferable to just having 'any' children), which I will not discuss here.

[22] As mentioned, increasing α and β as e_0 improves is not compulsory in *AIPS*. An alternative could be to raise β alone or not to change anything at all (but, in this case, both contribution rates c and $\tilde{c}$ will increase) or combine these options. I will not discuss this topic here: let me just say that adapting α and β is, by far, the simplest and, theoretically speaking, the most consistent way of contrasting the negative effects of ageing on the pension system.

permit the system to preserve all the substantive choices of the community: e.g. in the relative economic well-being of the old (and the young) with respect to the adults (π, χ) and in the share of life that we spend in the three basic phases $(\tilde{Y}, \tilde{A}, \text{ and } \tilde{O})$.

The adoption of an *AIPS* does not imply that everything is in the hand of 'experts' and that policy has no role, quite the opposite. There are several essential policy choices to make: on early or late retirement; on the relative amount of pension benefits (*and* pension contributions, of course); on the balance between actuarial equity and redistribution towards the poor (through the parameter Q); on the inclusion or exclusion of child benefits; etc. *AIPS* only guarantee a few basic things: future generations will not be left with pension imbalances to pay; the system will be viable, in principle, forever; a certain equilibrium will be guaranteed, in demographic and economic terms; etc. Each of these options reflects collective preferences and is indeed a policy choice, in the best possible sense: it models very important societal dimensions but does so explicitly and treats everybody in the same manner, now and in the years to come – at least, as long as the basic parameters of the system remain the same.

In a recent contribution, Aysan and Beaujot (2009) argue that each society follows its own preferred path in adjusting its pension system to the new scenarios opened by ageing and migration. I fully agree, but I add that these preferences and adjustments are not totally free: one must also take into account budget constraints and exogenous variables, economic and demographic in nature. This is what almost ideal pension systems explicitly do.

Allow me a final remark: Aysan and Beaujot (2009), as many others before them, remind us that the problems of the pension systems derive in part from the fact that there are implicit incentives for workers to retire early, frequently measured as an implicit tax levied on those who remain employed up until their late years. With *AIPS*, the problem is simply eliminated: no pension benefit is ever paid before the age β that the society itself has chosen. This may sound crude (see, however, the next section), but the message it conveys is simple and straightforward: one is free to stop working whenever he or she pleases, but an early retirement has a cost, that the society should not be obliged to pay, via pension benefits, because up to age β, everyone is considered an adult. Better still, retirement is never compulsory or encouraged in this system: after age β, a person receives his or her due in pension benefits regardless of his/her employment status. Those who work in their old age will receive both a wage and a pension benefit – and this is the strongest incentive I can imagine to keep people active until at least age β but also (most likely) beyond that.[23]

[23] Notice that older workers, too, pay pension contributions out of their labour earnings, even after age β: this raises the value of their lifetime contribution K_i, which will secure them a higher pension benefit in the following years.

1.7 What Role for Private Pension Provisions?

AIPS are not alternatives to private provisions in the pension system. Their aim is to create an efficient and transparent *PAYG* pension system, which, however, is also somewhat rigid. And this is precisely where private provisions could find their space. In my opinion, their role should be of two basic types: a 'traditional' and an 'innovative' one.

The traditional role of private provisions is that of complementing public pension provisions with additional ones, based on funding. Whether this should be compulsory or not, publicly subsidised or not, formed exclusively by the savings of individual workers, or with the financial support of their employers is something that does not fall within the scope of this chapter – and neither is the question of how much extra saving (and capital) would a funded system generate (Barr 2000), how much would be needed to raise labour productivity so as to counter population shrinking and ageing (the so-called second demographic dividend; Mason and Lee 2006), and why saving (and capital accumulation), if needed by the market, cannot be autonomously generated by demand, i.e. by sufficiently high interest rates. As a general remark, let me just note that *AIPS* could be adopted in a great variety of versions: 'light' or 'heavy' (i.e. with small contributions and small pension benefits or vice versa), Beveridgean or Bismarckian, with early or late retirement, etc. Each of these choices has its negative sides: for instance, low average pension benefits and greater emphasis on actuarial equity tend to increase the proportion of old people in economic difficulty.[24] And the role of private actors in this domain should be defined consistently with each of these choices – or perhaps, why not just left to market forces: once the skeleton (the public system) is strong, let the private initiative do the rest.

But the private sector could also secure the flexibility around the age at retirement that the simple version of *AIPS* I rapidly sketched above does not.[25]

There are two main variants of this intervention, and they partially overlap. The first is this: let us assume that the standard retirement age is, for instance, $\beta = 64$ years, and imagine that some people, for various reasons, do not feel like working up to that age but want to secure the right to retire earlier, e.g. at age 60. What should they do? Very simply, buy a private insurance that will pay them a

[24] Therefore, an accompanying welfare system aimed at protecting the poor (including the poor old) should probably also be considered when thinking about how to reform a pension system. Matters like those discussed in this volume by Légaré and Cossette, by Lee, and by Motonishi would still continue to be a concern, even if *AIPS* were implemented.

[25] Currently, most public systems envisage the possibility of a flexible retirement age, with pension benefits that vary in a (more or less) actuarially fair way with the preferred age at retirement (OECD 2011). Of course, this would be possible with *AIPS*, too. But this flexibility is virtually never actuarially neutral, and, besides, it is costly. My contention is that if the private sector is assumed to be better than the public one and to be capable of managing annuities for an entire life, why can't it be trusted with a simple and time-limited business of securing the possibility of anticipating one's age at retirement of a couple of years?

predefined amount of money (private 'early-pension benefit') from age 60 to age 64, if they are still alive. Annuities are generally very costly because nobody knows for how long the insured individual will survive, and the risk of facing a long survival (and, therefore, very substantial payments) is high. But not in this case, where the insured period is typically short and, most importantly, known from the start with only a very limited margin of uncertainty.

Indeed, and this is the second case, with *AIPS*, the retirement age, β, is not fixed: instead, it varies in such a way as to maintain the reference shares of life spent in the three basic phases of life at their predefined values ($\tilde{Y}, \tilde{A}$, and $\tilde{O}$). The role of private insurance companies, thus, may extend to cover the period between today's and tomorrow's normal retirement age β. For instance, should things evolve as in the simulation of Sect. 5.2, β in Italy would gradually increase from 62.5 to 65 in year 2050 to 68.3 in year 2100. This span of life, the delay between today's and tomorrow's retirement age (whose length is uncertain but in all cases short), could be profitably covered by private, voluntary arrangements and would benefit all those who do not want to run the risk of being forced to work beyond the retirement age that they are (psychologically) accustomed to.

Acknowledgements Financial support from the MIUR (Italian Ministry of Education, University and Research – Research grant 2007S8JLFN_001) is gratefully acknowledged.

Appendix: Symbols and Formulae

A.1 Symbols

α age that separates the young from the adults
β age that separates the adults from the old ('retirement' age)
π (=*P*/*N*) level of the average pension *P*, *relative* to the net average wage per adult *N*
χ (=*B*/*N*) level of the child benefit, *relative* to the net average wage per adult (*N*)
A share of the adults in the population ($\tilde{A}$ = same, in the stationary population)
B child benefit
c $\left(=\frac{O\pi}{A+O\pi}\right)$ contribution rate $\left(=\frac{O\pi+\chi Y}{A+O\pi+\chi Y}\text{including child benefits}\right)$
e (=*E*/*A*) employment rate
E employed (number of)
G gross average wage per employed*
K_i current values of the contributions paid by *i* during his/her working life
K average of K_i, calculated on all pensioners
L_x years lived (stationary population) at age *x*
N net average wage per adult [=*W*(1 − *c*)]*
O share of the old in the population ($\tilde{O}$ = same, in the stationary population)
P average pension
T_x total number of years lived (total stationary population) from age *x* onwards

W gross average wage per adult (=Ge)*
Y share of the young in the population ($\tilde{Y}$ = same, in the stationary population)

[* Gross = before pension contributions; Net = after pension contributions but before income taxes]

A.2 Formulae

$$EGc = OP \tag{A.1}$$

(for the pension institute, EGc = revenues, and OP = expenditures)

$$P = \pi N \tag{A.2}$$

(the average pension P is a fixed proportion π of the net labour earnings per adult N)

$$N = W(1 - c) \tag{A.3}$$

(net labour earnings per adult N derive from gross wage W, less contributions, at rate c)

$$W = Ge \tag{A.4}$$

(gross labour earnings per adult W depend on gross labour earnings per employed G, but take into account the employment rate $e = E/A$)

From (A.4) and (A.3), we obtain

$$N = G\frac{E}{A}(1 - c) \tag{A.5}$$

From (A.2) and (A.5), we obtain

$$P = \pi G\frac{E}{A}(1 - c) \tag{A.6}$$

From (A.1) and (A.6), we obtain

$$EGc = O\pi G\frac{E}{A}(1 - c) \tag{A.7}$$

Simplifying and reordering (A.7), one obtains Eq. 1.1 in the text, i.e.

$$c = \frac{O\pi}{A + O\pi} \tag{1.1}$$

A.3 A Schematisation of AIPS

Table 1.A.1 A schematisation of policy choices, constraints, and consequences in an almost ideal pension system (*AIPS*)

Level	Policy choices	Constraints (exogenous variables)	Consequences (dependent variables)
(1)	Only one, unique transfer system		
(2)	$\tilde{Y}$, $\tilde{A}$, $\tilde{O}$ (target shares of life spent in youth, adulthood, and old age)	Survival conditions (e_0 and L_x, reference age structure)	α, β (threshold ages)
(3)		Actual age structure	*Y*, *A*, *O* (proportions of young, adults, and old in the population)
(4)		*E*, *G* (employment, average gross wage)	*W* (average gross wage of the adults)
(5)	π, χ (relative pension, relative child benefit)		$\tilde{c}$ (target contribution rate) *c*, *N*, *P*, *B* (contribution rate, average net wages of the adults, average pension, child benefit)
(6)	*Q* (actuarial equity vs. redistribution)	K_i, *K* (individual and average cumulated contributions – only for pensioners)	P_i (individual pension benefit)

References

Aysan, M. F., & Beaujot, R. (2009). Welfare regimes for ageing populations: No single path for reform. *Population and Development Review, 35*(4), 701–720.

Barr, N. (2000). *Reforming pensions: Myths, truths and policy choices* (IMF Working Papers, WP/00/139). Washington, DC: Fiscal Affairs Department, International Monetary Fund.

Billari, F., Liefbroer, A. C., van de Kaa, D. J., Coleman, D., Bernhardt, E., & Micheli, G. (2004). Is the second demographic transition a useful concept for demography? In *Vienna yearbook of population research* (Vol. 2, pp. 1–34). Vienna: Publisher of the Austrian Academy of Sciences.

Caselli, G., & Egidi, V. (1992). New frontiers in survival: The length and quality of life. In *Proceedings of the conference on human resources in Europe at the dawn of the 21st century*, Luxembourg, November 27–29, 1991 (pp. 95–120). Luxembourg: EUROSTAT and the Government of Luxembourg.

Cigno, A., & Werding, M. (2007). *Children and pensions*. Cambridge/London: MIT Press.

De Santis, G. (1995). L'equità nei trasferimenti tra generazioni. In O. Castellino (Ed.), *Le pensioni difficili* (pp. 39–79). Bologna: Il Mulino.

De Santis, G. (1997). Welfare and ageing: How to achieve equity between and within the generations, *Proceedings of the 23rd IUSSP Conference*, Beijing (China). (Vol. 1, pp. 185–201).

De Santis, G. (2003). The demography of an equitable and stable intergenerational transfer system. *Population, 58*(6), 587–622.

De Santis, G. (2006). *Previdenza: A ciascuno il suo?* Bologna: Il Mulino.

De Santis, G. (2012). Can immigration solve the ageing problem in Italy? Not really.... *Genus, 67*, 37–64.

Gonnot, J. P., Keilman, N., & Prinz, C. (1995). *Social security, household and family dynamics in ageing societies*. Dordrecht/Boston/London: Kluwer Academic Publishers.
Guillot, M., & Kim, H. S. (2011). On the correspondence between CAL and lagged cohort life expectancy. *Demographic Research, 24*, 611–632.
Hagemann, R. P., & Nicoletti, G. (1990). Le financement des retraites publiques face à la transition démografique dans quatre pays de l'OCDE. *Economie et Statistique ("L'avenir des retraites"), 223*, 39–51.
Hansson, Å. (2010). In this world nothing is certain but death and taxes: Financing the elderly. In T. Bengtsson (Ed.), *Population ageing. A threat to the welfare state? The case of Sweden* (pp. 23–45). Heidelberg: Springer.
Human mortality database. University of California, Berkeley (USA), Oct. 2011 and Max Planck Institute for Demographic Research (Germany). Available at www.mortality.org or www.humanmortality.de. Accessed on Oct 2011.
Immergut, E. M., Anderson, K. M., & Schulze, I. (Eds.). (2007). *The handbook of West European pension politics*. Oxford: Oxford University Press.
ISTAT. (2010a). *I bilanci consuntivi degli enti previdenziali dal 1999 al 2007*, Rome. http://www.istat.it/dati/catalogo/20100521_00/
ISTAT. (2010b). *Forze di lavoro – Media 2008* (Labour force statistics – 2008), Rome. http://www3.istat.it/dati/catalogo/20100217_00/
Kohli, M., & Arza, C. (2011). The political economy of pension reform in Europe. In R. H. Binstock & L. K. George (Eds.), *Handbook of aging and the social sciences* (7th ed., pp. 251–264). Amsterdam: Elsevier.
Kruse, A. (2010). A stable pension system: The eighth wonder. In T. Bengtsson (Ed.), *Population ageing. A threat to the welfare state? The case of Sweden* (pp. 47–64). Heidelberg: Springer.
Lee, R. D. (1980). Age structures, intergenerational transfers and economic growth: An overview. *Revue économique ("Démographie économique"), 6*, 1129–1156.
Lee, R. D., & Goldstein, J. R. (2003). Rescaling the life cycle: Longevity and proportionality. *Population and Development Review, 29*(Suppl), 183–207.
Lee, R. D., & Mason, A. (2011). *Population aging and the generational economy. A global perspective*. Cheltenham/Northampton: Elgar.
Lefèbvre, M. (2007, March). *The redistributive effects of pension system in Europe: A survey of evidence* (Luxembourg Income Study Working Paper Series, Working Paper No. 457). Luxembourg: Cross-National Data Center.
Livi Bacci, M., & Tapinos, G. (1999). Economie et population. In J. P. Bardet & J. Dupâquier (Eds.), *Histoire des populations de l'Europe Vol III Les temps incertains: 1914–1998* (pp. 93–124). Paris: Fayard.
Mason, A., & Lee, R. D. (2006). Reform and support systems for the elderly in developing countries: Capturing the second demographic dividend. *Genus, 62*(2), 11–35.
Musgrave, R. A. (1981). A reappraisal of financing social security. In F. Skidmore (Ed.), *Social security financing* (pp. 89–127). Cambridge: MIT Press.
OECD. (2011). *Pensions at a glance 2011: Retirement-income systems in OECD and G20 countries*. Paris: OECD. www.oecd.org/els/social/pensions/PAG
Shkolnikov, V. M., Jdanov, D. A., Andreev, E. M., & Vaupel, J. (2011). Steep increase in best-practise cohort life expectancy. *Population and Development Review, 37*(3), 419–434.
Takayama, N. (2003). *Taste of pie. Searching for better pension provisions in developed countries*. Tokyo: Maruzen.
Takayama, N. (2005). *Pensions in Asia. Incentives, compliance and their role in retirement*. Tokyo: Maruzen.
United Nations. (2011). *World population prospects: The 2010 revision*, New York: United Nations. http://www.un.org/esa/population/unpop.htm

Chapter 2
Ageing and Policies: Pension Systems Under Pressure

Fernando Gil-Alonso

2.1 Introduction

In the last two decades, a considerable amount of research has been devoted to examining the economic consequences of ageing (see, e.g. Lee et al. 2001; Lesthaeghe 2002; Mason 2005), including, among other important issues, its impact on the labour market (Coleman 1992, 2004; Feld 2000; Fotakis and Gil-Alonso 2002; Bijak et al. 2007; D'Addio et al. 2010), human capital and productivity (Skirbekk 2004; Lutz et al. 2004; OECD 2006; Prskawetz et al. 2005, 2008; Bloom et al. 2010), health/disability (Lutz and Scherbov 2005; Breyer et al. 2010), and elderly care (Murphy et al. 2006; Gaymu et al. 2007). Obviously, the sustainability of pension systems is a particularly relevant topic, with far-reaching economic, social, and policy implications: see, e.g. Franco and Munzi (1996), Fotakis (2000), Heijdra and Romp (2009), Meier and Werding (2010), Zaidi (2011), European Commission (2006, 2009), and OECD (2007a, b, 2009b, 2011). In Europe, most of the public pension schemes are of the pay-as-you-go (PAYG) type, where current workers pay the pension of today's retired people (Whitehouse 2007; OECD 2007b, 2009a): in these schemes, population ageing may constitute a serious threat. And all the demographic projections indicate that, over the next decades, the European populations will age even more than they have done thus far, due to increasing life expectancy, low fertility, and, especially, the ageing of the baby boom cohorts.

The analysis of the economic implications of ageing on the financial sustainability of pension systems cannot be limited only to the effect of demographic factors. It also needs to take into account other variables such as employment and productivity (here measured in terms of GDP per employed person).

F. Gil-Alonso (✉)
Human Geography Department, Universitat de Barcelona,
c. Montalegre, 6, 08001 Barcelona, Spain
e-mail: fgil@ub.edu

G. De Santis (ed.), *The Family, the Market or the State?: Intergenerational Support Under Pressure in Ageing Societies*, International Studies in Population 10,
DOI 10.1007/978-94-007-4339-7_2, © Springer Science+Business Media Dordrecht 2012

Besides, the main characteristics of the pension systems deserve consideration, in particular the level of contributions and the relative level of pensions.

In the majority of the European Union member states, there are already several sophisticated models for forecasting pensions, and each of them takes into account the specificities of the national system. Nevertheless, inter-country comparison is very difficult, due to the differences in the models used, particularly in terms of their structures and basic assumptions and, of course, the different types of pension systems that exist across EU countries. A few attempts have also been made in the past to provide a common framework at the European level (see, for instance, Franco and Munzi 1996; European Commission 1997), but their complexity and the lack of comparability between countries limit the usefulness of their results.

Some years ago, when I was working at the European Commission Social and Demography Analysis Unit, we were asked to write an internal report about the future impact of ageing on the pension systems of EU member states. In order to overcome the obstacles posed by the lack of comparability between national pension systems, we built a very simple model, following Calot's (1995) idea. This model, which has been later improved, expanded, and updated (Gil-Alonso and Math 2000; Gil-Alonso 2005, 2009), does not take into account the specificities of each national pension system and, therefore, does not intend to give precise pension expenditure forecasts for each of the analysed countries. Consequently, no firm policy recommendations can be derived from the simulations. Rather, by using the same variables and indicators for all countries, they permit readers to assess in a comparative way the demographic effect of ageing on the balance between contributions and benefits, keeping all other factors unchanged. At the same time, although the model's results (which, as in all projections, depend on the hypothesis used) should be interpreted with caution, they shed light on the implications of a range of economic and demographic measures—increasing international immigration among them—that could be used to reduce the ageing burden.

2.2 What Parameters Ensure Sufficient Comparability Between Countries While Keeping the Model Simple?

The present, improved version of the model incorporates both new input data and an enlarged geographical scope, with four non-European developed countries (Canada, Japan, South Korea, and the United States) and the 27 European Union ones. Like the previous versions of the model, the current one reports the necessary key parameters to assess pension funding sustainability and is based on the same principle: a PAYG system is in equilibrium when there is a balance between contributions and pension benefits. If the number of retired people increases due to ageing, the volume of pensions will tend to increase, and the system will be put under strain unless the other variables of the model change to restore the initial financial equilibrium. These other variables or parameters of the model are (for a more detailed description, see Annex 1):

- The number of (autochthonous or immigrant) people in employment
- The average effective age at exit from the labour market
- The so-called transfer ratio or the ratio of average pension to average gross domestic product per employed person
- The so-called contribution rate or proportion of GDP spent on pensions

This is a somewhat more complex model than the purely demographic one proposed by the United Nations in their famous publication on 'replacement migrations' (United Nations 2001), where the only variable compensating a declining and ageing population was an increase in the number of immigrants.

The rationale behind our model is similar to De Santis' *AIPS* pension system (see Chap. 1, in this volume) in the sense that the parameters of both models have to change to keep its financial equilibrium across time, or using De Santis' words, 'all the relevant variables adapt automatically to changing circumstances (exogenous variables in the system)'. Even some of the parameters used in both models are similar: employment rates, contribution rates, effective retirement age, etc.

The present model uses Eurostat demographic projections (convergence no-migration and convergence with-migration scenarios) for the EU countries and the UN World Population Prospects 2008 Revision (zero-migration and medium scenarios) for the other developed countries, for the period 2008–2050, to foresee the future evolution of the retired. This is the initial input of the model (for a more detailed description of the assumptions for the variables and parameters of the model, see Annex 1). The implications of ageing on the balance between contributions and benefits, keeping all other factors unchanged, are examined, as well as the change(s) required in other key parameters of the model to ensure equilibrium between contributions and pension benefits. In this way, the model provides an insight on how the implications of ageing may be mitigated when examining possible evolutions of other key factors such as:

- Increasing the effective retirement age (which primarily leads to a lower number of retirees and, therefore, to lower pension expenditures and may secondarily increase the number of employed people and, consequently, contributions)
- Decreasing the pension level (and thus the expenditure)
- Increasing the number of people in employment—either through immigration or growing employment rates—and their productivity (which both imply an increase in the total contributions)
- Finally, increasing their average contributions to the pension system

These alternative compensatory measures are the outputs of the model. Among these, the number of employed immigrants that are needed from 2008 onwards (or their employed children) in order to compensate for the increasing size of the retired population will be emphasised in this chapter.

2.3 The Initial (2008) Situation Regarding Ageing and the Model's Parameters in 31 Countries

The values of the parameters of the model in (or around) 2008 for the 27 European Union countries plus Canada, Japan, South Korea, and the USA can be seen in Table 2.1. This table also shows the figures for related indicators such as the economic dependency ratio, the full-time equivalent employment rate, and the average effective retirement age, which is significantly lower than the 'legal' retirement age in most countries. Table 2.1 shows a wide range of 2008 'starting' positions in the different parameters:

- The initial ageing situation in each country is summarised in column *R* (number of retired persons, i.e. people over average effective retirement age, *ERA*), which depends on the national population size and on the level of *ERA*, and column *EDR* (economic dependency ratio or number of retired persons per 100 employed people). The lowest *EDR* in the EU can be found in Ireland (28%) and the highest in Italy (68%), well above the EU-27 average (52%). Non-European countries show on average lower *EDR*, although large differences exist between the very low Korean figure (15%) and the high Japanese one (40%).
- The average effective retirement age (ERA) is already above 64 years in Romania, Bulgaria, and Ireland, followed by Sweden (at 63.8), whereas, at the other end, in Slovakia it is just below 59, followed by France and Poland. The EU average is around 61, whereas workers retire later in the non-European countries: at almost 63 in Canada, more than 64 in the USA, 68 in Japan, and almost 70 in South Korea!
- Current employment levels are shown in column *E* (number of employed people, in full-time equivalents) and column *ER* (full-time equivalent employment rate, i.e. employed persons per 100 at working age). There are extremely different employment rates within the EU, varying between the lowest values of Malta (52.9%) and Hungary (55.1%) and the highest ones in Latvia (69.6%), Estonia (69.5%), Denmark (69.1%), and Sweden (67.7%). The EU average is about 61%. Regarding non-EU countries, values are close to 67% in Canada and Japan and close to 63% in South Korea and the USA.
- Parameter '*c*' (public expenditure on pensions, as a percentage of *GDP*), which has remained quite stable in the EU as a whole at around 12% in the last years, varies widely in the EU, from just 4.8% in Ireland and around 5% in the Baltic countries to 13.3% in Austria and 15.6% in Italy. Values are generally lower in the other non-European developed countries (where private pension schemes are more significant) and extremely low in Korea at 1.6%.
- Finally, the transfer ratio *t*, which relates the average pension to the *GDP* per employed, is significantly below the European average in Lithuania, Estonia, and Latvia and relatively high in Sweden, the Netherlands, Cyprus, and Austria. This parameter is again much lower in Korea, due to lower pension levels.

Table 2.1 Main parameters of the model in 2008 (or more recent available data) in the EU member states and in Canada, Japan, South Korea, and the USA

	R	*E*	*c*(%)	*t*	*EDR*	*ER*	*ERA*	*wap*
Belgium	2,217,148	4,020,898	12.7	0.23	55.1	57.1	61.6	7,038,546
Bulgaria	1,408,830	3,323,156	7.5	0.18	42.4	62.8	64.1	5,294,755
Czech Republic	2,117,398	4,884,818	7.9	0.18	43.3	66.4	60.6	7,354,503
Denmark	1,130,016	2,495,797	10.7	0.24	45.3	69.1	61.3	3,612,833
Germany	19,289,306	33,132,404	11.5	0.20	58.2	60.9	61.7	54,414,768
Estonia	266,968	632,808	5.4	0.13	42.2	69.5	62.1	910,343
Greece	2,545,204	4,423,849	12.4	0.22	57.5	58.8	61.4	7,525,155
Spain	8,633,067	18,934,813	8.5	0.19	45.6	60.8	62.6	31,143,415
France	14,083,834	24,031,994	13.1	0.22	58.6	59.6	59.3	40,323,500
Ireland	528,769	1,895,041	4.8	0.17	27.9	62.7	64.1	3,021,540
Italy	14,827,007	21,800,481	15.6	0.23	68.0	55.6	60.8	39,229,823
Cyprus	109,943	367,646	8.5	0.28	29.9	66.0	63.5	556,782
Latvia	443,299	1,089,679	5.0	0.12	40.7	69.6	62.7	1,566,455
Lithuania	694,717	1,474,032	6.5	0.14	47.1	63.6	59.9	2,316,290
Luxembourg	94,522	186,188	7.1	0.14	50.8	57.1	59.4	326,231
Hungary	2,222,671	3,805,920	9.6	0.16	58.4	55.1	59.8	6,912,606
Malta	85,588	151,664	9.4	0.17	56.4	52.9	59.8	286,877
Netherlands	2,773,053	6,470,872	10.8	0.25	42.9	58.5	63.2	11,055,061
Austria	1,790,715	3,576,608	13.3	0.27	50.1	63.6	60.9	5,627,532
Poland	7,255,575	15,145,607	10.7	0.22	47.9	55.9	59.3	27,083,387
Portugal	2,128,559	4,869,202	11.7	0.27	43.7	68.2	62.6	7,138,991
Romania	3,333,188	8,992,216	6.0	0.16	37.1	60.1	64.3	14,968,729
Slovenia	433,132	948,428	9.7	0.21	45.7	67.0	59.8	1,416,458
Slovakia	995,285	2,401,558	6.8	0.16	41.4	61.6	58.7	3,901,358
Finland	1,113,272	2,358,836	9.5	0.20	47.2	66.8	61.6	3,529,982
Sweden	1,757,862	4,082,200	11.9	0.28	43.1	67.7	63.8	6,032,781
United Kingdom	11,222,452	25,182,890	11.1	0.25	44.6	61.9	63.1	40,659,760
EU 27	103,501,379	200,679,605	11.7	0.23	51.6	60.2	61.4	333,248,461
EU 25	98,759,362	188,364,233	11.7	0.22	52.4	60.2	61.3	312,984,977
EU 15	84,134,785	157,462,073	11.9	0.22	53.4	60.4	61.5	260,679,918
Canada	5,395,821	15,551,500	4.1	0.12	34.7	67.2	62.6	23,154,622
Japan	22,684,139	56,290,000	8.7	0.22	40.3	67.9	68.0	82,936,683
South Korea	3,387,204	22,156,000	1.6	0.10	15.3	63.7	69.6	34,801,068
United States	41,662,156	132,694,500	6.0	0.19	31.4	63.6	64.3	208,590,929

Definitions and sources of data:

R Retired persons (people over average effective retirement age). Source: Calculated by the author from Eurostat data for the EU (2008) and UN World Population Prospects. The 2008 Revision, for Canada, Japan, S. Korea, and the US (2008)

E Employed people in full-time equivalents. Source: Calculated by the author from Eurostat Labour Force Survey data for the EU (2008) and OECD data for the other four countries (2008)

c(%) Public expenditure (% of GDP) on old age and survivors' pensions. Source: Eurostat ESSPROS database for the EU (2007) and OECD data for the other four countries (2005)

t Transfer ratio calculated as in formula (2.5) in order to ensure equality in Eq. 2.1

EDR Economic dependency ratio (number of retired persons per 100 employed people)

ER Employment rate (employed persons per 100 persons of working age) in full-time equivalents

ERA Average effective retirement age. Source: Eurostat 2007 data on average exit age from the labour market for the EU (2008 or more recent available data) and OECD data for the other four countries (2007)

wap Working-age population (persons aged 15–64 years old). Source: 2008-based Eurostat demographic projection for the EU and UN World Population Prospects. The 2008 Revision, for the other four countries

We will now asses the future (up to the year 2050) impact of ageing or, in other words, how the increasing number of people over the average effective retirement age will impact on these initial parameters of the model.

2.4 Results: A Classification of Countries by the Best Suitable Measure to Counter Ageing

The model examines the impact of ageing on the equilibrium of the pension system between 2000 and 2050, keeping all other key factors constant. The exact number of retired people, R', is determined by the value of the effective retirement age (*ERA*, which in this first step is kept constant between 2008 and 2050) and the variation of the age structure determined by demographic projections. The model's outputs show the magnitude of the changes needed in the different parameters in order to maintain the model in equilibrium and thereby counterbalance the effect of ageing. These compensatory changes are examined one by one (*ceteris paribus*): the variation of the parameter, to a certain extent, reflects each country's degree of freedom and flexibility when confronted by the ageing process.

Let us suppose that a country's population is closed to migration, as in the no-migration Eurostat convergence scenario and in the zero-migration UN scenario, and that the effective retirement age is fixed at its 2008 value. Then, on top of mortality, the number of retired people between 2008 and 2050 will only be determined by the ageing process. Table 2.2 shows the number of retired people in 2050 (R') under these conditions and some of the compensatory changes needed in the key factors to counter the increase in the number of retired people and maintain the model in equilibrium.

For instance, under the assumptions of a constant effective retirement age of 61.4 years, the number of retired people in the whole European Union will pass from 103.5 million in 2004 (Table 2.1) to 163.4 million in 2050 (Table 2.2, first column). If the number of employed people does not change (as do parameters t and c, *ceteris paribus* approach), then the economic dependency ratio in 2050 (EDR') will suffer a dramatic increase: from 51.6 to 81.4 retired people per 100 employed, with national values ranging from 56.2% in Latvia to 95.1% in Italy.

The most direct measure to keep the model in equilibrium and to fix the economic dependency ratio up to 2050 would be to increase the number of employed people at the same growth rate as R. The resulting number of the employed in 2050 is shown in Table 2.2 as E'. The value for the EU-27 is 322 million employed people in full-time equivalents, compared to 200.7 million in 2008. This means an increase in employment of about 120 million (+60%). The annual growth rate of employment (column Eg') should be 1.13%, which is somewhat less than the average employment growth that was required by the EU between 2000 and 2010 in order to fulfil the Lisbon employment targets (estimated at around 1.2% p.a.) and practically the same growth rate as the one experienced by

Table 2.2 Parameters of the model in 2050 when the increase in employment through immigration is the only compensatory action (ceteris paribus approach)

No-migration scenario

	R	*EDR* (%)	*E'*	*Eg'* (%)	*wap*	*Eg'* (%)	*Imm'*
Belgium	3,372,349	83.9	6,115,907	1.00	5,665,062	108.0	1,867,110
Bulgaria	1,957,851	58.9	4,618,191	0.79	3,247,403	142.2	2,182,638
Czech Republic	3,463,340	70.9	7,989,893	1.18	4,642,080	172.1	4,508,333
Denmark	1,660,556	66.5	3,667,567	0.92	3,081,779	119.0	1,356,233
Germany	26,273,672	79.3	45,129,146	0.74	34,076,817	132.4	19,571,533
Estonia	384,651	60.8	911,757	0.87	674,478	135.2	405,899
Greece	3,846,534	86.9	6,685,707	0.99	4,855,274	137.7	3,044,252
Spain	16,370,896	86.5	35,906,109	1.54	20,205,875	177.7	20,751,703
France	21,993,770	91.5	37,529,137	1.07	36,877,529	101.8	9,870,990
Ireland	1,484,640	78.3	5,320,755	2.49	2,958,925	179.8	3,101,562
Italy	20,730,666	95.1	30,480,764	0.80	24,574,736	124.0	12,049,712
Cyprus	269,077	73.2	899,783	2.15	447,994	200.8	563,787
Latvia	611,980	56.2	1,504,314	0.77	1,038,211	144.9	725,656
Lithuania	1,044,436	70.9	2,216,057	0.98	1,636,533	135.4	988,657
Luxembourg	173,919	93.4	342,583	1.46	258,255	132.7	148,892
Hungary	3,143,983	82.6	5,383,499	0.83	4,545,102	118.4	1,974,672
Malta	143,557	94.7	254,388	1.24	204,583	124.3	100,951
Netherlands	4,974,198	76.9	11,607,204	1.40	8,934,884	129.9	4,906,041
Austria	2,893,907	80.9	5,780,022	1.15	3,853,308	150.0	2,890,041
Poland	13,541,140	89.4	28,266,373	1.50	18,522,760	152.6	14,374,303
Portugal	3,452,069	70.9	7,896,809	1.16	4,768,451	165.6	4,320,471
Romania	5,827,661	64.8	15,721,764	1.34	10,139,476	155.1	8,117,157
Slovenia	722,490	76.2	1,582,036	1.23	868,625	182.1	930,567
Slovakia	1,970,150	82.0	4,753,844	1.64	2,631,447	180.7	2,780,259
Finland	1,616,149	68.5	3,424,350	0.89	2,883,180	118.8	1,261,965
Sweden	2,662,159	65.2	6,182,208	0.99	5,149,162	120.1	2,320,337
United Kingdom	18,788,861	74.6	42,161,717	1.23	35,199,017	119.8	15,762,454
EU 27	163,374,662	81.4	322,331,885	1.13	241,940,946	133.2	140,876,175
EU 25	155,589,149	82.6	301,991,930	1.13	228,554,067	132.1	130,576,380
EU 15	130,294,345	82.7	248,229,986	1.09	193,342,254	128.4	103,223,296
Canada	11,041,705	71.0	31,823,712	1.72	18,554,759	171.5	17,907,643
Japan	34,030,823	60.5	84,446,450	0.97	49,684,670	170.0	47,182,947
South Korea	12,073,833	54.5	78,976,002	3.07	24,201,184	326.3	60,825,114
United States	86,011,451	64.8	273,947,569	1.74	204,970,774	133.7	120,219,488

Definitions:

R Retired persons (people over average effective retirement age) in 2050 determined by Eurostat no-migration convergence scenario

EDR Economic dependency ratio (number of retired persons by 100 employed people) in 2050 if total employment (in full-time equivalents) does not change

E' Employed people in full-time equivalents maintaining the model in equilibrium in 2050

Eg' Annual employment growth (in %) between 2008 and 2050 maintaining the model in equilibrium

wap Working-age population (persons aged 15–64 years old) in 2050 determined by Eurostat no-migration convergence scenario

ER' Employment rate (employed persons/working-age population) in full-time equivalents maintaining the model in equilibrium in 2050

Imm' Number of (employed) immigrants and their descendants maintaining the model in equilibrium in 2050

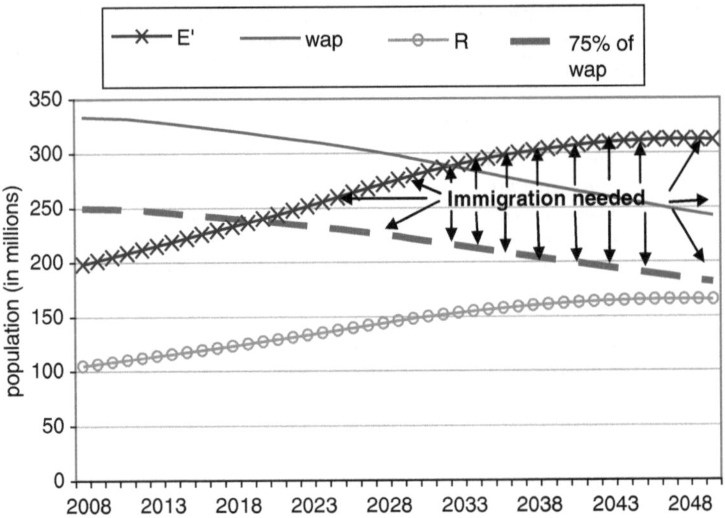

Fig. 2.1 Changes in the numbers of retired people (*R*) and working-age population (*wap*) in the EU-27 between 2008 and 2050 and number of employed persons (*E'*) maintaining the model in equilibrium (Source: Elaborated using Eurostat no-migration convergence scenario)

the EU-27 during the last decade (1997–2007), in a period of economic expansion. But here employment should increase for more than 40 years and should reach an 'impossible' employment rate in 2050 ($ER' = 133\%$). In other words, the decrease of the population of working age—from 333 million in 2008 to 242 million in 2050—will constitute an additional constraint in the adjustment process.

Figure 2.1 illustrates these numbers, showing the change in the number of retired people (*R*) determined by the demographic scenarios without migration and the number of employed persons maintaining the model in equilibrium (*E'*) for the EU-27 between 2008 and 2050. These growing numbers are compared with the decreasing size of the working-age population (*wap*). If we assume that an employment rate of 75% (in full-time equivalents) is a plausible ceiling of employability in the European Union (where the highest employment rate is currently in Latvia, at <70%), a deficit in the EU workforce emerges, from the year 2020 onwards.

The magnitude of the increase in employment required to compensate for ageing is so important that international (extra-EU) immigration appears as a natural candidate. Let us estimate the number of required immigrants (including their descendants) as the difference between *E'* (total employment in full-time equivalents maintaining the system in equilibrium) and a level of 75% of the working-age population projected by the convergence scenario (Fig. 2.1). The workforce deficit will reach its maximum in 2050, when *E'* will pass its ceiling (75% of the native working-age population) by more than 140 million. This is the number of additional workers, (immigrants and their descendants) necessary to fully compensate for ageing. Notice that the model assumes that all these immigrants and their children are employed so that the actual number of foreigners would in fact be much higher. Moreover, immigrants will eventually age and retire as well, resulting in an additional increase of E' to compensate for the growing numbers of R' and to keep the model in equilibrium.

However, even if we stick to the conservative estimate of 140 million employed foreigners (immigrants and their children) by the year 2050, the EU needs an average entry of more than 3.3 million net migrants per year. Now, the number of immigrants in the EU between 2002 and 2008 (a period of high immigration) has fluctuated between 1.6 and 2.0 million per year (Eurostat data, net migration including corrections). This result shows that employment growth alone will not be able to counter ageing, even if complemented with immigration, as both the amount of new employment required and the level of immigration needed are clearly not sustainable over a period of about 40 years.

Results are even more dramatic if we use the more ‘realistic’ Eurostat convergence scenario with migration—and the UN medium scenario, also including migration, for the non-EU countries (Table 2.3). In this case, the projection estimates a net influx of 49.4 million immigrants for the EU-27 between 2008 and 2050, whereas the number of retired people increases to 171 million, and the working-age population reaches 294 million in 2050. Therefore, the required number of employed immigrants (and their children) to compensate for ageing is ‘only’ 116 million. However, this scenario already includes a net migration of about 50 million immigrants for the whole EU during the projected period (a 1.2 million average per year), so the total number of required employed immigrants and their descendants under this scenario would in fact be more than 160 million.

We have just seen that the first alternative measure, increasing the number of employed persons (E'), does not suffice to counter ageing, given the future reduction of the EU working-age population and the high amount of employment creation required. Table 2.4 shows the alternative compensating changes required in the other parameters of Formula (2.4) to counter the impact of ageing for the period ending in 2050 (*ceteris paribus*):

- The average effective retirement age, which is estimated at 61.4 years in 2008 in the EU-27, should increase by more than 10 years by 2050 to reach a level of 71.6 years (see column ERA' in Table 2.4) in order to maintain the model in equilibrium—by fixing the number of retired people at nearly 104 million like in 2008, all other parameters remaining equal. This is, without doubt, a very important increase, but not all that different from the observed growth in life expectancy since 1960 which developed at a pace of about two additional years per decade.
- The share of pensions to the *GDP* (c') should increase, on average for the EU, from 11.7% in 2008 to 18.5% in 2050 (column c', Table 2.4). Therefore, there should be a change of nearly 7 percentage points in 42 years (column *cc*). This would be a very important increase as the current value for Italy, the country with the highest GDP share devoted to pension payments, is 15.6%. Note, however, that we are assuming here the *GDP* in the EU-27 area will not increase, which is unlikely in the long term. Therefore, the effort needed to finance the future pension burden will realistically be lower than that predicted by the model.

Table 2.3 Parameters of the model in 2050 when the increase in employment through immigration is the only compensatory action (ceteris paribus approach)

Scenario with migration

	R	*EDR* (%)	*E′*	*Eg′* (%)	*wap*	*Eg′* (%)	*Imm′*
Belgium	3,621,321	90.1	6,567,429	1.17	7,143,908	91.9	1,209,498
Bulgaria	1,935,420	58.2	4,565,279	0.76	3,340,560	136.7	2,059,859
Czech Republic	3,676,736	75.3	8,482,196	1.32	5,584,236	151.9	4,294,019
Denmark	1,677,207	67.2	3,704,343	0.94	3,492,621	106.1	1,084,877
Germany	26,972,140	81.4	46,328,875	0.80	41,857,001	110.7	14,936,125
Estonia	378,009	59.7	896,012	0.83	686,451	130.5	381,174
Greece	4,110,059	92.9	7,143,743	1.15	6,334,651	112.8	2,392,755
Spain	18,637,201	98.4	40,876,771	1.85	29,119,926	140.4	19,036,827
France	22,676,214	94.4	38,693,627	1.14	40,736,917	95.0	8,140,939
Ireland	1,617,986	85.4	5,798,653	2.70	3,837,819	151.1	2,920,289
Italy	23,094,150	105.9	33,955,847	1.06	33,726,904	100.7	8,660,669
Cyprus	315,483	85.8	1,054,963	2.54	772,172	136.6	475,834
Latvia	605,378	55.6	1,488,084	0.74	1,042,386	142.8	706,295
Lithuania	1,046,441	71.0	2,220,312	0.98	1,589,182	139.7	1,028,425
Luxembourg	202,984	109.0	399,836	1.84	423,938	94.3	81,883
Hungary	3,304,629	86.8	5,658,576	0.95	5,232,017	108.2	1,734,564
Malta	151,874	100.1	269,126	1.37	242,162	111.1	87,504
Netherlands	4,860,468	75.1	11,341,818	1.35	9,878,591	114.8	3,932,874
Austria	3,035,260	84.9	6,062,349	1.26	5,321,505	113.9	2,071,220
Poland	13,542,677	89.4	28,269,581	1.50	18,900,392	149.6	14,094,287
Portugal	3,788,634	77.8	8,666,719	1.38	6,511,600	133.1	3,783,019
Romania	5,829,680	64.8	15,727,209	1.34	10,394,013	151.3	7,931,700
Slovenia	744,084	78.5	1,629,320	1.30	1,027,671	158.5	858,567
Slovakia	2,022,609	84.2	4,880,423	1.70	2,771,351	176.1	2,801,909
Finland	1,678,600	71.2	3,556,673	0.98	3,133,248	113.5	1,206,737
Sweden	2,794,032	68.4	6,488,449	1.11	6,294,311	103.1	1,767,716
United Kingdom	18,818,899	74.7	42,229,122	1.24	45,046,728	93.7	8,444,076
EU 27	171,138,175	85.3	336,955,336	1.24	294,442,261	114.4	116,123,641
EU 25	163,373,075	86.7	316,662,848	1.24	280,707,688	112.8	106,132,082
EU 15	137,585,156	87.4	261,814,255	1.22	242,859,668	107.8	79,669,504
Canada	12,679,176	81.5	36,543,129	2.05	26,145,713	139.8	16,933,845
Japan	34,209,692	60.8	84,890,307	0.98	51,790,129	163.9	46,047,711
South Korea	12,058,537	54.4	78,875,950	3.07	23,980,976	328.9	60,890,218
United States	90,634,582	68.3	288,672,299	1.87	247,924,860	116.4	102,728,654

Definitions: See Table 2.2

- Finally, the transfer ratio (t') should be multiplied, at the EU level, by 0.63 (coefficient *ct*, Table 2.4), i.e. the average pension should decrease by 37% (column cp) in relation to the *GDP* for each employed person. Or in other words, increasing productivity by 58% in the same period—which means an average growth of 1.1% per year—if pensions remain constant (column *cGDP*/*e*). That means that productivity should increase more rapidly than monetary pensions between 2008 and 2050. An annual *GDP* growth of 1.1% is feasible: for instance, it has been surpassed every year at the EU-27 level during the period 1999–2007. However, it should also be kept in mind that the growth needed will

Table 2.4 Alternative compensatory actions (ceteris paribus approach) to maintain the model in equilibrium in 2050

No-migration scenario

	ERA'	*cERA*	*c'* (%)	*cc* (%)	*t'*	*ct*	*cp* (%)	*cGDP/e* (%)
Belgium	71.2	9.6	19.3	6.6	0.15	0.66	−34.3	52.1
Bulgaria	70.1	6.0	10.4	2.9	0.13	0.72	−28.0	39.0
Czech Republic	71.0	10.4	12.9	5.0	0.11	0.61	−38.9	63.6
Denmark	70.7	9.4	15.7	5.0	0.16	0.68	−31.9	46.9
Germany	69.4	7.7	15.7	4.2	0.15	0.73	−26.6	36.2
Estonia	68.7	6.6	7.8	2.4	0.09	0.69	−30.6	44.1
Greece	71.1	9.7	18.7	6.3	0.14	0.66	−33.8	51.1
Spain	75.1	12.5	16.1	7.6	0.10	0.53	−47.3	89.6
France	70.2	10.9	20.5	7.4	0.14	0.64	−36.0	56.2
Ireland	78.8	14.7	13.5	8.7	0.06	0.36	−64.4	180.8
Italy	70.6	9.8	21.8	6.2	0.16	0.72	−28.5	39.8
Cyprus	77.4	13.9	20.8	12.3	0.12	0.41	−59.1	144.7
Latvia	68.4	5.7	6.9	1.9	0.09	0.72	−27.6	38.1
Lithuania	67.8	7.9	9.8	3.3	0.09	0.67	−33.5	50.3
Luxembourg	73.9	14.5	13.1	6.0	0.08	0.54	−45.7	84.0
Hungary	67.8	8.0	13.6	4.0	0.12	0.71	−29.3	41.5
Malta	70.4	10.6	15.8	6.4	0.10	0.60	−40.4	67.7
Netherlands	75.5	12.3	19.4	8.6	0.14	0.56	−44.3	79.4
Austria	72.3	11.4	21.5	8.2	0.16	0.62	−38.1	61.6
Poland	70.9	11.6	20.0	9.3	0.12	0.54	−46.4	86.6
Portugal	72.7	10.1	19.0	7.3	0.17	0.62	−38.3	62.2
Romania	73.3	9.0	10.5	4.5	0.09	0.57	−42.8	74.8
Slovenia	71.3	11.5	16.2	6.5	0.13	0.60	−40.1	66.8
Slovakia	71.5	12.8	13.5	6.7	0.08	0.51	−49.5	97.9
Finland	69.9	8.3	13.8	4.3	0.14	0.69	−31.1	45.2
Sweden	72.6	8.8	18.0	6.1	0.18	0.66	−34.0	51.4
United Kingdom	73.5	10.4	18.6	7.5	0.15	0.60	−40.3	67.4
EU 27	71.6	10.2	18.5	6.8	0.14	0.63	−36.6	57.8
EU 25	71.6	10.3	18.4	6.7	0.14	0.63	−36.5	57.5
EU 15	71.8	10.3	18.4	6.5	0.14	0.65	−35.4	54.9
Canada	74.8	12.2	8.4	4.3	0.06	0.49	−51.1	104.6
Japan	73.7	5.7	13.1	4.4	0.14	0.67	−33.3	50.0
South Korea	81.8	12.2	5.7	4.1	0.03	0.28	−71.9	256.5
United States	75.2	10.9	12.4	6.4	0.09	0.48	−51.6	106.4

Definitions:

ERA'	Average effective retirement age in 2050 maintaining the model in equilibrium
cERA	Increase in years in the average effective retirement age between 2004 and 2050 maintaining the model in equilibrium
c' (%)	Public expenditure (% of GDP) on old age and survivors' pensions in 2050 maintaining the model in equilibrium
cc (%)	Increase (in % points) in public expenditure on old age and survivors' pensions in 2050 maintaining the model in equilibrium
t'	Transfer ratio in 2050 maintaining the model in equilibrium
ct	Coefficient multiplying 2008 transfer ratios maintaining the model in equilibrium in 2050
cp	% Change in average pension between 2008 and 2050 maintaining the model in equilibrium (if productivity remains constant)
cGDP/e (%)	% Change in GDP per employed (productivity) between 2008 and 2050 maintaining the model in equilibrium (if average pension remains constant)

probably be higher because pension benefits are also likely to increase in the future. This future growth could only be mitigated at the EU level through indexing pensions to prices (as it is done, for instance, in Spain) rather than to wages. By doing this, the transfer ratio should decrease (as average pensions would probably increase less, over the long term, than the GDP per employed), and the sustainability of pension systems could be more easily achieved.

These compensatory changes have been estimated using the Eurostat no-migration convergence scenario, but results are similar to those obtained when using the scenario with migration (not presented here). The changes required are even slightly more important, as the number of retired people in the scenario with migration is also larger. For instance, the average effective retirement age in Europe should increase up to 72 years, instead of 71.6, to maintain the model in equilibrium; public expenditure on pensions should increase by 7.7 percentage points instead of 6.8; and the transfer ratio should be 0.60 instead of 0.63.

Obviously, the changes required to ensure the equilibrium of the model must be seen as extreme values since the real evolutions are likely to be a mix of smaller changes in all the factors, resulting from the implementation of different policies. For instance, in most EU countries, in order to alleviate the pension burden, a future decrease in transfer ratios (lower pension benefits) and an increase of *ERA* (later retirement) are virtually certain.

Even though a policy mix is the best way to attenuate the consequences of ageing, each combination of measures should be adapted to each country's specific characteristics. For instance, a further increase in the retirement age can be hard to achieve where this age is already high, while reducing transfer ratios (t') could be difficult if the average pension benefits are already low.

Similarly, implementing (either of) these policies should be easier in those countries where the ageing process between 2008 and 2050 will be less pronounced. This is the case of countries like Germany, Belgium, Italy, Greece, or the Scandinavian ones, where ageing levels (measured by the *EDR*) are already relatively high and will likely not increase very much. This is also the case in countries like Bulgaria, Hungary, and the Baltic ones, where the number of retired people (which is at present relatively low) will increase less, due to their relatively lower life expectancy and their peculiar age structure. At the other end, there are South Korea, Ireland, Cyprus, the United States, Canada, Slovakia, Spain, Poland, Luxembourg, and the Netherlands, where ageing will be more rapid.

Owing to differences between the ageing process and other relevant factors, some compensatory measures might be more appropriate for some countries rather than others. Therefore, the results of the models at the national level (see Tables 2.2 and 2.4 again) have been used to classify our 31 developed countries into five groups, according to the most appropriate measure needed to compensate for ageing:

- The Scandinavian countries (Denmark, Sweden, and Finland) and the Baltic ones (Estonia, Latvia, and Lithuania), together with some new member states like Bulgaria and Hungary, and some former ones (Belgium and Germany) are going to experience less pronounced ageing processes. Therefore, raising the local population's employment rates together with relatively moderate foreign immigrant entries (in the Scandinavian countries, Belgium, and Italy) and/or other secondary measures (such as increasing the *ERA* in Hungary or Lithuania, where the current effective retirement age is low, or in Germany, Bulgaria, Estonia, and Latvia, where minor growths in ERA will be required) should be enough to maintain their public pension systems in equilibrium.

- Countries like Slovenia, Poland, France, Malta, and Italy currently have a very low average exit age from the labour market (around 60 years, or less) so that increasing the effective retirement age should be the primary measure there. Other countries like the Czech Republic, Slovakia, Austria, or Luxembourg also have a low *ERA*, but the required growth to compensate for ageing (more than 10 years) will be very hard to achieve, so other policies should also be considered there.
- Non-EU countries like Canada, Japan, South Korea, and the United States, together with other EU countries like the Czech Republic, Ireland, Luxembourg, Romania, or Slovakia, currently have low or very low contribution rates (c). Therefore, increasing the public expenditure on pensions (measured as GDP share) should be the most convenient measure here. Even so, in 2050, c' will be at 13% or lower. Similar measures could be implemented in the Baltic countries and Bulgaria, where current contribution rates are very low too. However, as we have seen, other less unpopular policies, such as increasing employment levels, can be implemented there instead.
- The transfer ratio (t) or ratio of average pension to *GDP* per employed person is currently high in countries like Portugal, Austria, the Netherlands, and the United Kingdom and could be reduced in the future. Relatively minor transfer ratio diminutions could also maintain the public pension system in equilibrium in Germany, Italy, or the Scandinavian countries. However, as we have seen, other measures can also be applied here. In other countries such as Bulgaria, Hungary, and the Baltic countries, this measure could also be implemented, but current t' levels are already very low (due to low average pensions) so that decreasing them even more seems unrealistic.
- Finally, there are three countries, Spain, Greece, and Cyprus, where no specific measure by itself seems to be enough as they will experience very significant ageing processes. There, the number of jobs needed to keep pensions in equilibrium will not be met by a decreasing working-age population. Moreover, their average effective retirement age is not especially low, the contribution rate in 2050 (c') will be relatively high—between 16% (Spain) and 21% (Cyprus)—and their transfer ratio allows for less margin of manoeuvre than in other countries. Therefore, to compensate for ageing and keep their public pension systems in equilibrium, these three countries will necessarily have to rely on a combination of several policies.

2.5 Conclusions

As the model shows, the impact of ageing on the sustainability of pension systems up to the year 2050 will be significant both at the European Union level, for each of the 27 EU member states, and for the other four non-European developed countries analysed here. Indeed, none of the developed countries can expect to escape ageing. 'Baby boomers' will sooner or later reach their retirement age, and, despite national differences in fertility rates, the younger cohorts entering the labour market will be unable to compensate for the high numbers of older people who will retire in the near future. As most public pension schemes are pay-as-you-go (PAYG) where currently employed people pay the pensions of today's retired people, future demographic trends threaten the schemes' future viability.

The model's results show that the long-term sustainability of pension systems appears to be a challenge which can only be overcome by an appropriate mix of policies and measures in the next 40 years. Employment must be raised, and immigration will be helpful in this respect but not sufficient; retirement must be deferred, and the average pension benefit must be lowered in real terms. Therefore, all the developed countries require a policy framework promoting economic growth with increasing productivity and more jobs, together with policies encouraging people to remain longer in work.

Within this general framework, it is, however, worth stressing that the ageing challenge will differ in each country: in part because of its pace and in part because of the initial (2008) levels in the model's key variables (employment, effective retirement age, contribution rate, transfer ratio). Therefore, the measures required to preserve equilibrium will not have the same impact everywhere. The countries with a high average effective retirement age and high employment rates may need to adjust the GDP contribution and pension levels. In other cases, labour market participation must be increased, as well as the effective age at retirement. Immigration, a very sensitive issue in most countries, can be used (as a secondary or complementary policy and in combination with the other ones) to alleviate ageing, but it is not sufficient in itself: the number of immigrants needed to compensate for the increasing number of retired people would be extremely high. Readers will note that this conclusion coincides in practice with that of the United Nations (2001) report on 'replacement migration'.

In summary, future public pension system sustainability will only be achieved by combining different employment, immigration, retirement age, economic productivity, and pension policies. A proper policy mix that would only require relatively small changes in each of the variables is probably the best way of assuming the varying social costs of the different policies, although this does not guarantee that the process will be easy to implement.

Acknowledgements This research is a result of the R+D Project CSO2008-06217/SOCI. I would like to acknowledge the Spanish Ministry of Science and Innovation for funding this project through the *National R+D+i Plan 2008–2011*. I would also like to thank Ms. Eva Jiménez-Julià for revising the English text.

Annex 1: How the Model Works

Formal Description of the Model

At the macroeconomic level, the funding of pensions is a question of gross domestic product (*GDP*) redistribution from those who are participating in economic life to those who are already retired. A pension system can be described as in equilibrium when the volume of contributions levied on workers equals the amount of pensions paid to retired people.

$$\text{Contributions} = \text{Pension benefits} \tag{2.1}$$

or

$$GDP \cdot c = R \cdot p \tag{2.2}$$

where:

- GDP = the wealth produced (gross domestic product).
- c = the 'contribution rate' or the share of gross domestic product necessary to finance pensions, comprising all forms of contribution to the system, i.e. employer and employee contributions, taxes, and other contributions. This broad definition of 'c' results from the underlying assumption that people in employment are the only producers and contributors within the system, and hence, there is no difference between systems financed more through taxation and systems financed more through social contributions.
- R = the number of retired people.
- p = the average pension.

(2.2) is equivalent to

$$E \cdot GDP/E \cdot c = R \cdot t \cdot GDP/E \tag{2.3}$$

where:

- E = the number of people in employment (in full-time equivalents), i.e. the people producing the *GDP* from which the pensions are financed
- GDP/E = the average gross domestic product per employed person (*GDP* divided by the number of people working)
- t = the 'transfer ratio', defined here as the ratio of average pension to average gross domestic product per employed person $\left(t = \frac{p}{GDP/E}\right)$

(2.3) can be simplified further and then is equivalent to

$$E \cdot c = R \cdot t \tag{2.4}$$

As the number of the retired (R), the number of the employed (E), and the share of contributions to the GDP (c) are known for any particular year, t can be estimated for 2008 (initial year of the projection model) by assuming equilibrium between expenditures and receipts:

$$t = E/R \cdot c \tag{2.5}$$

In this model, pension sustainability is achieved when total resources equal total expenditures at the macroeconomic level during the considered period (in this case, 2008–2050). Within this framework, it is not relevant whether pension schemes are based on a pay-as-you-go (PAYG) or funding since the current *GDP* is shared every year between those who receive income directly from their participation in economic life and those who do not. If there are more retired people, the share of pensions in *GDP* is likely to be greater, whatever the funding base of the pensions: contributions, taxes, or financial yields.

Assumptions for the Variables and Parameters Used in the Model

The model works on the basis of the following assumptions:

- Pension schemes are assumed to be in financial equilibrium in the starting year (2008). Therefore, all findings should be related to this year as the reference point.
- The only external shock unbalancing the system is assumed to be the change in the number of retired people (defined as the number of persons aged over the average pension age in each country) due to population ageing.
- Data on population by age for the period 2008–2050 are taken from Eurostat demographic projections (convergence no-migration and convergence with-migration scenarios) for the EU member states and from UN World Population Prospects 2008 Revision (zero-migration and medium scenarios) for Canada, Japan, South Korea, and the United States. Two different sets of scenarios have been developed by Eurostat and UNPD: with migration and without migration from 2009 onwards (therefore, in zero-migration scenarios, population growth and structure is only determined by births and deaths). The latter has been preferably used here, as the number of (employed) immigrants (and their descendants) compensating ageing is one of the main outputs of the model. However, the more realistic scenario with migration has also been used to compare results and to assess the compensatory effect of migration levels forecasted by Eurostat and UNPD.
- E, the number of people employed and contributing to the system, is calculated by using the full-time equivalents (FTE). They have been calculated for each country by multiplying the number of people working part-time times the ratio of the average number of usual weekly hours of work of those working part-time

to the average number of weekly working hours of those who are employed full-time. This ratio is around 0.5, but significant variations exist among countries. The resulting figures, plus the number of people currently working full-time, give the total number of full-time equivalents employed. Taking the FTE rate provides a better and more comparable insight, between countries and over time, of the ability of employed people to create wealth and to contribute to pension system funding, as part-time workers contribute less than full-time ones regardless of the type of pension system funding: directly through social contributions (since those are mostly more or less proportional to earnings) or indirectly through general taxation. Furthermore, using FTE allows for a more reliable comparison between countries, given the wide dispersion in the prevalence and average duration of part-time employment.

- *c*, the share of *GDP* levied to finance pensions, is estimated for the EU countries from the total expenditure on old age and survivors' benefits, as given by Eurostat ESSPROS (European System of Social Protection Statistics) database. For the other developed countries, I used OECD data.
- *R*, the retired population, is assumed to be the part of the population above the average effective retirement age (ERA, as defined by Eurostat: average exit age from the labour market, weighted by the probability of withdrawal from the labour market). This assumption is acceptable as most elderly people actually have direct or derivative rights to pensions. The average effective retirement age has been estimated for each EU country by Eurostat from EU Labour Force Survey data on age-specific activity rates. For the four other developed countries, OECD statistics on average effective retirement age have been used (OECD 2009b).
- *t*, the transfer ratio, is equal to $E/R \cdot c$ when the system is in equilibrium (see Eq. 2.5) and provides a proxy measure to assess the evolution of the relative pension level. It is similar to the 'net replacement rate' used in other models, which is the ratio of the average pension to the average wage. However, *t* puts the average pension in relation to the average *GDP* per employed person, which is a direct measure of productivity—indeed, '*t*' can decrease because the average pension diminishes or because productivity increases. Therefore, maintaining the relative level of average pension implies that the absolute level of the average pension should evolve at the same pace as productivity.
- Finally, as the model assumes that *GDP* is entirely produced by employed people and pensions are distributed among the retired population (as defined in *R*), it disregards people who are neither employed nor retired. It is hence assumed, for the sake of simplicity, that those people are neither contributing nor costing anything to *GDP*, although some of them may benefit from different forms of government transfers. A more complex model could incorporate the impact of other forms of government transfers and social policies—e.g. health-care contributions and expenditures, which are distributed across ages in a similar way as pensions or unemployment benefits.

Annex 2: Results for the EU and the 29 Countries Analysed in This Chapter

Figures 1–31. Retired people (*R*) and working-age population (*wap*) projected in the analysed country between 2008 and 2050 and number of employed persons (E') maintaining the model in equilibrium

Bulgaria

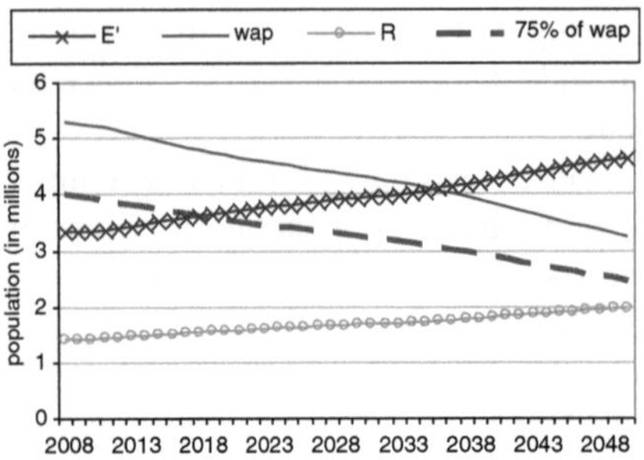

Belgium

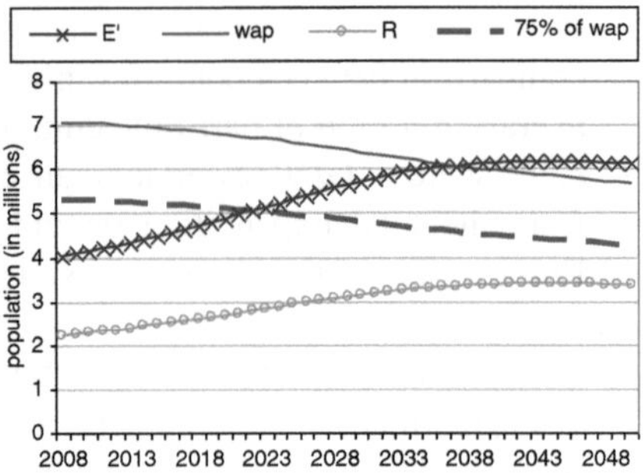

Canada

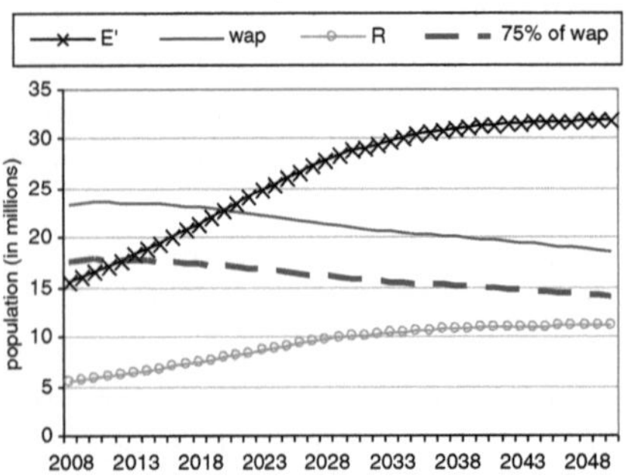

Czech Republic

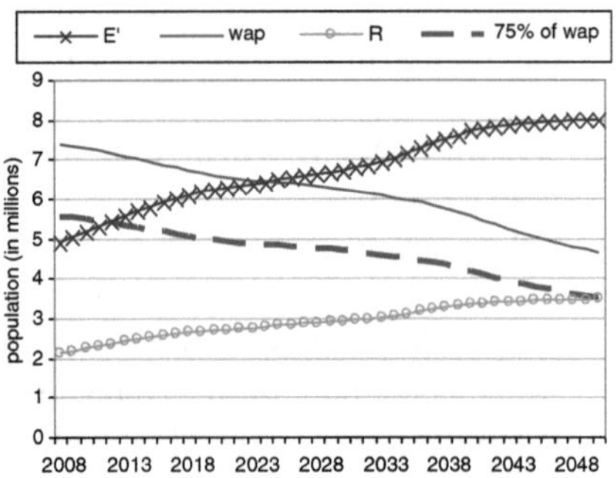

Denmark

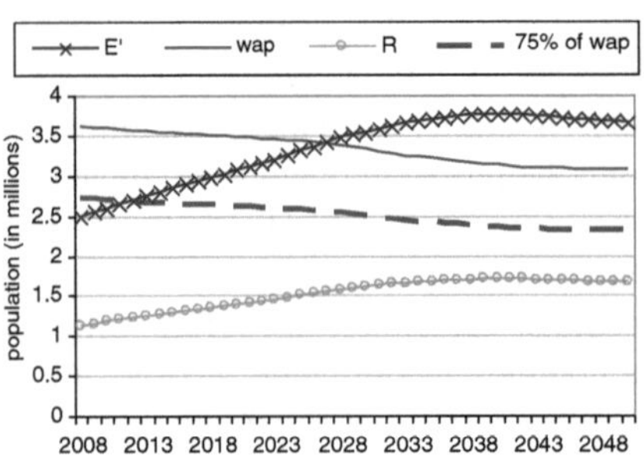

Germany

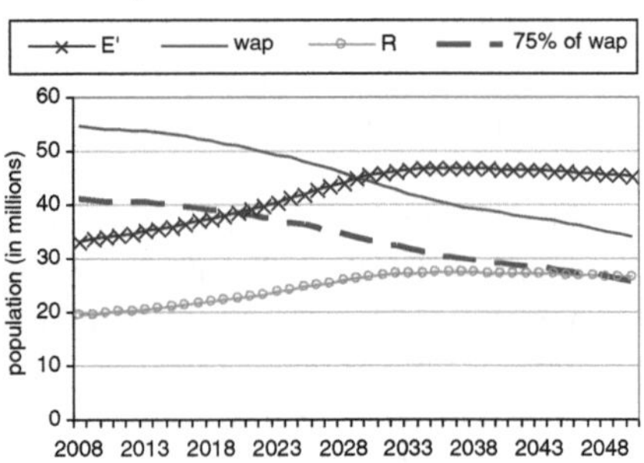

Estonia

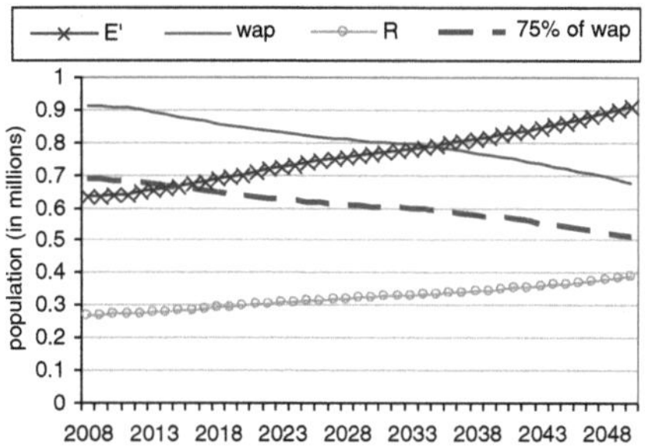

Greece

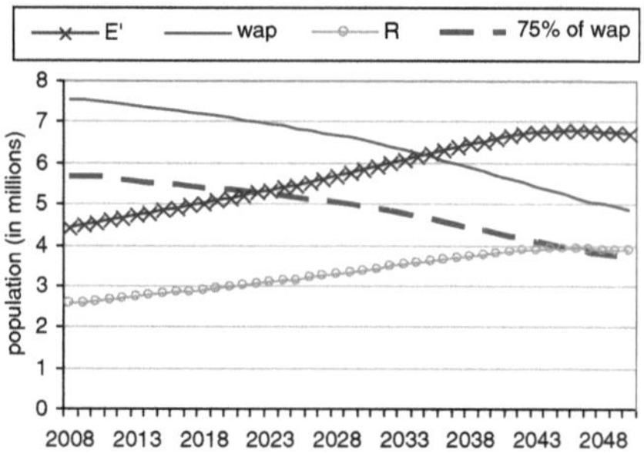

Spain

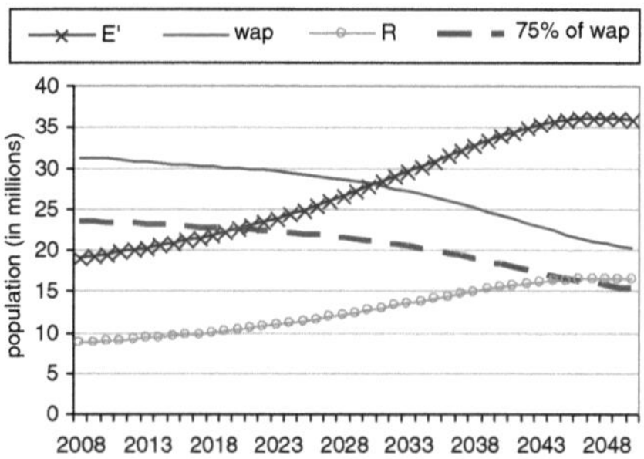

France

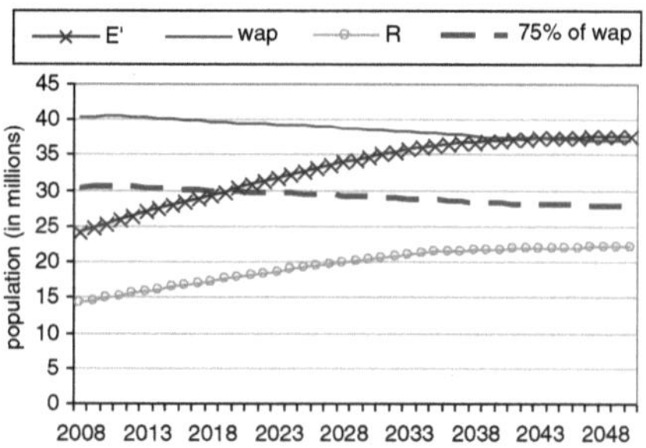

Ireland

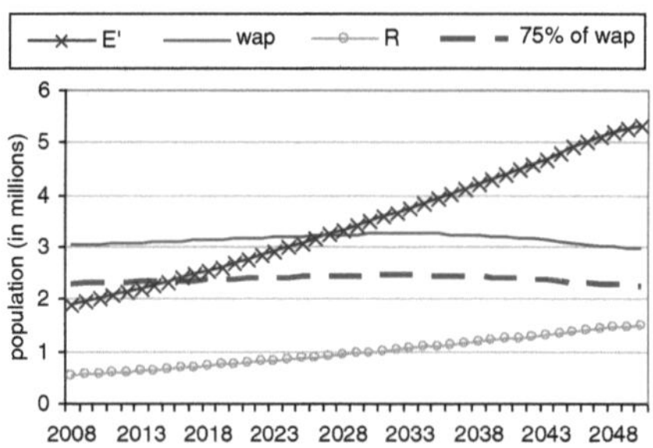

Italy

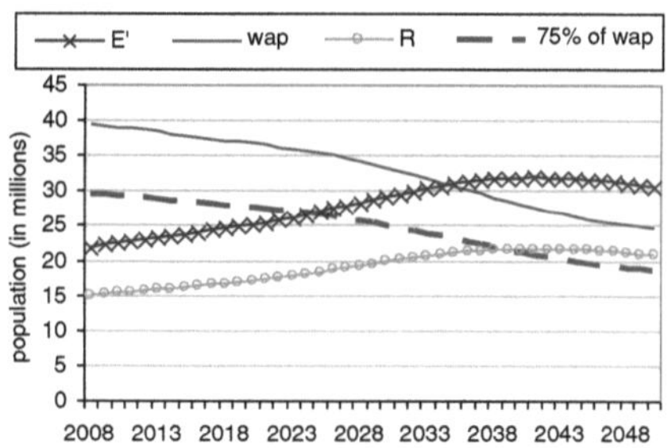

Japan

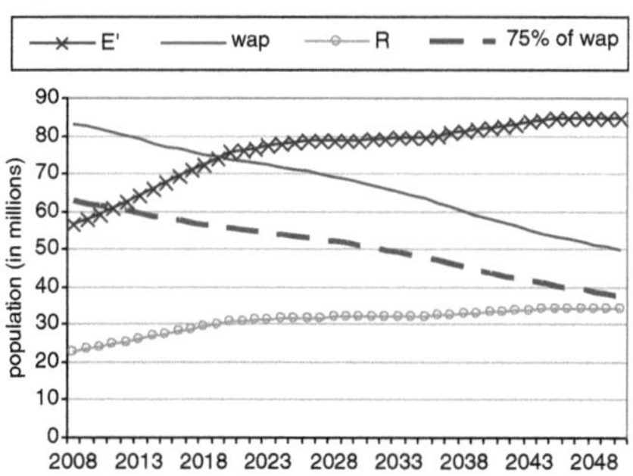

Cyprus

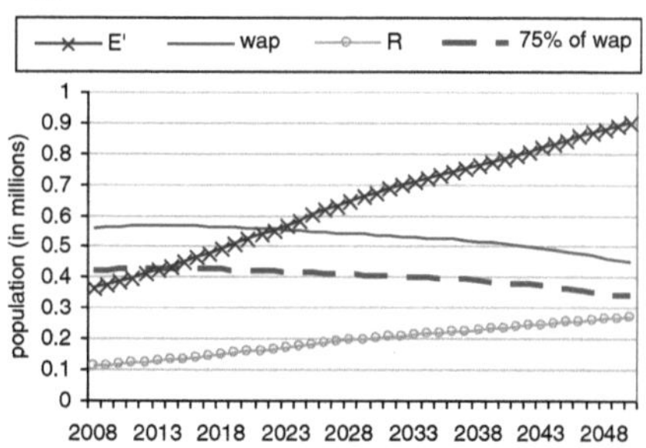

Latvia

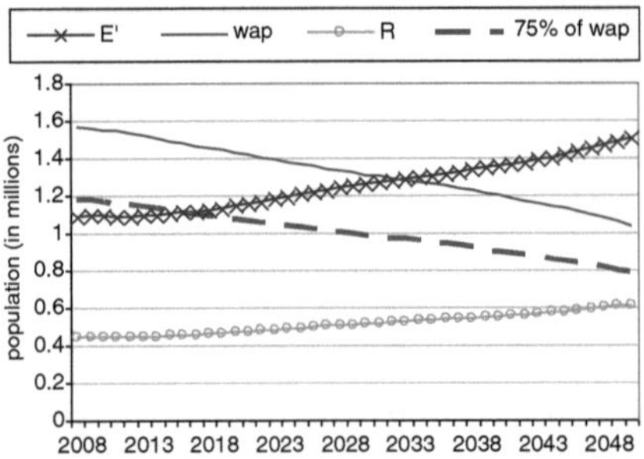

Lithuania

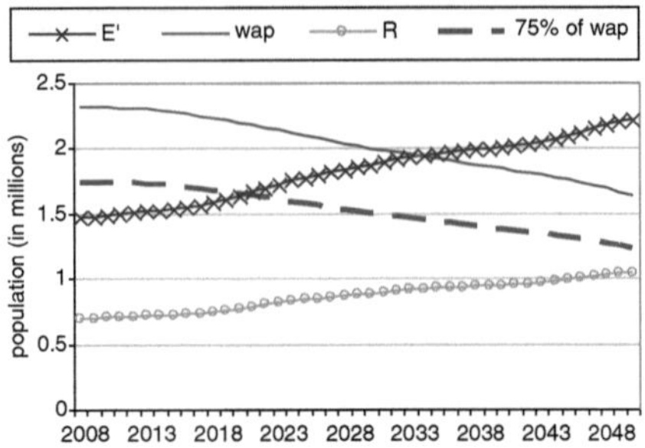

Luxembourg

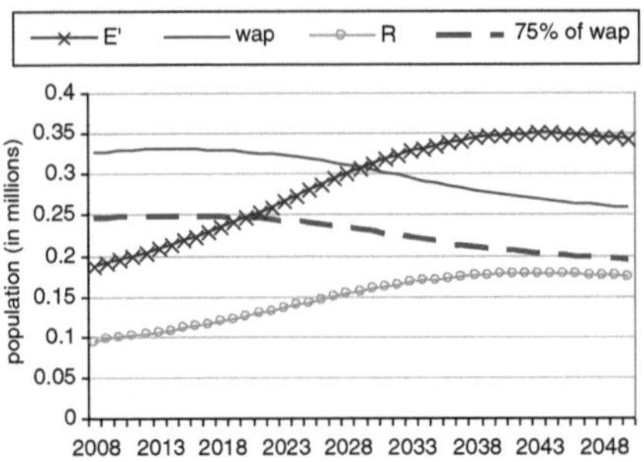

Hungary

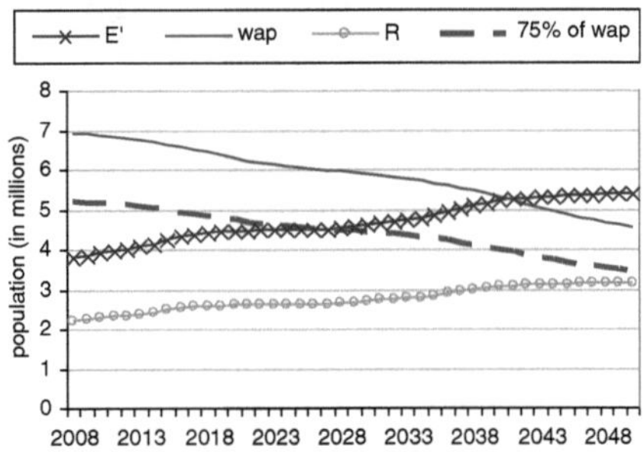

Malta

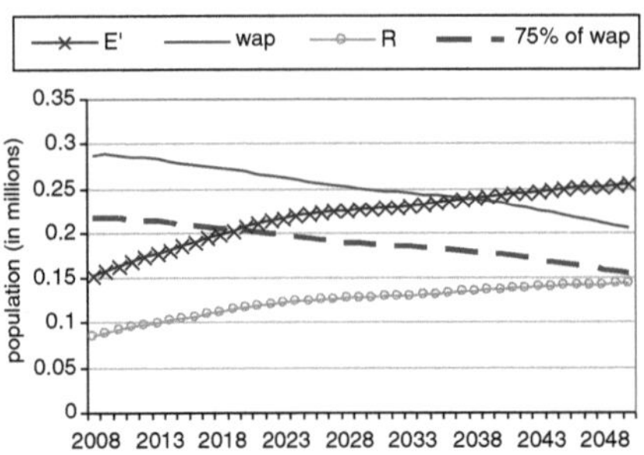

Netherlands

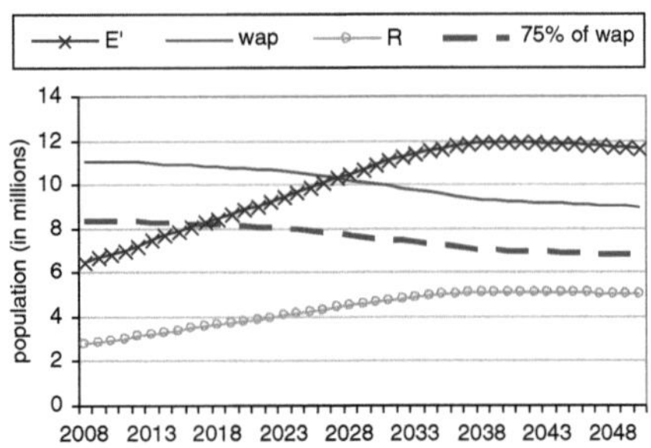

Austria

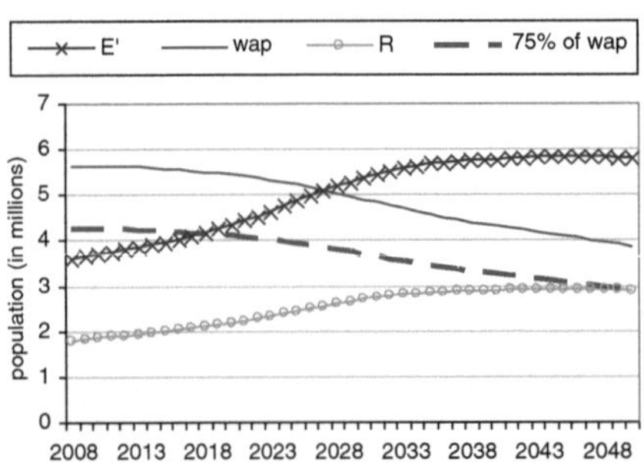

Poland

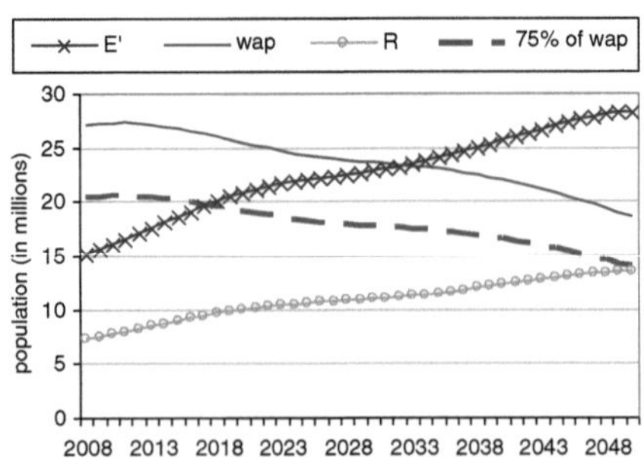

Portugal

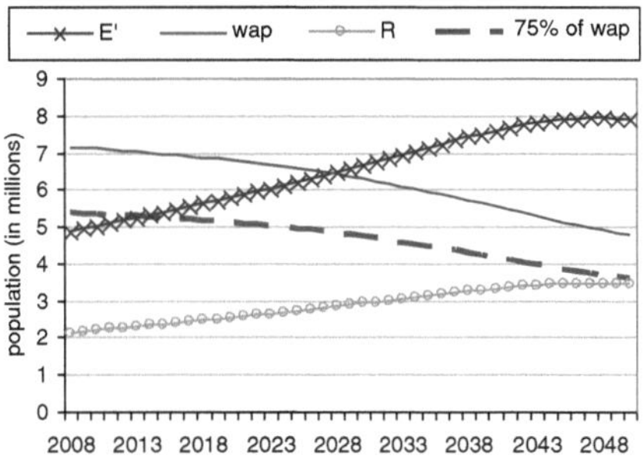

Romania

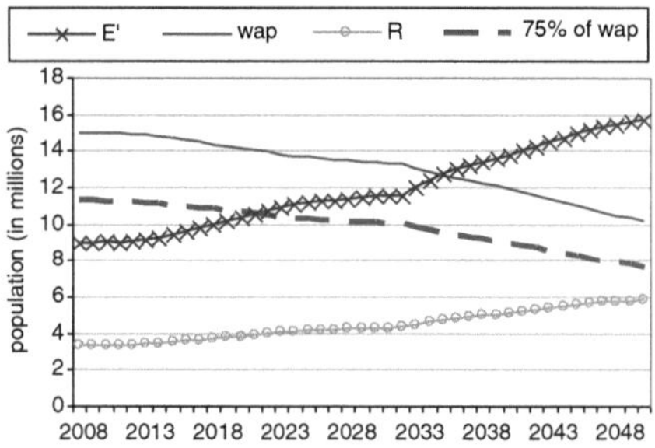

Slovenia

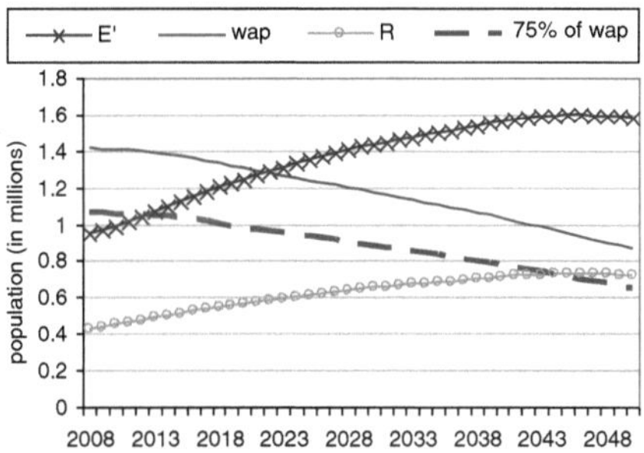

Slovakia

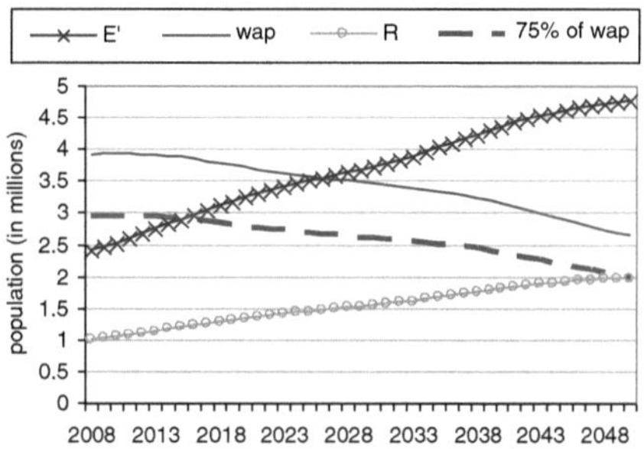

South Korea

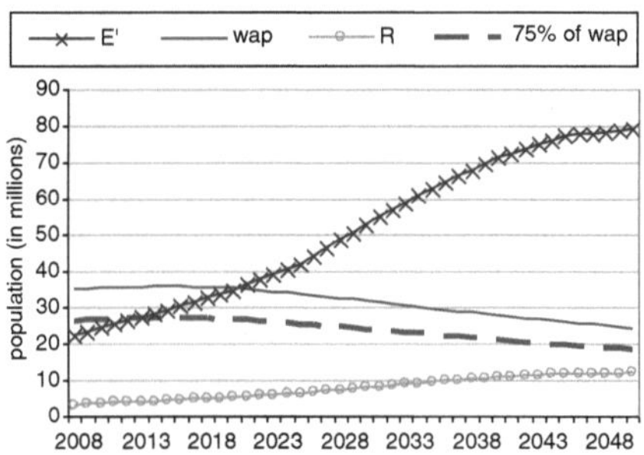

Finland

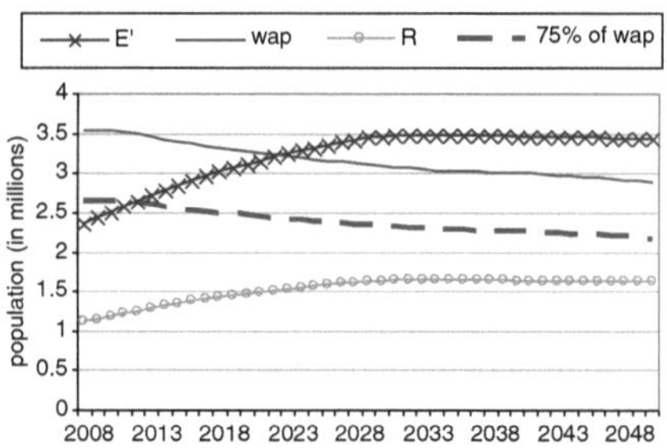

Sweden

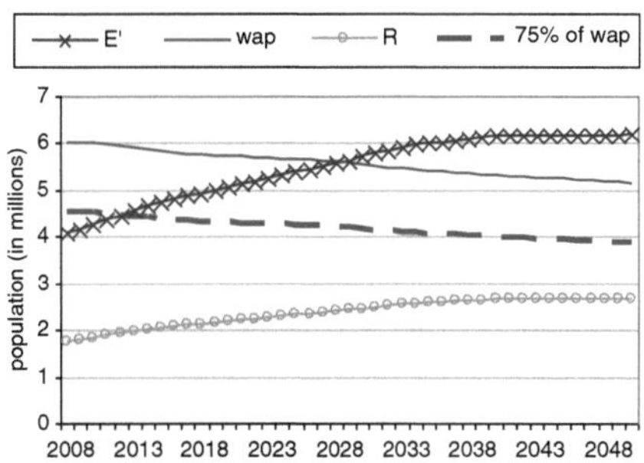

United Kingdom

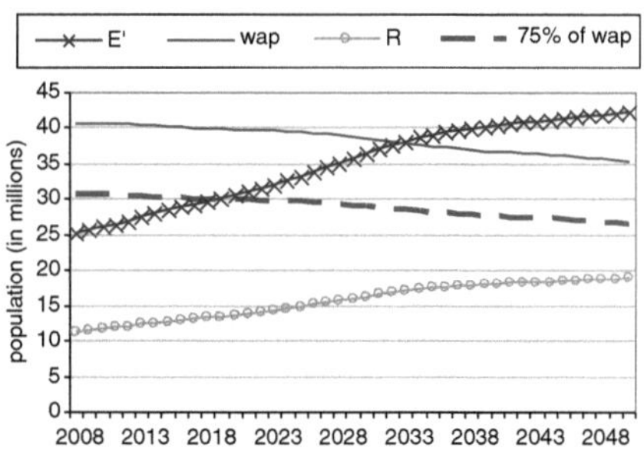

United States

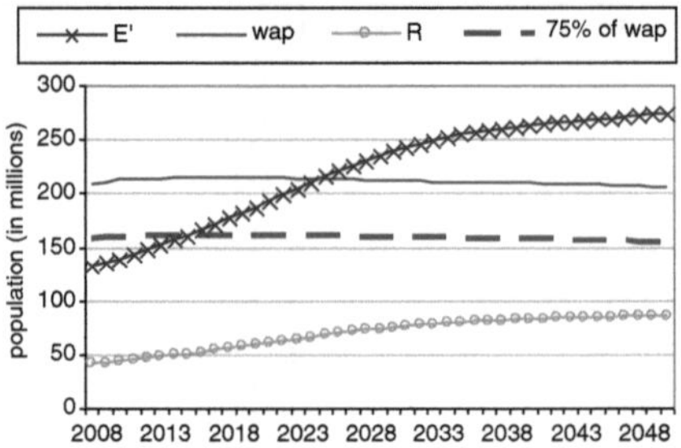

References

Bijak, J., Kupiszewska, D., Kupiskewski, M., Saczuk, K., & Kicinger, A. (2007). Population and labour force projections for 27 European countries, 2002–2052: Impact of international migration on population ageing. *European Journal of Population, 23*(1), 1–31.

Bloom, D. E., Canning, D., & Fink, G. (2010). Implications of population ageing for economic growth. *Oxford Review of Economic Policy, 26*(4), 583–612.

Breyer, F., Costa-Font, J., & Felder, S. (2010). Ageing, health, and health care. *Oxford Review of Economic Policy, 26*(4), 674–690.

Calot, G. (Dir.). (1995). *Le vieillissement démographique dans l'Union Européenne à l'horizon 2050. Étude d'impact du viellissement démographique*. Directorate-General Employment and Social Affairs, European Commission, Brussels.

Coleman, D. A. (1992). Does Europe need immigrants? Population and work force projections. *International Migration Review, 26*(2), 413–461.

Coleman, D. A. (2004). Europe at the cross-roads – Must Europe's population and workforce depend on new migration? In V. Ionsev (Ed.), *International migration: ICPD+10, scientific series "International migration of population: Russia and contemporary world"* (Vol. 12, pp. 19–33). Moscow: Max Press.

D'Addio, A. C., Keese, M., & Whitehouse, E. (2010). Population ageing and labour markets. *Oxford Review of Economic Policy, 26*(4), 613–635.

European Commission. (1997). Franco & Munzi (1996). Ageing and fiscal policies in the European union. In Franco & Munzi (Eds.), *European economy, no. 3, the welfare state in Europe – challenges and reforms* (pp. 239–388). Luxembourg: OPOCE.

European Commission. (2006). *The demographic future of Europe. From challenge to opportunity*. Luxembourg: Office for Official Publications of the European Communities.

European Commission. (2009). *Demography report 2008: Meeting social needs in an ageing society*. Commission Staff Working Document, D.G. for Employment, Social Affairs and Equal Opportunities, E.1 unit. Luxembourg: Office for Official Publications of the European Communities.

Feld, S. (2000). Active population growth and immigration hypotheses in Western Europe. *European Journal of Population, 16*, 3–40.

Fotakis, C. (2000, October 16–18). Demographic ageing, employment growth and pensions sustainability in the EU: The option of Migration. *Expert group meeting on policy responses to population ageing and population decline*. New York: United Nations.

Fotakis, C., Gil-Alonso, F., et al. (2002). Le marché européen de l'emploi sous l'angle de l'évolution démographique. In F. Gendreau, D. Tabutin, & M. Poupard (Eds.), *Jeunesses, vieillesses, démographies et sociétés* (pp. 43–60). Louvain-la-Neuve/Paris: Académia – Bruylant/L'Harmattan.

Franco, D., & Munzi, T. (1996). Public pension expenditure prospects in the European Union: A survey of national projections. In *European economy – Ageing and pension expenditure prospects in the Western World* (pp. 1–126). Brussels: Directorate-General for Economic and Financial Affairs of the European Commission.

Gaymu, J., Ekamper, P., & Beets, G. (2007). Qui prendra en charge les Européens âgés dépendants en 2030? *Population, 62*(4), 789–822.

Gil-Alonso, F. (2005, July 18–23). *Building a simplified model to assess the impact of population ageing, employment trends and immigration levels on pension sustainability in the EU-25 Member States.* Presented at the IUSSP international population conference 2005, Tours.

Gil-Alonso, F. (2009). Can the rising pension burden in Europe be mitigated by immigration? Modelling the effects of selected demographic and socio-economic factors on ageing in the European Union, 2008–2050. In D. Coleman & D. Ediev (Eds.), *Vienna Yearbook of Population Research, special issue on: Impact of migration on demographic change and composition in Europe* (pp. 123–147). Vienna: Austrian Academy of Sciences.

Gil-Alonso, F. & Math, A. (2000). *Pension sustainability, ageing and labour supply* (Internal Working Paper No. 2). Brussels: DG Employment and Social Affairs, European Commission.

Heijdra, B. J., & Romp, W. E. (2009). Retirement, pensions and ageing. *Journal of Public Economics, 93*(3–4), 586–604.

Lee, R. D., Mason, A., & Miller, T. (2001). Saving, wealth, and population. In N. Birdsall, A. C. Kelley, & S. W. Sinding (Eds.), *Population does matter: Demography, poverty, and economic growth* (pp. 137–164). Oxford: Oxford University Press.

Lesthaeghe, R. (2002). Europe's demographic issues: Fertility, household formation and replacement migration. *Population Bulletin of the United Nations. Special issue. Policy responses to population ageing and decline* (Vols. 44–45, pp. 385–423).

Lutz, W., & Scherbov, S. (2005). Will population ageing necessarily lead to an increase in the number of persons with disabilities? Alternative scenarios for the European Union. In W. Lutz & G. Feichtinger (Eds.), *Vienna Yearbook of Population Research* (pp. 219–234). Vienna: Publishing House of the Austrian Academy of Sciences.

Lutz, W., Sanderson, W. C., & Scherbov, S. (Eds.). (2004). *The end of world population growth in the 21st century. New challenges for human capital formation and sustainable development.* London/Sterling: IIASA/Earthscan.

Mason, A. (2005, August 31–September 2). *Demographic transition and demographic dividends in developed and developing countries.* Presented at the United Nations expert group meeting on social and economic implications of changing population age structures, Mexico.

Meier, V., & Werding, M. (2010). Ageing and the welfare state: Securing sustainability. *Oxford Review of Economic Policy, 26*(4), 655–673.

Murphy, M., Martikainen, P., & Pennec, S. (2006). Demographic change and the supply of potential family supporters in Britain, Finland and France in the period 1911–2050. *European Journal of Population, 22–3*, 219–240.

OECD. (2006). *Live longer, work longer.* Paris: OECD Publishing.

OECD. (2007a). *Ageing and the public service. Human resource challenges.* Paris: OECD Publishing.

OECD. (2007b). *OECD pensions at a glance 2007. Public policies across OECD countries.* Paris: OECD Publishing.

OECD. (2009a). *OECD private pensions outlook 2008.* Paris: OECD Publishing. http://www.oecd.org/daf/pensions/outlook

OECD. (2009b). *OECD pensions at a glance 2009. Retirement-income systems in OECD countries.* Paris: OECD Publishing.

OECD. (2011). *Pensions at a glance 2011. Retirement-income systems in OECD countries and G20 countries.* Paris: OECD Publishing. www.oecd.org/els/social/pensions/PAG

Prskawetz, A., Skirbekk, V., & Lindh, T. (2005). Demographic debate: Will population ageing decrease productivity? In: *Vienna Yearbook of Population Research* (Supplement to Vol. 34, pp. 1–15).

Prskawetz, A., Bloom, D. E., & Lutz, W. (Eds.). (2008). *Population aging, human capital accumulation, and productivity growth. Population and development review* (Supplement to Vol. 34). New York: Population Council.

Skirbekk, V. (2004). Age and individual productivity: A literature survey. In G. Feichtinger (Ed.), *Vienna Yearbook of Population Research* (Vol. 2, pp. 133–154). Vienna: Austrian Academy of Sciences.

United Nations. (2001). *Replacement migration. Is it a solution to declining and ageing populations?* New York: UN Population Division, Department of Economic and Social Affairs.

Whitehouse, E. (2007). *Pension panorama. Retirement – Income systems in 53 countries.* Washington, DC: The World Bank.

Zaidi, A. (2011). Population ageing and financial and social sustainability challenges of pension systems in Europe: A cross-national perspective. In L. Bovenberg, C. van Ewijk, & E. Westerhout (Eds.), *The future of multi-pillar pensions*. Cambridge: Cambridge University Press.

Chapter 3
Quebec's Public Finances Between Demographic Changes and Fiscal Sustainability

Luc Godbout, Suzie St-Cerny, Pier-André Bouchard St-Amant, and Pierre Fortin

3.1 Background

In this chapter, we assess the fiscal sustainability of Quebec's provincial government budget over the 46-year horizon 2010–2056 in light of expected major demographic and economic changes.[1] Broadly speaking, fiscal sustainability requires that the public debt does not ultimately grow faster than the economy – in other words, that the ratio between the two does not follow an explosive path. Our assessment therefore involves projecting the government's debt-to-GDP ratio over the long term based on assumptions about current programme spending commitments and tax-transfer rules, given demographic and economic trends. This allows us to calculate to what extent the current fiscal structure of Quebec's provincial government is in fact sustainable.

One can think of two reasons why running this kind of exercise is particularly important for a Canadian province such as Quebec. First, Quebec's population is ageing rapidly. While the 65-and-over population will have taken 50 years or more to rise from 12% to 24% of total population in most of Europe, the United States, and Australia, the current projection is that it will take just over 30 years for Quebec to get through this passage.[2] If so, this will be the third fastest transition among advanced societies, Korea (17 years) and Japan (22 years) being in the lead.

[1] Quebec is the second largest of the ten Canadian provinces. In 2009, its population was 7.8 million (23.2% of the Canadian total), and its GDP was C$304 billion (20% of the Canadian total).

[2] Based on data from OECD (2011) and ISQ (2009).

L. Godbout (✉) • S. St-Cerny • P.-A. Bouchard St-Amant
Taxation and Public Finance, Université de Sherbrooke, Campus de Longueuil, 150, Place Charles-Lemoyne, bureau 200, Longueuil, QC J4K 0A8, Canada
e-mail: luc.godbout@usherbrooke.ca; suzie.st-cerny@usherbrooke.ca; pabsta@pabsta.qc.ca

P. Fortin
Département des sciences économiques, Université du Québec à Montréal, Case postale 8888, succursale Centre-ville, Montréal, QC H3C 3P8, Canada
e-mail: fortin.pierre@uqam.ca

G. De Santis (ed.), *The Family, the Market or the State?: Intergenerational Support Under Pressure in Ageing Societies*, International Studies in Population 10,
DOI 10.1007/978-94-007-4339-7_3,

Second, Canada provinces have full jurisdiction over health care and education. Consequently, provincial budgets are large[3] and age-sensitive: their long-term sustainability is a key current concern.

We find that the current fiscal structure of Quebec's provincial government is indeed unsustainable. This is by no means a prediction that its debt-to-GDP ratio will actually follow an explosive path over time. It is an indication that, if the assumed demographic and economic trends make sense, there is an inherent long-term disequilibrium in the current fiscal structure that ought to be corrected through changes in programme commitments and/or tax-transfer rules in the not-too-distant future if the debt situation is not to get out of control. Our projection implies that it would take a permanent increase of tax revenues amounting to 2.2% of GDP for the present discounted value of primary deficits generated by demographic-economic change over the 45-year horizon to be nullified and, hence, for intergenerational equity to be restored.

We proceed as follows. Section 3.2 mentions some relevant theoretical and empirical developments in the literature. Section 3.3 describes the demographic, economic, and budgetary assumptions on which our analysis of sustainability is based. Section 3.4 presents the resulting projection of the government's revenues, expenditures, and budget deficits over the 2010–2056 horizon, as well as implications for fiscal sustainability and intergenerational equity. Section 3.5 indicates how sensitive our projection is to changes in key demographic and economic assumptions. Section 3.6 explores the impact of an alternative scenario where health expenditure shifts with life expectancy due to the high cost of end-of-life health care. Section 3.7 concludes.

3.2 Literature

Blanchard et al. (1990) define fiscal sustainability as 'essentially about whether, based on the policy currently on the books, a government is headed towards excessive debt accumulation'. In what follows, we will take the fiscal structure to be sustainable if its programme spending commitments and tax-transfer rules do not lead to sustained growth in the debt-to-GDP ratio over the long-term horizon of 45 years that we consider.

Blanchard et al. (1990) show that under general conditions, a necessary condition for sustainability over the long term is that the present discounted value of current and future primary budget surpluses be large enough to repay the current outstanding level of the public debt. They go on to define the 'sustainable tax rate'

[3] In 2008, federal government spending amounted to 27% of total public sector expenditure in Quebec. The rest was shared among provincial government ministries and agencies (56%) and local governments (17%). In turn, local governments are under the authority of the provincial government.

as that tax-to-GDP ratio which, if constant, would achieve an unchanged debt-to-GDP ratio over the relevant horizon, given the assumed fiscal structure and projected demographic and economic trends. Their approach to fiscal sustainability has been very influential. It is currently put into practice by the Congressional Budget Office (2011) in the United States, the Office for Budget Responsibility (2011) in the United Kingdom, and the Parliamentary Budget Office (2011) in Canada, among other fiscal agencies.[4]

Our definition of fiscal sustainability follows Blanchard et al. (1990), but we take a slightly different approach to maintaining sustainability (and restoring intergenerational equity). We determine the constant amount by which the tax-to-GDP ratio would have to be raised from 2010 to 2056 to offset the present discounted value of current and future primary budget deficits generated by our assumptions over this period. The additional tax revenues would initially be set aside in a 'demographic fund', would accumulate with interest over a certain period, and would later be disbursed as needed so as to restore budget balance.

3.3 Demographic, Economic, and Budgetary Assumptions

We begin our quantitative assessment of the consequences of the demographic transition on Quebec's budget by setting out our demographic, economic, and budgetary assumptions. In Sect. 3.4, these will be fed into our projection model of government revenues and expenditures from 2010 to 2056, which will allow fiscal sustainability to be judged.

3.3.1 Demographic Assumptions

In a previous paper (Godbout et al. 2007), we provided an assessment of the consequences of the demographic transition on Quebec's public finances over the next 50 years. Two main results stood out: (1) health will consume an ever-increasing share of public spending, and (2) budget deficits will appear in 2013 and grow continuously until 2051.

After that, the Statistical Institute of Quebec published a new demographic reference scenario projecting the population until 2056 (ISQ 2009). Instead of projecting an absolute decline in the population beginning in 2031 as in the

[4] Although it has broad intergenerational consequences, the approach of Blanchard et al. (1990) is mainly concerned with fiscal sustainability in a macroeconomic sense. It differs from Kotlikoff's (1992) generational accounting framework, which proposes a cohort-by-cohort microeconomic analysis of tax payments and transfer receipts over the life cycle.

Table 3.1 Quebec's population by age group. Real data for 1971 and ISQ reference scenario for 2010 and 2056

				Variations			
				1971–2010		2010–2056	
Age group	1971	2010	2056	Abs	%	Abs	%
0–14	1,799,614	1,233,555	1,334,798	−566,059	−31.5	101,243	8.2
15–64	3,919,243	5,436,459	5,294,848	1,517,216	38.7	−141,611	−2.6
65+	418,448	1,210,910	2,583,179	792,462	189.4	1,372,269	113.3
Total	6,137,305	7,880,924	9,212,825	1,743,619	28.4	1,331,901	16.9

Sources: ISQ (2009) and Statistics Canada (2011), Table 051-0001

previous exercise (ISQ 2003), the new scenario suggests that the population will continue to grow until 2056, due to increases in assumed fertility, net migration, and life expectancy. As reported in Table 3.1, Quebec's population is now expected to grow from 7.9 million in 2010 to 9.2 million people in 2056, instead of declining to 7.8 million by 2051 as in the earlier projection.

A closer look at Table 3.1 reveals that the population increase will be concentrated in the 65-and-over age group. The latter is projected to rise from 1.2 to 2.6 million people between 2010 and 2056, that is, from 15% to almost 28% of the total population. Conversely, the size of the 0–64 population is set to remain almost unchanged.

The 15–64 adult population, which had always increased in previous decades (from 3.9 million in 1971 to 5.4 million in 2010), is now projected to decline somewhat in the next 46 years. Since this group is the main contributor to the labour force and economic activity, its shrinking in absolute and relative terms will not be without consequences on economic growth and government revenues. This trend in Quebec will likely be unique in North America. While the ISQ reference scenario sets the 15–64 population to decline by 3.3% between 2010 and 2030, the same age group is projected to increase by 5.6% in the other Canadian provinces and by 10% in the United States, in the same period.[5] As a result of this ISQ scenario, Quebec's old-age dependency ratio (P_{65+}/P_{15-64}) would increase by 20 percentage points over the next two decades (to 42.4% in 2030 from 22.3% in 2010). It would turn out to be the largest increase in the dependency ratio among the G7 countries, for which the second largest increase projected by the United Nations (UN 2008) would be 17.7 points in Japan. The Quebec situation is compounded by the fact that Quebec workers retire earlier than other North Americans: in 2007, the average retirement age was 59.9 years in Quebec, 61.6 years in Canada, and 64 years in the United States.[6]

[5] Sources: Statistics Canada (2011), Table 052-0004; US Census Bureau, Population Division.

[6] Sources: Statistics Canada (2011), Table 282-0051, ISQ and OECD.

Table 3.2 Change in the components of economic growth, Quebec 1981–2008 (annual rates of growth)

(1)	Population	0.75
(2)	Employment rate	0.29
(3)	Labor productivity	0.96
(4) = (1 + 2 + 3)	Real GDP	2.00

Source: Statistics Canada (2011) and author's calculations

3.3.2 Economic Assumptions

In the last quarter of a century (from 1981 to 2008), net of inflation, the real annual economic growth in Quebec averaged 2.0% (Table 3.2). This growth is attributable in almost equal measure to, on the one hand, the change in hours worked arising from the juxtaposition of population growth and the rise in employment rates[7] and, on the other, the change in productivity per hour worked.

Since the change in the population aged 15–64 (pool of potential workers), the employment rate, and productivity are the three factors that determine the rate of economic growth, assumptions on how they change over time are fundamental.

3.3.2.1 Population

In this analysis, we use as a reference demographic scenario the one provided by the Statistical Institute of Quebec (ISQ 2009: 20). Here are its most important assumptions:

(a) Life expectancy will reach 85.5 years for men and 89.0 years for women in 2051.
(b) The total fertility rate will be of 1.65 as of 2013 (and constant afterwards).
(c) There will be a net migration of 30,000 people as of 2015 (and constant afterwards).

While economic growth in the past quarter century was boosted by a marked increase in the population aged 15–64, the reference demographic scenario points instead to a decline in this age group, both in the first part of the projection (between 2010 and 2030) and in the second part (between 2030 and 2050).

3.3.2.2 Productivity

The annual growth rate of labour productivity (per hour worked) in Quebec was 0.96% on average from 1981 to 2008, while the average between 2000 and 2008 amounts to 1%. In our baseline scenario, we will make it grow linearly from 1% to 1.5% in 2031, at which point the annual rate increase will remain constant.

[7] The employment rate is defined here as the total number of hours worked in a year, per capita.

Table 3.3 Assumptions about employment rates by sex and age group, Quebec, 2005 and 2031

	2005		2031 and on	
Age group	Men	Woman	Men	Woman
15–19	40.0	44.4	46.0	46.0
20–24	70.1	72.6	73.0	73.0
25–29	81.5	74.9	85.0	82.0
30–34	83.7	77.9	90.0	86.0
35–39	84.1	76.2	90.0	86.0
40–44	84.3	77.7	90.0	86.0
45–49	85.7	78.1	90.0	86.0
50–54	81.1	71.4	86.0	82.0
55–59	67.6	48.6	75.0	65.0
60–64	43.5	26.1	55.0	45.0
65–69	16.0	9.2	28.0	17.0
70–79	5.1	2.0	9.0	4.0
80+	0.0	0.0	0.0	0.0
		2006	*2036*	*2056*
Global employment rate		59.3	55.3	53.7

Sources: Table 282-0002 (Statistics Canada 2011), ISQ (2009) and author's computations

A large literature has explored possible feedbacks from demographic change to productivity but so far remains inconclusive at the macroeconomic level (e.g. Feyrer 2007). This is why we have chosen to treat productivity growth as an exogenous factor, unreactive to demographic change.

3.3.2.3 Employment Rate

Turning to the labour market, the employment rates of almost all age groups have risen since the 1970s. It seems plausible that in most cases, they will continue to rise since Quebec might be catching up with its neighbouring economies and, notably, Ontario.

Based on a detailed analysis of rates by age group and sex, we assume that our employment rates will rise linearly over a period of 25 years to reach those of Ontario and will remain constant afterwards. This is not unreasonable; for example, the employment rates among older women have made an amazing leap in the last 25 years, and, in 2009, women aged between 25 and 44 had an employment rate of 80% whereas only 20 years ago it was less than two-thirds.

Table 3.3 describes these assumptions. The bottom line indicates the overall (weighted) employment rate for the population aged 15 or over. It can be seen that, despite increases in the employment rate for each age category, the ageing of the population will nonetheless reduce the employment rate for the total population because the effect of the increase in the population aged 65 or over, whose employment rates are low or zero, is dominant.

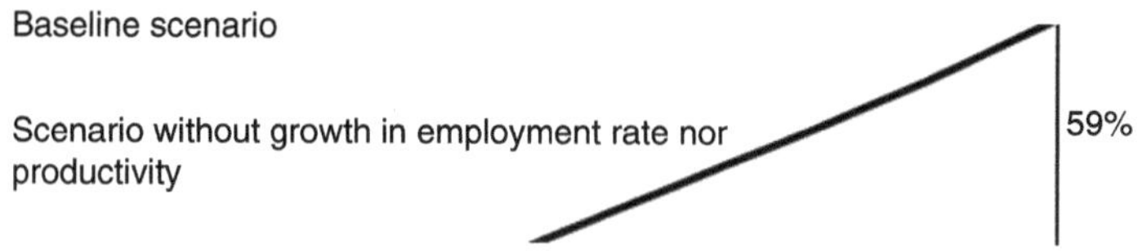

Fig. 3.1 Index of real GDP with or without improvement in employment and productivity growth rates, 2006 index = 100 (Source: Author's calculations)

3.3.2.4 Inflation

Since the 1990s, the Bank of Canada's inflation target has been 2%. This target will be revised in 2011, but we do not anticipate any change to a policy that has been in effect for 15 years now. This target will be used as part of our projections.

To illustrate the expected impact of our assumptions, Fig. 3.1 shows the possible evolution of the real GDP, both in the baseline scenario and in an alternative scenario that holds employment rates and productivity growth rates constant. This shows the sensitivity of our economic assumptions: without any improvement in them, the real GDP would be 59% lower in 2056.

3.3.3 Budgetary Assumptions

3.3.3.1 Health

Each year, the Canadian Institute for Health Information (CIHI 2009) publishes data on average per capita health spending by age group, which, not surprisingly, increased with age both in 2007 (Table 3.4) and in previous years (not shown here). With the traditional projection method of health expenses, population ageing, with its increase in the relative weight of older age groups, has an upward effect on health spending.[8] The projection of public health spending applies the foreseen demographic structure to per capita spending by age and sex as observed in the recent past. It then submits the result to an annual rate of increase in real per capita spending, which is of 1.7% in this case. This projected increase attempts to incorporate both technological advances and growth in demand.

3.3.3.2 Education and Childcare Services

The method used to project education and childcare services expenditures is similar to the one used for health expenditures. The foreseen young population is applied to

[8] Section 3.6, however, will also consider an alternative approach, by which health expenses depend instead on how close to death each person is.

Table 3.4 Per capita health spending by the Quebec government by age group and sex, 2007 (Canadian dollars)

Age group	Total	Woman	Men
<1	5,771	5,380	6,143
1–4	1,019	986	1,050
5–9	944	905	981
10–14	813	806	819
15–19	988	1,067	912
20–24	1,246	1,468	1,034
25–29	1,359	1,718	1,014
30–34	1,314	1,709	940
35–39	1,460	1,632	1,295
40–44	1,509	1,546	1,473
45–49	1,678	1,705	1,650
50–54	2,062	2,024	2,100
55–59	2,620	2,465	2,781
60–64	3,131	2,925	3,348
65–69	4,880	4,593	5,189
70–74	7,454	7,139	7,822
75–79	10,659	10,401	10,998
80–84	13,552	13,726	13,269
85–89	24,148	25,516	21,244
90+	23,207	23,085	23,613
All ages	*2,840*	*3,142*	*2,533*

Source: CIHI (2009)

recently recorded spending per child, per pupil, and per student, and the result is increased by an estimate of the annual growth in real per capita spending that varies with the group.

3.3.3.3 Other Spending

Under our projection, other budgetary expenditures rise at the same pace as the nominal GDP.

3.3.3.4 Debt

The Quebec government debt contracted to acquire assets (fixed assets, investments in government corporations, etc.) is the primary debt. Between 1998 and 2005, an annual average of about 1% of GDP was devoted to such acquisitions of assets. This rate of increase of the debt is maintained, in our assumptions, until 2056. We assume an average annual interest rate of 6.3%.

3.3.3.5 Pension Plans

The net taxation of pension plans is the balance of taxes levied on withdrawals from registered retirement savings plans (RRSP) and registered pension plans (RPP) less tax deductions granted on contributions to these plans. The analysis takes explicit account of the fact that the ageing population increases withdrawals faster than contributions, thereby enhancing the yield of income tax. These effects are calculated in the same way as health-care expenses. We project expenses by age, to find out the average net contribution/deduction by age. We then assume that this distribution by age is stationary over time.

3.3.3.6 Own-Source Revenue and Federal Transfers

Except for the tax treatment of retirement plans, we assume that the government's own-source revenues (taxes, fees, and revenues of government corporations) and federal transfers are proportional to nominal GDP. This implies that own-source revenues and federal transfers grow at the same rate as nominal GDP. We assume that the feedback of the changing age structure of taxpayers on tax revenue is negligible. Indeed, a few simulation tests of this assumption, which we based on Quebec tax statistics for the year 2008 (Finances Quebec 2010), suggest that it is consistent with the current tax structure.

The demographic transition is taken into account in the projection of economic growth and the budgetary balance. We keep government revenue constant in proportion to GDP, but we allow spending to increase because of the changes in the age structure of the population. In this way, we can assess whether the budgetary sustainability of public finances will be maintained in time and whether intergenerational equity will be safeguarded. A lack of budgetary sustainability would mean either of the following:

(a) That future generations will be in deficit, if they want to have the same public services at a comparable level of taxation
(b) That to keep the budget balanced, they will have to accept fewer public services for a comparable level of taxation
(c) That they will have to increase taxation to maintain the same public services

3.4 Projection Results and Implications

Based on the economic and budgetary assumptions described above, Table 3.5 shows our baseline scenario and makes it possible to assess the budgetary sustainability of public finances.

Our assumptions lean towards optimism on the revenues side, while they are unclear on the expenses side. Productivity growth gradually accelerates, and employment rates rise for all age categories. Health-related spending increases more slowly than during the period 1997–2010, expenditures in education and childcare services rise at a slower pace than GDP, and other current spending remains stable as a percentage of GDP.

Table 3.5 Quebec's budget in our baseline scenario (millions of Canadian dollars, unless otherwise indicated)

	2016	2026	2036	2046	2056	*g*
Revenues						
Autonomous revenues (excl. retirement plans)	74,068	105,551	152,639	216,516	305,215	3.6
Tax from retirement plans	363	1,723	3,288	5,445	8,180	–
Federal transfers	16,821	23,971	34,666	49,172	69,317	3.6
Total revenues	*91,252*	*131,245*	*190,593*	*271,133*	*382,712*	3.6
Expenses						
Health care	39,057	68,004	115,595	181,705	268,032	4.9
Education	15,644	20,915	27,604	36,144	48,227	2.9
Kindergarten services	2,200	2,625	3,051	3,936	4,753	1.9
Interest on debt	9,869	13,073	17,703	24,317	33,641	3.1
Other expenses	27,281	38,877	56,220	79,747	112,417	3.6
Total expenses	*94,051*	*143,494*	*220,174*	*325,849*	*467,070*	4.1
Budget balance	*(2,799)*	*(12,248)*	*(29,581)*	*(54,717)*	*(84,358)*	
GDP	417,350	594,748	860,079	1,220,004	1,719,802	3.6
Deficit/GDP (%)	0.7	2.1	3.4	4.5	4.9	

Source: Author's calculations

g Average yearly growth rate, 2016–2056

Note 1: The debt service shown here is the service on the primary debt. It is equal to the interest expense on debt incurred to acquire assets (fixed assets, investments in government corporations, etc.) only. This excludes interest payable on the debt that would accumulate because of forecast chronic deficits if the baseline scenario were to materialise

Note 2: In accordance with the definition of service on the primary debt, the budgetary balance shown here is the primary budgetary balance. It does not include interest payable on the debt that would accumulate because of forecast chronic deficits if the baseline scenario were to materialise

Note 3: Traditionally, public finance data are presented in current rather than constant dollars. The authors opted for this presentation. Obviously, the ratios, such as the deficit/GDP, remain the same as the data are presented in current or constant dollars. The same result would occur for health spending. In current dollars, health expenditures in 2056 represent 15.6% of GDP ($ 268,032/$ 1,719,802). In constant dollars, health expenditures in 2056 represent 15.6% of GDP ($ 97,628/$ 626,426)

Nonetheless, on the whole, economic growth slows markedly. Real GDP growth (nominal economic growth minus inflation, 2% per year in this scenario) averages 1.6% from 2010 to 2056, compared with an annual average of 2.0% from 1981 to 2008.

This expected slowdown in economic growth combined with the pressures of demographic change and the growth rate of expenses undermines budgetary sustainability. In particular, the growth in health spending fuels the overall growth in public spending at a faster pace than economic growth.

The second feature of the projection is that it shows a rapid accumulation of ever larger deficits over time. These deficits reach 4.9% of GDP in 2056. Furthermore, it should be noted that the primary budgetary balance shown in Table 3.5 voluntarily excludes interest payable on debt that would accumulate as a result of the forecast chronic deficits if the baseline scenario were to materialise. Indeed, the debt service shown in the table represents only the interest expense on the debt contracted to acquire assets. But, ultimately, what matters is the debt-GDP ratio. Thus, the current budgetary policy could not be maintained indefinitely. Inevitably, changes in budgetary orientations, consisting of tax increases or spending cuts or both, would be needed to avoid a continual increase in debt as a percentage of GDP.

3.4.1 Intergenerational Equity

The analysis of budgetary sustainability makes it possible to introduce the notion of intergenerational equity. For the analysis of intergenerational equity, it should be noted that the present value of the forecast budget deficits from 2010 to 2056, under the assumptions of our baseline scenario, would amount to $193.5 billion.

Obviously, there has been no reserve set up to provide for this amount. On this basis, to restore intergenerational equity, the approach is to determine the amount by which taxes and fees would have to be raised by a constant and uniform percentage from now until 2056. These new tax revenues would be set aside in a fund to accumulate with interest over a certain time and then spent at a later date for the benefit of future generations. Accordingly, what would be needed is to set up a 'demographic fund' whose disbursement terms would depend on pre-established demographic parameters.

From 2010 to 2056, the increase in tax revenues required by this approach would be equal to 2.2% of GDP. This is a considerable amount.

3.5 Sensitivity Analysis

Based on the demographic scenarios of the ISQ, five determinants of the sustainability of public finances relating to the demographic transition will be studied. They are the change in population in connection with fertility, net migration and life expectancy, employment, and productivity rates. We will go over the assumptions made regarding each of these determinants one at a time so as to measure budgetary sensitivity to these assumptions.

3.5.1 Fertility

Higher fertility affects total population projections. For instance, using a total fertility rate (TFR) of 1.85 children per woman, rather than 1.65 as used in the ISQ reference scenario, the population would rise from 9.2 million to 9.8 million in 2056. From now to 2031, this increased fertility would raise the number of births per year by roughly 10,000.

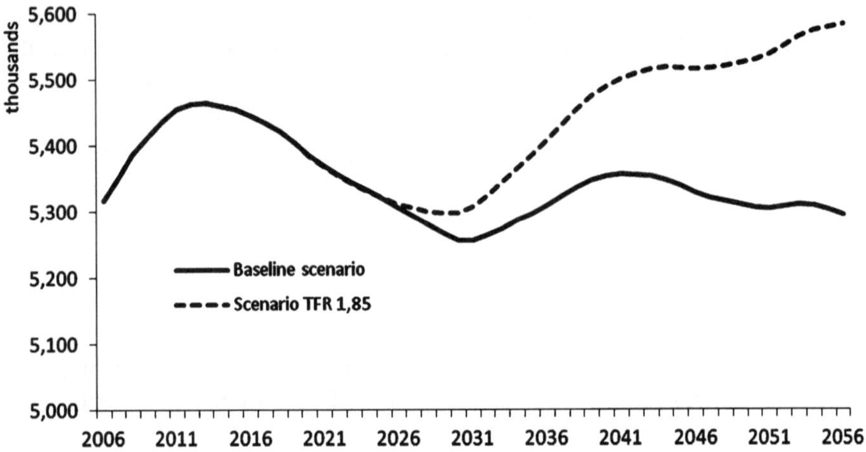

Fig. 3.2 Effect of higher fertility on the pool of workers, Quebec, 2006–2056 (Source: Author's calculations)

Greater fertility does not have an immediate positive effect on public finances. Initially, it even has the opposite effect: it increases pressure on spending, particularly for public childcare and education. The impact thus takes longer to be felt on revenues, which flow through the economy. Ultimately, the impact will be experienced through an increase in the pool of potential workers (population age 15–64). Figure 3.2 shows that using a TFR of 1.85 instead of 1.65 would gradually increase the population age 15–64 years starting in the mid-2020s, eventually offsetting the decrease of this population group that emerges from the baseline scenario.

3.5.2 Net Migration

A change in net migration also has an effect on the projections of population of working age. The effect of net migration on the expected change in the pool of potential workers is important. Figure 3.3 shows the effect on the pool of potential workers in this scenario (no net migration) as compared with the baseline (a yearly influx of 30,000 people). If net migration were zero rather than 30,000 people per year, the number of adults would drop to 3.9 million in 2056 rather than stay at 5.3 million.

3.5.3 Life Expectancy

The third main assumption of the ISQ reference demographic scenario concerns life expectancy. The ISQ assumes that life expectancy will improve to 85.5 years for men and 89.0 years for women in 2051. Figure 3.4 illustrates the effect of this

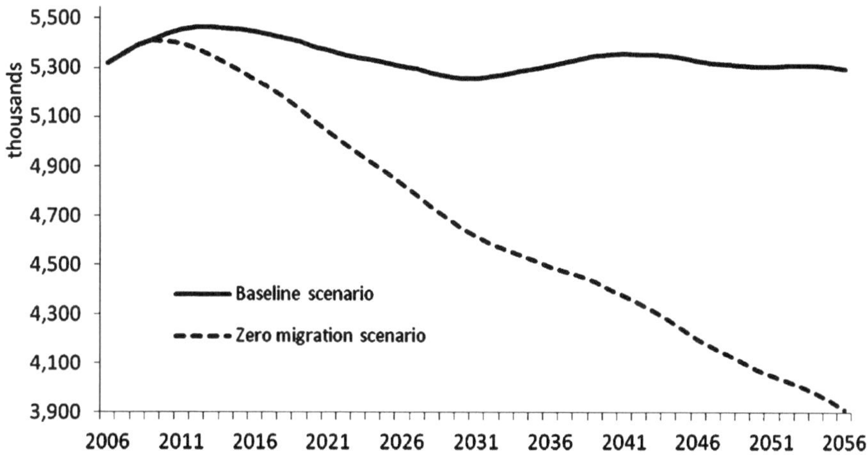

Fig. 3.3 Effect of migration on the pool of potential workers, Quebec, 2006–2056 (Source: Author's calculations)

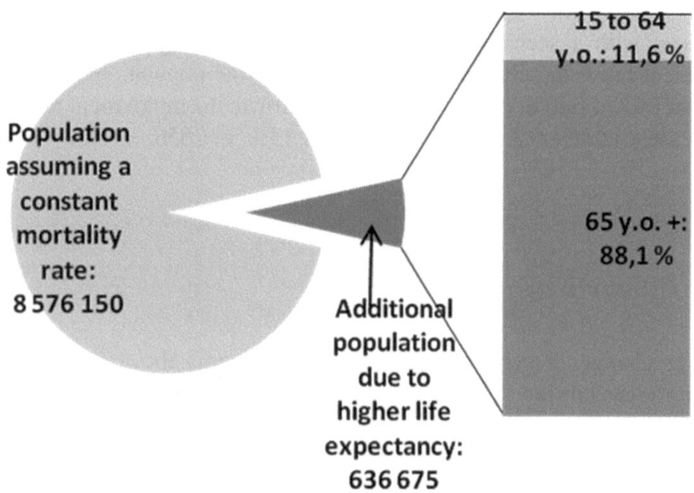

Fig. 3.4 Distribution of the additional population arising from the expected improvement in life expectancy compared to holding life expectancy constant, Quebec, 2056 (Source: Author's calculations)

assumption on Quebec's population by comparing the results with the baseline (constant life expectancy). The lengthening of life expectancy increases population projections by 637,000 people in 2056, but these are primarily the elderly: 88% of this difference would be due to people aged 65 and over.

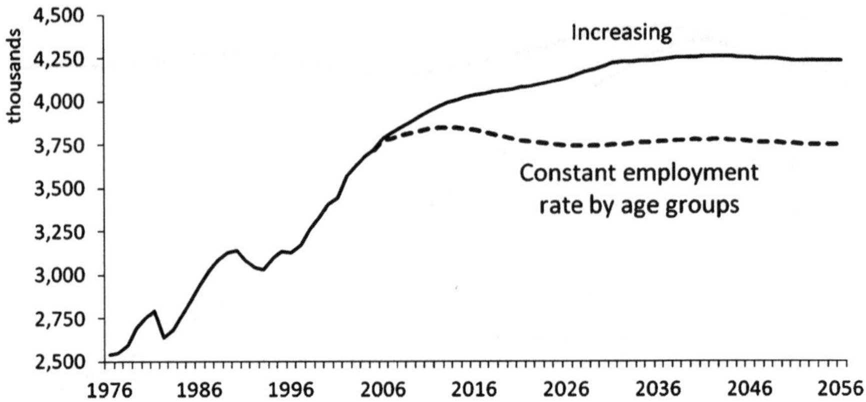

Fig. 3.5 Employed persons in Quebec, in two scenarios (1976–2056) (Source: Author's calculations)

3.5.4 Employment Rates

Figure 3.5 shows the effect of the assumption of a rise in employment rates in comparison with a scenario where they remain unchanged. Without growth in employment rates, the change in the structure of the population would cause the number of jobs to start declining in 2014. The growth in employment rates increases the forecasted number of jobs by 483,000, or 13%, in 2056.

3.5.5 Productivity

The other change in economic assumptions concerns the improvement of the productivity growth rate. Figure 3.6 shows the change in real GDP per job when the productivity growth rate rises from 1.0% to 1.5% by 2031 and then remains constant rather than holding it steady at 1.0% for the entire period. This assumption of an improvement in productivity growth alone raises expected real GDP per job by 19% in 2056.

Obviously, the projection of the sustainability of public finances varies according to changes in economic and budgetary assumptions. The sensitivity analysis, summarised in Table 3.6, measures the effect of these changes.

A change in the assumption on fertility initially affects spending, in particular through increased public spending on education and childcare. Next, the increase in population of working age will have a positive effect on economic activity and government revenues. However, the effect on the ratio of deficit/GDP over the period extending until 2056 remains limited. The ratio would be 5.0% with a lower fertility and 4.7% with a higher fertility. Only in the longer term will the increasing

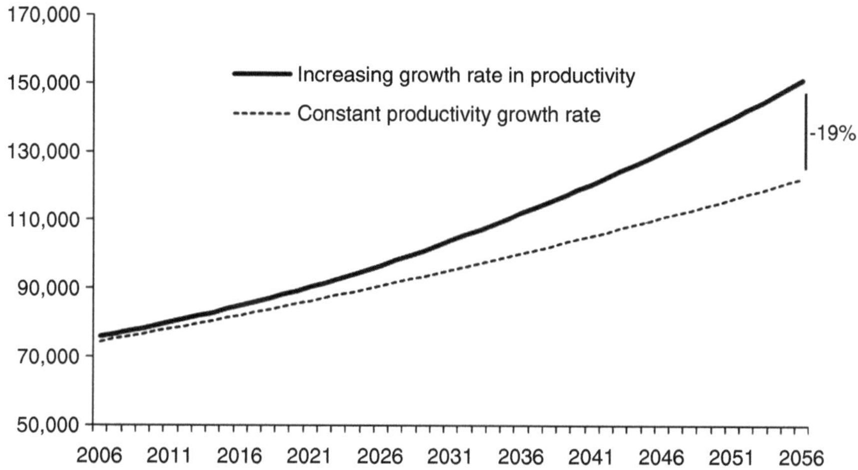

Fig. 3.6 Real GDP per employed, in two scenarios (Source: Author's calculations)

Table 3.6 Effects of changes in assumptions on the determinants of the sustainability of public finances – the budgetary balance as a proportion of GDP

Factor	Hypothesis	Deficit/GDP in 2056 (%)
Fertility	TFR: 1.65 (baseline)	−4.9
	TFR: 1.45	−5.0
	TFR: 1.85	−4.7
Net migration	30,000 (baseline)	−4.9
	15,000	−6.3
	45,000	−3.5
Life expectancy	Man 85.5 and woman 89.0 (baseline)	−4.9
	Constant life expectancy	−2.1
Interest rate	6.3% (baseline)	−4.9
	5.3–1% less	−4.6
	7.3–1% more	−5.2
Employment rate	Increasing employment rate (baseline)	−4.9
	Constant employment rate	−7.3
Productivity	Linear increase in the productivity growth rate from 1% to 1.5% in 2031 and constant afterwards (baseline)	−4.9
	Constant productivity growth rate	−9.1

Source: Author's calculations

effects of a higher birth rate on the number of people aged 15–64 have positive effects on budgetary sustainability.

Migration also has a significant effect on budgetary sustainability, particularly as regards economic activity and government revenue. The effect on the deficit as a proportion of GDP of moving from net migration of 30,000 people as in the ISQ reference scenario to 45,000 people would lead to a reduction in the deficit as a proportion of GDP from 4.9% to 3.5% by 2056.[9]

Improving life expectancy increases the projected deficit as a proportion of GDP in 2056 from 2.1% to 4.9%. A comparison with the effect of changes in fertility or net migration shows that the population component has the greatest influence on budgetary sustainability. The increased number of people age 65 or over has a direct effect on health spending.

A change in the assumption of 100 points (i.e. 1%) on interest rates would affect the baseline ratio of deficit/GDP of 4.9% by ±0.3%, thus ranging from −4.6% with a lower interest rate to −5.2% with a higher interest rate.

The effect of an improvement in employment rates is significant. The forecast deficit as a proportion of GDP of 4.9% in 2056 would be 7.3% without any increase in employment rates.

Budgetary sustainability is also sensitive to the assumption on productivity growth. The forecasted ratio of deficit/GDP of 4.9% in 2056 would be 9.1% without any improvement in the productivity growth rate.

3.6 Alternative Assumptions for Projection of Health Expenditures

The analysis has shown that improved life expectancy has a significant effect on budgetary sustainability, by increasing the deficit as a proportion of GDP in 2056 from 2.1% to 4.9%. According to our baseline scenario, the increased number of people aged 65 or over together with gains in life expectancy adds 0.6% to the average annual rate of increase of health spending (4.9% versus 4.3%).

In the Quebec government's budget, health spending accounted for more than 40% of total budgetary expenditure in 2010. However, under our baseline scenario, this proportion will increase to more than 57% in 2056. The assumptions used to project its growth are therefore crucial.

In a context where life expectancy rises, a simple proportional projection of health spending based on data by age and sex, which assumes a stationary distribution of health expenses, could lead to an overestimation of future health spending. Zweifel et al. (1999) and Serup-Hansen et al. (2002) have sought to clarify this issue. By breaking down health spending into 'ordinary' spending and spending at the end of life, they show that the size of morbidity expenditure is greater than expenditures by age group as such.

To compare our assumptions and the potential effects of increased life expectancy in the projection of health spending, we can consider an exploratory health

[9] The model applies the same employment and productivity rates for people joining the pool of potential workers regardless of their origin.

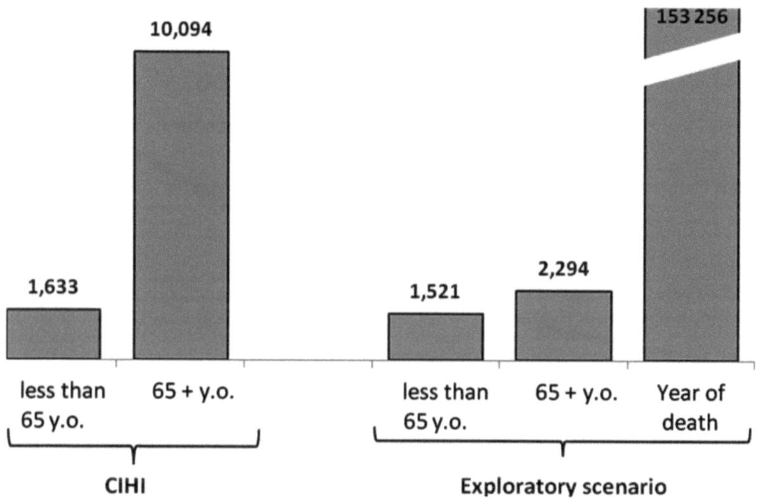

Fig. 3.7 Health-care costs at the beginning of projection (dollars) – exploratory health scenario (Sources: CIHI 2009; Pollock 2001, and author's calculations)

scenario based on the only Canadian study available (Pollock 2001), whose approach is similar to that of Zweifel et al. (1999). The analysis is based on the assumption that the link between increasing age and increasing health spending can at least in part be explained by the fact that health expenditures tend to be relatively small and distributed fairly evenly up to the final stages of life (last year or last 2 years), when spending rises substantially, regardless of the person's age. Since the probability of being in the last year of life increases with age, for the population as a whole health costs are higher at higher ages. But this tendency is lessened when life expectancy increases because these costs are deferred to a later time.

Using Canadian data, Pollock determines average costs by age according to sex of $362 and $430 for men and women under age 65 compared with $666 and $545 when they are 65 or over. For all ages, the cost of death was $29,181 for men and $50,956 for women.

To estimate the scope of this approach on our projection of health spending and its impact on budgetary sustainability, Pollock's costs by age and year of death were scaled so as to obtain the same overall cost of health in Quebec as given by the Canadian Institute for Health Information (CIHI). On this basis, Fig. 3.7 compares health costs by age and sex according to the CIHI data and our exploratory health scenario. Given the higher proportion of deaths among people age 65 or over, there was a sharp decrease in the cost, for those who are not in their last year of life, using the exploratory health method.

To test the effect of using either method of projecting health-care costs, the first step is to project health spending in a demographic framework leaving life expectancy unchanged. Figure 3.8 confirms that in the absence of improvement in life expectancy, health spending, whether using the baseline scenario

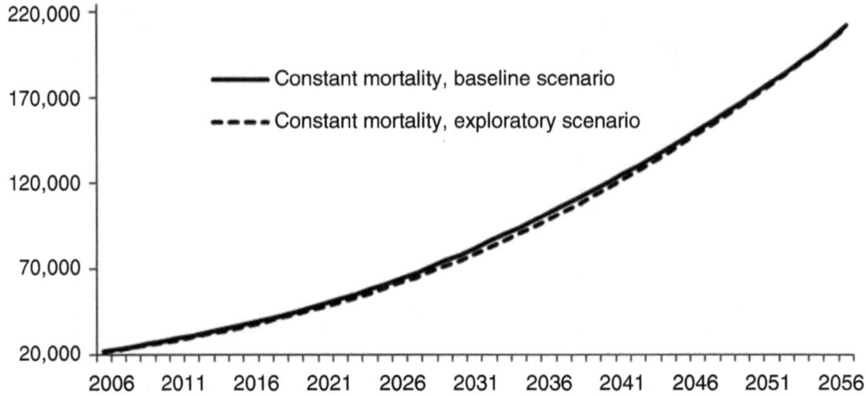

Fig. 3.8 Health spending according to the baseline scenario and the exploratory health scenario at constant mortality (Quebec, 2006–2056, million dollars) (Source: Author's calculations)

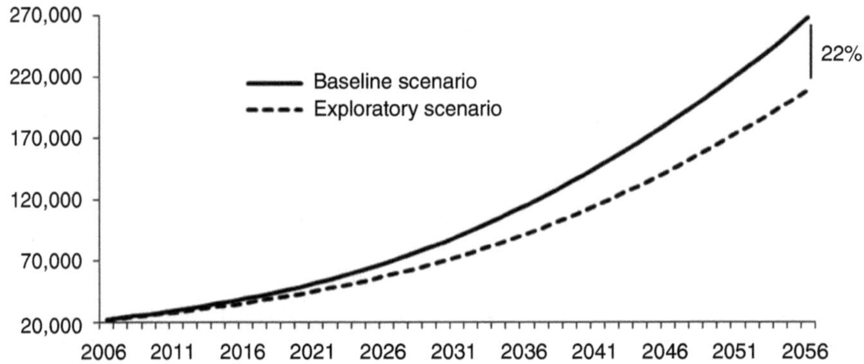

Fig. 3.9 Health spending according to the baseline scenario and the exploratory health scenario (millions of dollars) (Source: Author's calculations)

relying on CIHI data or those of the exploratory health scenario, follows the same trajectory until 2056.

By applying the exploratory health scenario to the reference demographic framework, where longer life expectancy is anticipated, predicted health spending is lower than with the baseline scenario (with CIHI data). In the baseline, costs increase as life expectancy lengthens because there are more elderly to care for. Figure 3.9 shows that growth in projected health spending differs depending on the scenario. In 2056, the difference reaches 22%. The average annual growth rate of health spending over the projection period would decline from 5.0% to 4.6% with the exploratory health scenario, and in 2056, the deficit/GDP ratio would drop to 1.4% instead of 4.9% in the baseline scenario (Fig. 3.10).

However, this figure fails to show that, by assumption, these expenses are not saved: merely deferred to after 2056. Thus, if the exploratory health scenario is a

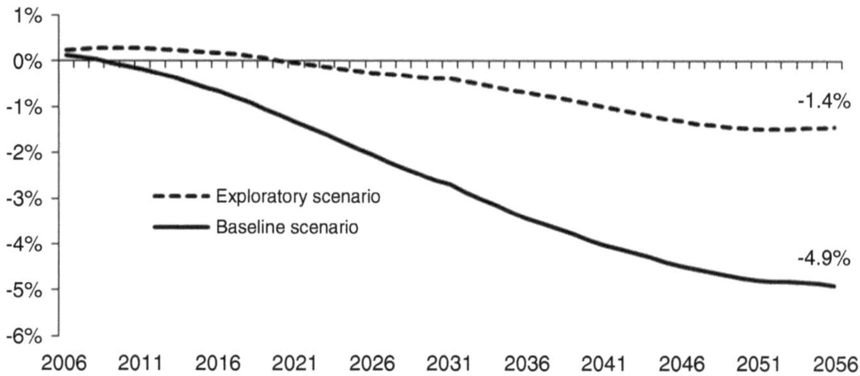

Fig. 3.10 Effect on the budgetary balance as a proportion of GDP of a change in the assumption on health costs (Source: Author's calculations)

better representation of how the expenses are made, the problem of budgetary sustainability needs to be evaluated over a longer period of time. Since these costs would be deferred beyond our projection horizon (2056), it is impossible for us to determine whether this alternative improves or worsens the financial sustainability of the government in the long run.

We note that choosing one method or the other is not without consequences on the determination of budgetary sustainability. The crucial difference lies therefore in the variations in spending due to longer life expectancy, combined with the demographic structure of the population. If life expectancy rises, per capita health costs calculated with CIHI data for elderly groups implicitly take into account current mortality rates, which are higher than in the future. For example, take those of age 75–79, where the number of deaths will decline by almost 9% from an estimate of nearly 8,100 in 2006 to <7,400 in 2056, even though the population of this age group will have risen from 225,000 to 446,000. Without the increase in life expectancy, the number of deaths would instead reach almost 15,000 in 2056.

Knowing the assumption of longer life expectancy projected in the ISQ population scenario, it is doubtless reasonable to indicate that the CIHI data overstate health spending over the projection period while the exploratory health method (Pollock) defers part of this spending to a later date.

Note, however, that the latter approach is not necessarily closer to reality than the standard one. Moreover, since Pollock's estimated results are only briefly presented in a government report, it is difficult to assess their robustness. Indeed, some scholars believe that this approach could result in overstating the expenses at the end of life (e.g. Hogan and Hogan 2002). Scitovsky (1994), for instance, estimates that end-of-life spending in the United States is 4–11 times higher than health spending unrelated to the final year. But, in some cases, the estimate of the exploratory health scenario becomes 100 times as high. In addition, in Europe and North America, Stooker et al. (2001) and Emmanuel (1996) have estimated that end-of-life spending represents roughly 10–12% of total health spending. But when the exploratory health scenario is applied in 2006, end-of-life health spending represents 40% of total health spending.

Although the results obtained with the exploratory health scenario are far from being proven, they nevertheless show the importance of further analysis of health costs by age and sex according to whether or not the main costs occur in the last year of life.

3.7 Conclusion

The projection of the sustainability of Quebec's public finances, developed using a series of relatively optimistic assumptions, with improvements in employment and productivity, reveals a problem of budgetary sustainability in the medium and long term. Sensitivity analysis exposes the importance not only of the assumptions on these economic variables but also of the main population parameters: an increase in fertility turns out to be positive only in the very long term, or outside the period of analysis; an increase in net migration has a greater impact during the observation period; and improvements in life expectancy tend to exacerbate the problem of budgetary sustainability, except if they come along with improvements in health conditions and, therefore, lower health-related expenses at each age.

Indeed, the discussion surrounding the projection of health spending, the government's largest expenditure item and a variable greatly influenced by the demographic transition, shows that the choice of a method distinguishing whether or not health-care costs occur mainly in the last year of life profoundly affects the determination of budgetary sustainability. The crucial difference lies in the variations in health spending due to longer life expectancy, combined with the demographic structure of the population. Although the results obtained under the exploratory scenario are still far from being proven, they nevertheless show the importance of further analysis of how health costs are actually determined.

Acknowledgements We thank the *Research Chair in Taxation and Public Finance* of the Université de Sherbrooke for financial support and Matthieu Arseneau for helpful comments.

References

Blanchard, O., Chouraqui, J. C., Hagemann, R. P., & Sartor, N. (1990, Autumn). The sustainability of fiscal policy: New answers to an old question. *OECD Economic Studies, 15*, 7–36.

CIHI – Canadian Institute for Health Information. (2009). *National health expenditure trends, 1975 to 2009*. Ottawa: CIHI.

Congressional Budget Office. (2011). *CBO's 2011 long-term budget outlook*. Available at www.cbo.gov/ftpdocs/122xx/doc12212/06–21-Long-Term_Budget_Outlook.pdf

Emmanuel, E. J. (1996). Cost savings at the end of life. What do the data show? *Journal of the American Medical Association, 275*(24), 1907–1914.

Feyrer, J. (2007). Demography and productivity. *Review of Economic and Statistics, 89*(1), 100–109.

Finances Québec. (2010). *Statistiques fiscales des particuliers, Année d'imposition 2008*. Quebec.

Godbout, L., Fortin, P., Arseneau, M., & St-Cerny, S. (2007). Choc démographique et finances publiques: Comment relever le défi de l'équité intergénérationnelle. *Cahiers Québécois de Démographie, 36*(2), 159–182.

Hogan, S., & Hogan, S. (2002). *How will the ageing of the population affect healthcare needs and costs in the foreseeable future?* (Discussion Paper No. 25). Ottawa: Commission on the Future of Health Care in Canada (Romanow Commission).

ISQ – Institut de la statistique du Québec. (2003). *Perspectives démographiques, Québec et régions, 2001–2051*. Québec.

ISQ – Institut de la statistique du Québec. (2009). *Perspectives démographiques du Québec et des régions, 2006–2056*. Québec.

Kotlikoff, L. J. (1992). *Generational accounting*. New York: The Free Press.

OECD – Organisation for Economic Co-operation and Development. (2011). *OECD. stat databank*. www.oecd.org

Office for Budget Responsibility. (2011). *Fiscal sustainability report*. Available at budgetresponsibility.independent.gov.uk/fiscal-sustainability-report-july-2011/

Parliamentary Budget Office. (2011). *Fiscal sustainability report 2011*. Available at www.parl.gc.ca/pbo-dpb/documents/FSR_2011.pdf

Pollock, A. (2001). Compression of health expenditures. *Health Policy Research Bulletin* (1) Ottawa: Health Canada.

Scitovsky, T. (1994). Towards a theory of second-hand markets. *Kyklos, 47*, 33–52.

Serup-Hansen, N., Wickstrom, J., & Kristiansen, I. S. (2002). Future health care cost. Do health care costs during the last year of life matter? *Health Policy, 62*(2), 161–172.

Statistics Canada. (2011). *CANSIM data bank*. Available at www.statcan.gc.ca

Stooker, T., van Acht, J. W., van Barneveld, E. M., van Vliet, R. C. J. A., van Hout, B. A., Hessing, D. J., & Busschbach, J. J. V. (2001). Costs in the last year of life in The Netherlands. *Inquiry, 38*(1), 73–80.

UN – United Nations. (2008). *World population prospects: The 2008 revision*. New York: United Nations.

Zweifel, P., Felder, S., & Meiers, M. (1999). Ageing of population and health care expenditure: A red herring? *Health Economics, 8*(6), 485–496.

Part II
Economic Security in Old Age

Introduction to Part II

Economic Security in Old Age

In this part, the authors adopt the point of view of cohorts and individuals and consider the likely economic implications that ageing has in part already brought about and will further cause in the next few years.

Jacques Légaré and Amélie Cossette tell us that the worries about the future prospects of the baby boomers (how difficult it will be for them to face old age, since their large numbers might well depress their average pension) may be exaggerated. When compared to their 'fathers', i.e. the cohorts born 30 years before, these individuals can be seen to have enjoyed much higher standards of living – almost twice as high in real terms, at the same ages. The paper proves this claim only for Quebec and Ontario, but all indications are that this conclusion can be generalised to the rest of Canada and also, very likely, to all of the industrialised world. The basic message urges us to put things in the correct perspective: even if, after retirement, things should get somewhat worse for these generations (which, in all cases, remains to be seen), they will very likely still be substantially better off than all the preceding ones.

Jinkook Lee and Drystan Phillips refer to the Republic of Korea (or just Korea, for the sake of brevity), but the issues they raise are, actually, of more general interest and apply also to other newly developed countries. The problem is how to set up a welfare system for the elderly that will not cost a fortune, that will not leave the poor behind, that will not discourage private savings for old age, and, finally, that will not 'crowd out' private (i.e. family) assistance. The Korean case clearly shows that such a system cannot be implemented all at once, but must instead be phased in, little by little. In so doing, a close monitoring of the subgroups more in need is essential, so as to be (relatively) sure that targeting is correct. And what the empirical analysis reveals is that fears of crowding out are empirically unjustified, at least in Korea: when the public hand intervenes – which in some cases is essential for preserving a decent standard of living for the elderly – the parallel reduction in private support (e.g. from sons and daughters) is very limited.

Also, in Japan, as in Korea, family and traditional values are still widespread and binding, and there is a strong social pressure for adult children, especially adult sons, to provide for their aged parents, in case of need. However, the picture is in fact more complex than this, and Taizo Motonoshi suggests that having old parents (and, even more, living with old parents or parents in law) may be a cost or a benefit, depending on at least two main variables. The first, obvious one is how affluent the elderly parents are. If they are poor, they are a cost, but if they are rich, they can be an asset: their presence and contribution to household expenses sustain the (adult children's) family budget. But it is also important to consider culture and norms: rich elderly parents are in fact much more likely to transfer resources to their daughters than to their sons, everything else equal. The different economic roles of men and women in the Japanese society, as well as issues of norms, tradition, and perhaps also of transmission of family name, are the main reasons behind this attitude.

Chapter 4
Comparing the Economic Well-Being of Baby Boomers and Their Parents in Quebec and Ontario*

Jacques Légaré and Amélie Cossette

4.1 Our Research Question and Its Background

In the early 1990s, Easterlin and colleagues (1993) asked themselves, 'Will the baby boomers be less well off than their parents?' The question was intriguing because there seemed to be convincing theoretical reasons why larger cohorts could be at risk of faring worse than others throughout their lives. There were also a few empirical elements supporting this view, but since the baby boomers were barely at the middle of their working years by then, no firm conclusion could be reached at that time. Twenty years later, with the oldest baby boomers on the verge of retirement, one would expect scholars to be in a position to give a more complete and satisfactory answer.

In practice, however, the task is more difficult than it may appear at first sight for various reasons. In the past 200 years or so, the world economy has increased at an unprecedented pace, and the same has happened in Canada. Even if the growth has somewhat slowed down over the past 40 years (the time frame that interests us here), it remains impressive by historical standards: in real terms, the income of the average Canadian is about twice as high in 2006 as it was in 1971 (from 12.6 to 25.0 thousand 1990 International Geary-Khamis dollars; Fig. 4.1). Thirty years later (e.g. in 2001 as compared to 1971, or in 2006 as compared to 1976), real incomes are 70–80% higher.

If we imagine, for the sake of simplicity, that 30 years is the average age difference between parents and children, this increase of 70–80% is also the order of magnitude that we should expect in the income comparison between the

*Translated from French to English by Rufteen Shumanty.

J. Légaré (✉) • A. Cossette
Département de Démographie, Université de Montréal,
C.P. 6128, succursale Centre-ville, Montréal, QC H3C 3J7, Canada
e-mail: jacques.legare@umontreal.ca; amelie.cossette.1@umontreal.ca

G. De Santis (ed.), *The Family, the Market or the State?: Intergenerational Support Under Pressure in Ageing Societies*, International Studies in Population 10,
DOI 10.1007/978-94-007-4339-7_4, © Springer Science+Business Media Dordrecht 2012

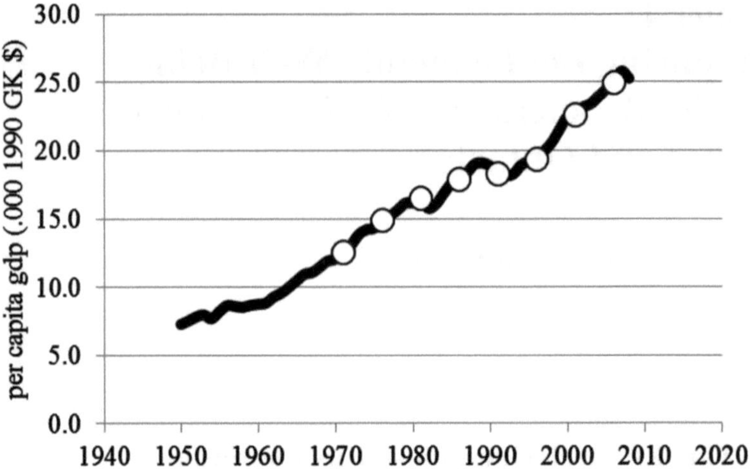

Fig. 4.1 Per capita GDP in Canada, 1950–2008 (1990 International Geary-Khamis dollars, thousands). Note: *White circles* indicate the census years, 1971–2006, analysed in this paper with reference to selected birth cohorts (Source: The Conference Board, Total Economy Database, http://www.conference-board.org/data/economydatabase/)

preceding generation ('parents') and the next one (children). How reasonable, then, is it to fear that 'the baby boomers will be less well off than their parents'? At most, this could emerge in terms of deviation from a trend: children tend to be better off than their parents, at any given age, but well-being also depends on the relative size of cohorts, and improvement is lesser for larger cohorts. By how much? This is probably a more sensible research question, but, unfortunately, it is not one that can be easily answered with our data, which are too rough to allow us to determine an expected value from which to calculate a deviation. We could, in theory, use some external benchmark, but unfortunately, we miss it: Maddison's data (the original source, from which those of Fig. 4.1 derive) are themselves little more than approximations and rough estimates.

Another major difficulty derives from data availability. Survey data on income only start to become available in the 1970s, but breaking them down by birth cohort typically results in too few observations. Besides, and most importantly, we are interested in life cycle income, not merely income at a given point in time.

Canada, however, is one of the few countries in the world where the census is taken every 5 years (not 10, as, for instance, in the United States) and where in the 'long' version of the questionnaire, administered to one-fifth of the respondents, there are specific questions on income. Luckily, these questions happen to be highly reliable (see Sect. 4.3) and comparable over time: this provides us with a unique opportunity to create pseudo panels based on a very large number of observations that effectively simulate individual income over the life cycle. This advantage comes at a cost, of course: we are interested in a specific topic (preparation for retirement of people in the final years of their working careers), but census data do not tell us what use is made of this income: how much has been saved over time or what assets have been accumulated?, nor do we know if the respondent participates in some (private or public) pension programme and how much this will yield in the future.

Incomes are asked of every individual, in the census (long) form, but we decided to work only on household income by pooling the individual incomes of all household members and dividing this sum by a proper equivalence scale. The reason is that it makes little sense to try to describe the economic situation of an individual without considering also the type of household he/she lives in, in terms of both needs and incomes. I may earn nothing, or very little, but if my wife (husband) is very rich, how can I be considered poor? Of course, there are also disadvantages in this operation: one is that the main provider of income may be in a stronger bargaining position within the family[1] (see, e.g. Browning et al. 1994), which may have income consequences if and when the family breaks up (e.g. after a divorce or when adult children leave the parental home).

The second difficulty is that equivalence scales are a poor approximation of the true economies of scale within a family: no one knows which is the best equivalence scale to apply and the choice of a specific one (the square root of household members, in our case) is frequently based more on convenience, or adherence to the standard practice, than on solid theoretical arguments.

In this chapter, we examine the financial situation of the oldest Quebecer and Ontarian baby boomers in terms of income and wealth, and we compare it with that of their parents at the same age. By 'parents' we mean 'members of the cohorts born 30 years before'.

In both cases, we focus on people aged between 45 and 55 years: what we get is therefore also an indication of how properly the baby boomers are preparing for their retirement, which is approaching quickly. This is an issue of great policy concern for various reasons. On the one hand, there are worries for the financial sustainability of the passage of a large cohort from being an asset to being a liability for public finances, essentially in terms of pensions and health expenditure (see, e.g. Chap. 3 by Godbout et al. in this volume; see also Lee and Mason 2011). On the other hand, from the point of view of the individuals concerned, the fear is that this passage may cause a certain (possibly, a sizeable) proportion of baby boomers to fall into poverty. This might be aggravated by the fact that informal assistance, too, will likely become more difficult to obtain in the future (see Chap. 7 by Keefe et al. in this volume): those who need it might well be forced to demand it of professional, but expensive, caregivers.

In analysing this individual-level concern, it is obviously important to keep in mind that the boomers are a heterogeneous category in terms of wealth and income, and some of them find themselves in a state of greater vulnerability, as we will see shortly.

[1] Families and households practically coincide in Canada. We will use the two terms (family and household) interchangeably in this chapter.

The objective of our study is therefore double: it aims at assessing the adequacy of retirement preparations on average, but it also aims at understanding who among the boomers lies in the left tail of the income distribution and how vulnerable his or her situation is. This chapter is an update of a previous study on this subject in Quebec (Légaré and Mo 2006; Mo and Légaré 2007): we now extend the time window by using the Canadian census data of 2006, which have recently become accessible. But we enlarge the picture by also considering Ontario. Quebec and Ontario, the most populated provinces in Canada, have traditionally been, and still are, very distinct from a socio-economic and cultural point of view: how do they compare in terms of economic growth across the generations and adequacy of financial means of their 'mature' workers, who also happen to be the first baby boomers?

4.2 Methodology

4.2.1 The Intergenerational Comparison

The intergenerational comparison is the essential approach of this study. According to the life cycle approach, wealth accumulated during the working years of an individual serves principally to finance his or her consumption in retirement. The more he (or she) has, the better financially prepared will he (or she) be for retirement. Unfortunately, as we will see shortly, our (census) data do not give us full information on the accumulated wealth of each individual or household. We will therefore need to use proxies: household income in the census year and home ownership.

Several important studies have been published since 1993 on the financial planning for retirement of the baby boomers in the United States. A recent one, conducted by the Congressional Budget Office of the United States (CBO 2003), stresses the importance of intergenerational comparison for shedding light on the financial perspectives of the seniors of tomorrow. This is the method that we will adopt here because it will permit us to examine the life cycle experience of successive birth cohorts. We will do this with the aim of comparing the current state of the boomers with that of their parents at the same age, some 30 years before. From there, we can infer the likely relative standards of living of the future retirees.

Baby boomers, in general, are identified by demographers as the cohort of individuals born between 1946 and 1966. However, our study focuses only on the situation of the oldest boomers (heretofore simply 'baby boomers'), born between 1946 and 1956, who will be the first to retire and who were relatively mature in 2006 (50–59 years). This constitutes an advantage of the present study over the American ones on the same subject because these were led in the 1990s on baby boomers who at the time were aged between 25 and 45 years (Easterlin et al. 1993; CBO 1993; Keister and Deeb-Sossa 2001).

A large number of cohorts gave birth to children born between 1946 and 1956. In order to keep things simple, we will consider as parents of the baby boomers the cohorts born between 1916 and 1926, i.e. 30 years before, on average. We chose this age interval both because it is a conveniently round figure and because in Quebec (as well as in the rest of Canada and in most other populations of the world), the average age at maternity was not far from 30 years for these birth cohorts: in fact it was about 29.5 years (ISQ 2004).

4.2.2 *The Interregional Comparison*

The comparison of the socio-economic evolution in Quebec and in Ontario is particularly interesting, at least for Canada. Both are populous (Ontario has about 13 million inhabitants and Quebec about 8 million, out of the 32 of the whole of Canada), and both are eastern provinces. But Quebec is mainly a French province, and Ontario is mainly an English one. Ontario has traditionally been richer, and it is not by chance that Ontario integrates within it a much larger number of immigrants, among whom some arrived at an advanced age or, anyway, did not study in Canada.

Given the social and cultural climate in which the baby boomers of both provinces lived in, how different is their economic situation?

4.2.3 *Measures of the Economic Well-Being*

We measure the economic well-being of our cohorts with two different indicators, the only ones that are available in the census: equivalent income and home ownership. As mentioned before, we expect these variables to be correlated with all the other provisions for retirement that the members of our cohorts may have made: e.g. buying equities and participating in private and public pension programmes.

As for income, we use household, not individual, income. Since income is typically shared among household members, individual income does not properly reflect the economic well-being of a person. In order to account for economies of scale within a household, we transform household income into an 'adjusted individual income' using an equivalence scale. The equivalence scale that we adopt is the one currently preferred by the OECD (2008, 2009): the square root of household size. As an example, for a family of four people with an income of 40,000 CDN dollars, the value of adjusted individual income is, for each member of this family, 20,000 CDN dollars $(40,000/\sqrt{4})$. Several scales have been proposed in the past (OECD 2009), but the 'square root' approach is presently the one that is used most frequently (Yamada 2002). In the present study, income is measured by the median of adjusted individual income in constant CDN dollars of 2005, so as to eliminate the effects of inflation.

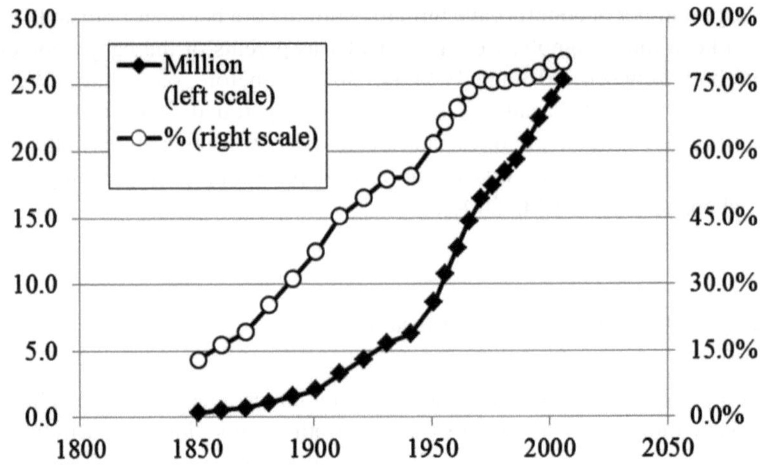

Fig. 4.2 Urban population in Canada, 1851–2006 (Source: Statistics Canada, http://www40.statcan.gc.ca/l01/cst01/demo62a-eng.htm)

As for wealth, we consider the dichotomous variable 'home ownership'. Unfortunately, we do not know the value of the dwelling or if there is a mortgage on it: merely whether the members of our cohort possess it or not. This is undoubtedly a limitation because houses can be of very differing monetary values, but it is the best that we can do with our data. And, in comparison to most other studies, where only income is considered, this inclusion can be considered an improvement. In general, we can say that the price of housing has increased in Quebec and Ontario (as well as in the rest of Canada) over time: this reflects both an increase in quality, with more and better equipment, and a 'Ricardian' effect of concentration of the population in urban areas, which now host 80% of the population in Canada, or 25 million people (up from 16 million and 76%, in 1971; Fig. 4.2). The increased demand for space in urban areas has led to a corresponding increase in rents and market price of real estate.

4.2.4 Gender Comparison

Women tend to have lower individual income than men in part because, since they are more engaged than men in indoor activities (see also Chap. 9 by Tanturri, in this volume), they work more frequently on a part-time basis and their working careers are less continuous (see, among others, Abowd and Killingsworth 1983; Silvera 1996; Makepeace et al. 1999; Stier and Mandel 2009). As a consequence, in old age, women's pension benefits are typically lower than men's. Does this pattern apply to female baby boomers too? Do they risk finding themselves in an unfavourable economic situation compared to their male counterparts?

4.2.5 The Vulnerable Socio-economic Categories

The heterogeneity of boomers in terms of income and accumulated wealth, by definition, puts some of them in a more vulnerable state, throughout their lives and also at the time of retirement. In addition to women, already discussed, there are also several other categories whose incomes are typically low or with scarce participation in public or private pension programmes: for instance, those with low education or immigrants. Consequently, it is to be expected that baby boomers belonging to disadvantaged socio-economic categories will be below the median. In this chapter, we will consider at risk of poverty those whose median (equivalent) income is lower than the median of all the boomers and also lower than the median of similar categories in their parent's birth cohort.

Unfortunately, our data do not permit us to compare exactly their parent's birth cohort at the same age. Therefore, in order to get a feeling of how things have evolved in this respect, we decided to compare baby boomers aged 50–59 years in 2006 with individuals of the same category and age 25 years earlier, in 1981, when sufficiently detailed data began to be collected in the census. The basic expectation is that each socio-economic category improves its income over a period of 25 years at a similar pace. When this does not occur, and we observe instead a worsening with respect to the situation of 25 years earlier, we consider these baby boomers as a vulnerable category in terms of their well-being shortly before retirement.

4.3 Data

Every 5 years, the Canadian census collects data on the income of individuals, families, and households, as well as on home ownership.[2] In Canada, unlike several other countries, the data on individual income from the census are very reliable. This is because they come from a pairing with data of the Canada Revenue Agency on annual individual tax reports, which are mandatory and closely controlled.

The data used here are the ones from the Canadian censuses from 1971 to 2006 – from the main data file and not from the PUMF (Public Use Micro-File): this means that we have, for each census, one-fifth of all the census questionnaires, which makes a very large data set. In 1971, the long form of the census questionnaires was

[2] The census questionnaire for 2006 (long form: the only one of interest for our study) can be found on the web page of Statistics Canada, currently at this address http://www12.statcan.ca/census-recensement/2006/ref/question-guide-eng.cfm. Note that income is recorded individually, but we decided to analyse it at the household level for reasons of opportunity (we feel that this reflects better one's real economic situation). Home ownership, instead, is reported collectively (the census question is 'Is this dwelling owned by you or a member of this household?'): working at the household level is, in this case, the only possible solution.

first distributed to a sample (20%) of the census population. It is only in this long form that we find, among other things, the detailed information on income and tenure that we need for our study.

In order to evaluate if the baby boomers are better off than their parents and by how much, we will make an intergenerational comparison using the life cycle profile of each of the cohorts. In fact, the cohorts can be followed from one census to another. For example, those who were born in 1946–1950 are aged 20–24 years in the census of 1971, 25–29 years in 1976, . . ., and 55–59 years in the census of 2006. By chaining census information, we can also study the life cycle profiles of several cohorts, and here we are particularly interested in those of the baby boomers and of their 'parents' (30 years older). Unfortunately, we are subject to truncation, both on the left (we do not have information prior to 1971) and on the right (our observation stops in 2006), and this limits our analysis, as we will see shortly.

4.4 Results

4.4.1 Equivalent Income

Income profile by age follows a typical curve: it increases up to about age 50 and decreases afterwards. Our data confirm this traditional trend, but they also show that, at every age, younger birth cohorts are advantaged, and the baby boomers are no exception (Figs. 4.3, 4.4 and 4.5). Between the ages of 45 and 54, for instance, the boomers had, on average, a considerably higher real income than their parents at the same age: between 40% and 60% higher.

The individual equivalent income of boomers born between 1946 and 1951, as measured by the median of the equivalent income, in constant 2005 CDN dollars, was more than 40,000 between the ages of 50 and 60 in Quebec. In comparison, the income of individuals belonging to cohorts of their parents, born in 1916–1920 (but measured at the same age), was <30,000.

A few things are worth noting. First, the trends are similar for Ontario and Quebec, but Ontarians enjoy higher standards of living, both among the baby boomers and their parents (Fig. 4.4). However, and this is the second observation, Quebec seems to be catching up: the relative increase in real income is more pronounced in Quebec (about +54%) than it is in Ontario (about +47%). The overlapping period is too short to draw any firm conclusion, but the indication seems to emerge consistently in our data.

Third, we do not really know how well the baby boomers are preparing for their retirement: income is one thing, but saving and capital accumulation, if we had the data, could tell a different story. Assuming, however, that the two are correlated, the most important conclusion that we can draw is that, contrary to the widespread negative vision of insufficient preparation for financial retirement of the baby boomers, the boomers will have to face fewer financial constraints than their

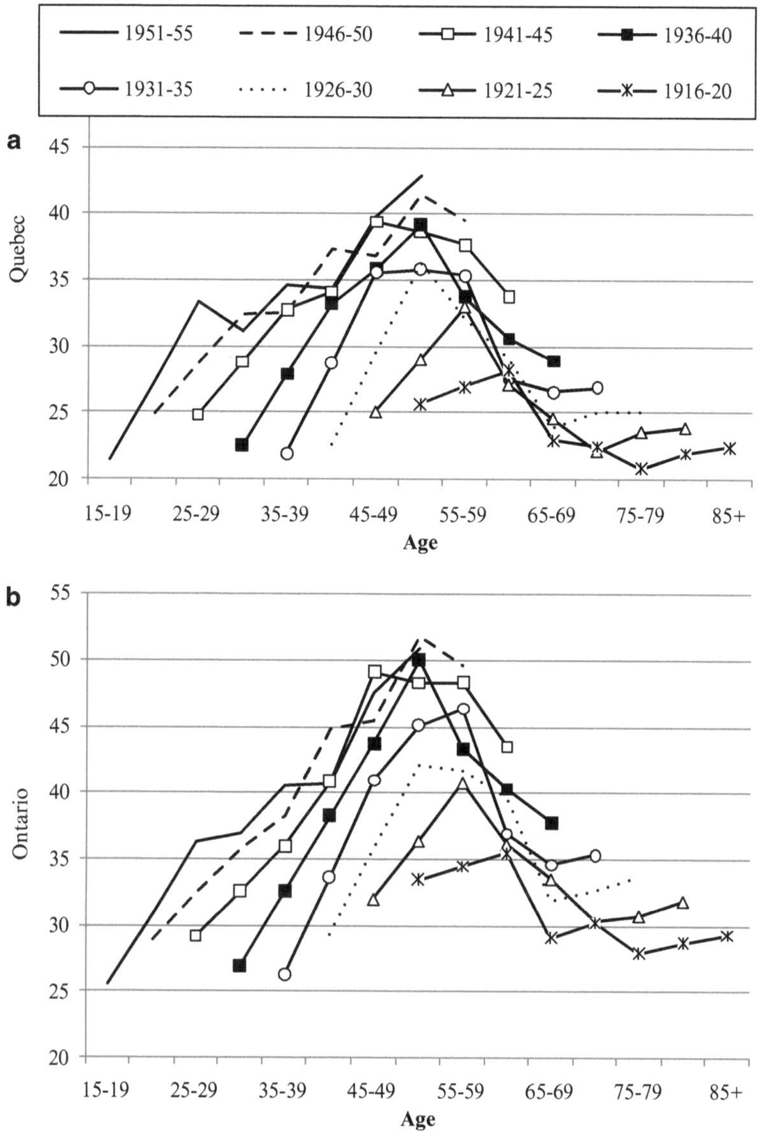

Fig. 4.3 Median of the equivalent income by age and birth cohort: (**a**) Quebec, (**b**) Ontario. Note: All values expressed in constant (2005) Canadian dollars (thousands). Cohorts of 1946–1950 and 1951–1955: baby boomers (Source: Own elaborations on census data)

parents (and also, incidentally, of every other birth cohort before them). Obviously, this is subject to a few conditions, among which the most important are that pension promises will be honoured in the future and that the value of whatever assets the boomers hold now (slightly before retirement) will not suffer from major declines in the future.

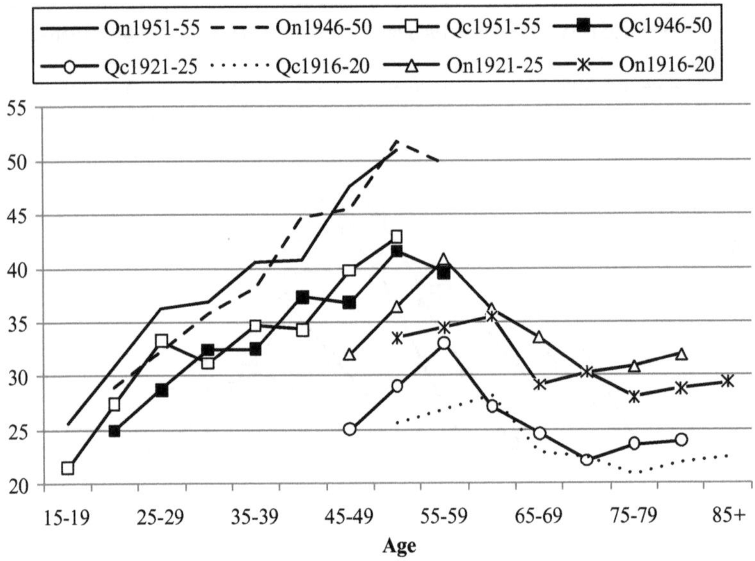

Fig. 4.4 Median of the equivalent income by age and selected birth cohort: Quebec and Ontario. Note: All values expressed in constant (2005) Canadian dollars (thousands) (Source: Own elaborations on census data)

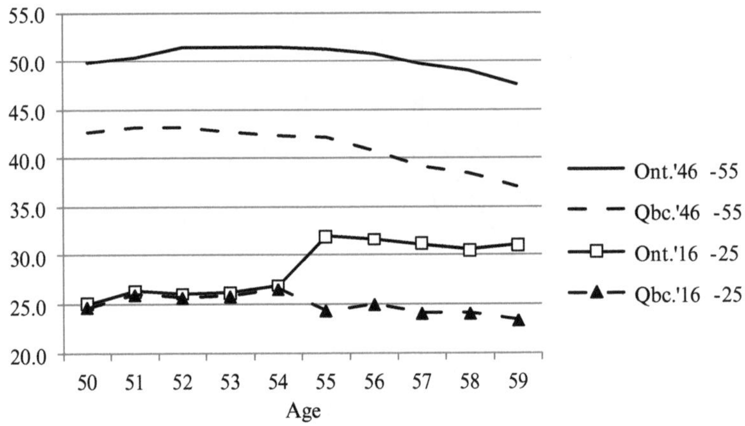

Fig. 4.5 Median of the equivalent income by selected age and birth cohort: Quebec and Ontario. Note: All values expressed in constant (2005) Canadian dollars (thousands) (Source: Own elaborations on census data)

Finally, note that the average income increase between the 'parents' and the boomers is somewhere between 40% and 60%, in real terms, which is lower than the 70–80% increase indicated by Maddison's data (see again Fig. 4.1). The two data sets are not comparable, to be sure, but we find here some indications that the boomers might be at some relative disadvantage, after all: their income did increase significantly but perhaps not as rapidly as that of the rest of the population.

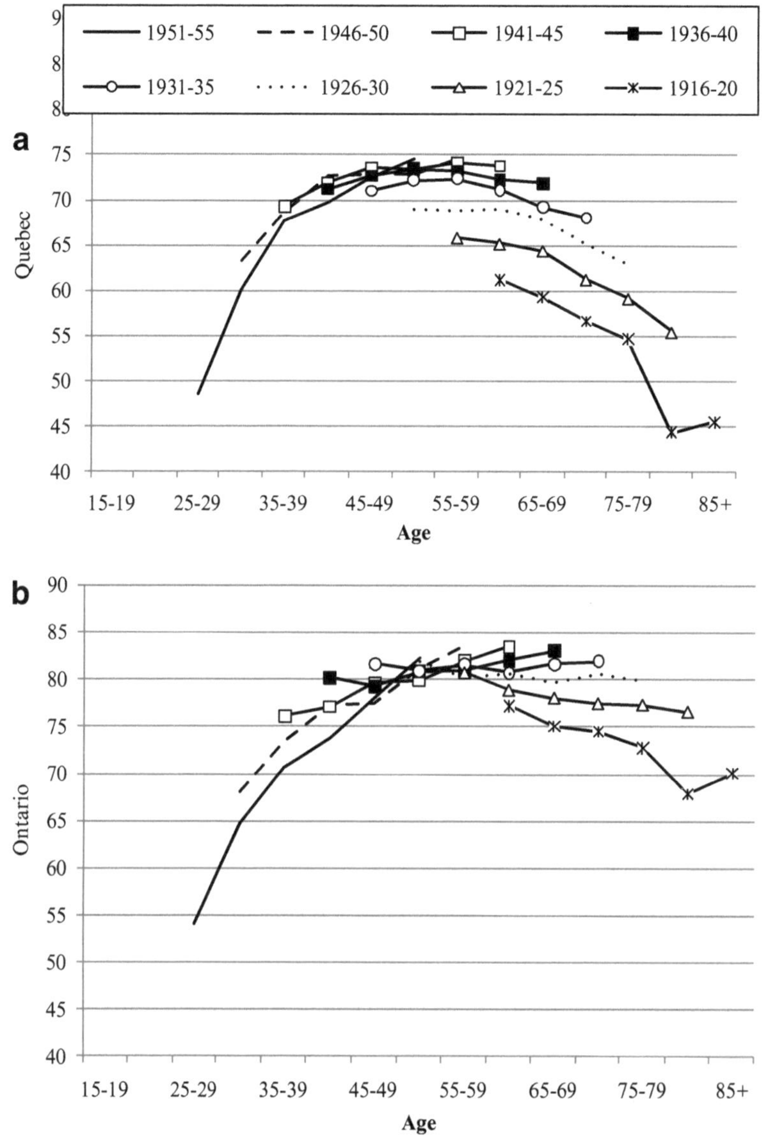

Fig. 4.6 Proportion of home owners*, by age and birth cohort: (**a**) Quebec, (**b**) Ontario. Note: *Individuals whose dwelling is owned by one of the members of their household. All values expressed in per cent (Source: Own elaborations on census data)

4.4.2 Wealth: Home Ownership

Compared to their parents, the baby boomers earn much more, in real terms and at the same age. What can we say of their wealth? In order to answer this question, we will examine home ownership of the boomers. Figure 4.6 shows the life cycle profile of home ownership for our birth cohorts. The first thing to remark is that, among birth cohorts born before 1941, the proportion of home owners (or better, of individuals whose dwelling is owned by one of the members of their household) has increased considerably from one birth cohort to the next. Among birth cohorts born between 1941 and 1956, instead, the trend is still positive, but the increase is smaller.

The proportion of home owners in Quebec is clearly higher among the boomers than among their parents at the same age, whereas in Ontario, there is very little difference between birth cohorts beyond 35 years of age, with the partial exception of the oldest cohorts (born between 1916 and 1921). But this is also due to the fact that Ontarians have traditionally been home owners, and proportions have a ceiling: they cannot exceed 100%. When levels are very high right from the start, further increases cannot, by definition, be very pronounced: in the case of Ontario, among the oldest, born in 1916–1920, 70% are home owners, and already among the cohorts of 1936–1940, the proportion reaches 85%.

Once again, then, we note the catch-up effect: the ancient cohorts were markedly better off in Ontario than in Quebec, but this difference has progressively eroded over time, and the young generations in the two Canadian provinces are now comparable in terms of home ownership (Fig. 4.7). And, once again, we note that the boomers are surely not worse off than their parents, quite the contrary: especially in Quebec, they are markedly wealthier (in terms of home ownership).

4.4.3 Gender Comparison

As mentioned earlier, our objective is to analyse the economic well-being of individuals in terms of equivalent income, which is, by definition, the same for each member of a household, whether male or female. Nevertheless, when we try to differentiate by gender, we systematically observe that, on average, men have an adjusted income that is slightly higher than that of women. This difference is due in large part to households headed by a single woman, whose financial situation appears to be worse, both in terms of equivalent income and in terms of home ownership (data not shown here).

Gender inequality can be observed for all the birth cohorts, but it is slightly lower among the baby boomers than among that of their parents[3]: once again, an indication that the boomers are not faring worse than their parents – not even in terms of income distribution and not only with reference to average levels.

[3] And it is also slightly lower in Ontario than in Quebec.

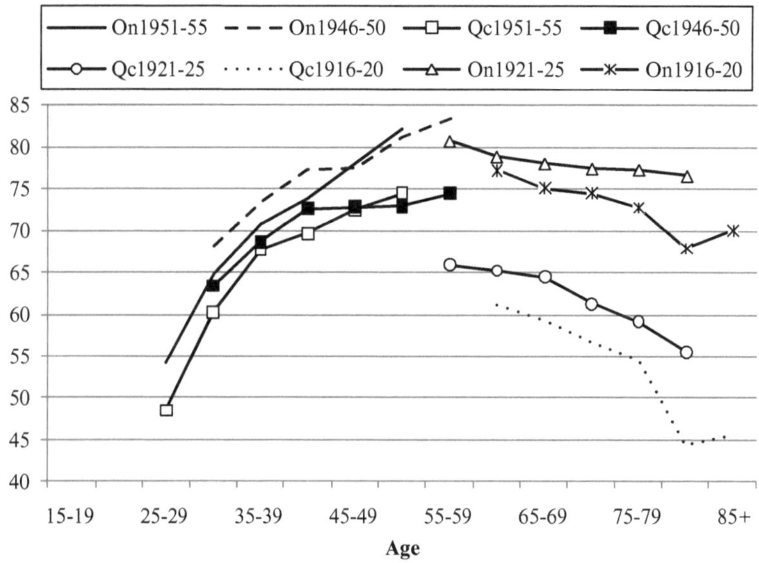

Fig. 4.7 Proportion of home owners*, by age and selected birth cohort: Quebec and Ontario. Note: *Individuals whose dwelling is owned by one of the members of their household. All values expressed in per cent (Source: Own elaborations on census data)

4.5 The Vulnerability of Some Boomers

As previously specified, the financial situation of the baby boomers is not homogeneous, and certain socio-economic categories are more vulnerable than others. According to our definition (Sect. 4.2.5), in year 2006, we can identify as many as ten vulnerable categories among Quebecer baby boomers and six among the Ontarian ones. Indeed, the latter, in general, fare better, and cases where the average income declines over time from 'parents' to 'children' are rarer and normally less intense (Fig. 4.8). Being an immigrant seems to be a serious handicap only in Quebec – in the sense that in Ontario their economic standing has not deteriorated in absolute terms, even if immigrants are generally poorer than natives (by about 16% in Quebec and 8% in Ontario; see Légaré and Bergeron Boucher (2012)) and may be characterised by a slower increase in their standard of living (data not shown here). However, the immigrants who have migrated relatively late in life, at the age of 35 years or more, or were unemployed in 2005, find themselves in a particularly vulnerable category, as much in Quebec as in Ontario: their equivalent income may be 30–50% lower than average in these cases. The same applies to people who are not home owners, or are single, or come from large families.

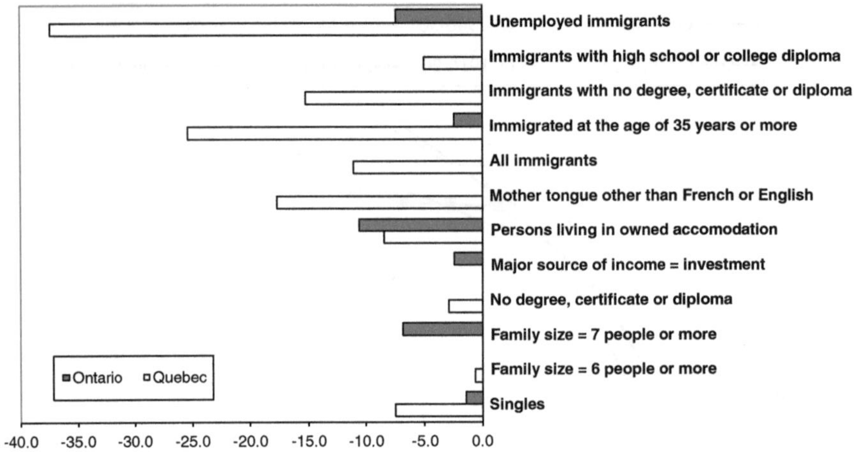

Fig. 4.8 Categories where the variation of equivalent income is negative for people aged between 50 and 60 years in 2006 compared to people of the same category and the same age in 1981, a Quebec-Ontario comparison (Source: Own elaborations on census data)

4.6 Conclusion

In order to predict the likely economic well-being of baby boomers in retirement, it is generally better to focus on a few specific variables, like participation in a pension plan, assets owned, and the like (Mo and Légaré 2007; Mo 2010). But the availability of recent data from the Canadian census of 2006 encouraged us to validate, on a different data set, the results that had been found before. Both sets of results point in the same direction: the well-being of the baby boomers is considerably higher than that of their parents, their wealth larger, and their preparation for their retirement years correspondingly better. The trends are the same in Quebec and Ontario: even if the starting levels differ, with the Ontarians slightly better off, the Quebecers are slowly catching up – and this holds for all the available variables.

Easterlin's concerns about the fate of larger birth cohorts do not find empirical support in Canada, at no stage of the life cycle. Of course, there are specific subgroups for whom the economic situation has not evolved as well as for the rest of the population (immigrants, members of very large families, . . .), and these will probably need special consideration in the public policies of the next years.

Apart from this, there is also the question, not discussed in this chapter, of how quickly expectations increase, with time and age: it is well possible that the worries that are frequently echoed with regard to the economic situation of our future elderly are deeply influenced by the rapidity with which these expectations have grown, possibly outpacing the remarkable increase in material life achievements. But this is a different matter that merits more thorough discussion in a separate chapter.

References

Abowd, J. M., & Killingsworth, M. R. (1983). Sex, discrimination, atrophy, and the male-female wage differential. *Industrial Relations. Journal of Economy and Society, 22*(3), 387–402.

Browning, M., Bourguignon, F., Chiappori, P. A., & Lechène, V. (1994). Income and outcomes: A structural model of intrahousehold allocation. *Journal of Political Economy, 102*, 1067–1097.

CBO – Congressional Budget Office. (1993). *Baby boomers in retirement: An early perspective*. Washington, DC: Congress of the United States.

CBO – Congressional Budget Office. (2003). *Baby boomers' retirement prospects: An overview*. Washington, DC: Congress of the United States.

Easterlin, R. A., Schaeffer, C. M., & Macunovich, D. J. (1993). Will the baby boomers be less well off than their parents? Income, wealth, and family circumstances over the life cycle in the United States. *Population and Development Review, 19*(3), 497–522.

ISQ – Institut de la statistique du Québec. (2004). *La situation démographique au Québec, bilan 2004*. Québec: Institut de la statistique du Québec. (www.stat.gouv.qc.ca)

Keister, L. A., & Deeb-Sossa, N. (2001). Are baby boomers richer than their parents? Intergenerational patterns of wealth ownership in the Unites States. *Journal of Marriage and Family, 63*(2), 569–579.

Lee, R., & Mason, A. (2011). *Population aging and the generational economy. A global perspective*. Cheltenham/Northampton: Elgar.

Légaré, J., & Bergeron Boucher, M. P. (2012). Qui seront les premiers nés du baby-boom à risque de vulnérabilité financière à la retraite? Une comparaison Québec-Ontario. *Canadian Journal of Ageing, 31*(2), 1–11.

Légaré, J., & Mo, L. (2006). *L'évaluation de la préparation financière à la retraite des premiers baby-boomers québécois: deux études comparatives*. Montréal: Rapport de recherche pour le fond québécois de recherche sur la société et la culture. (http://www.fqrsc.gouv.qc.ca/upload/editeur/RFJLegare%281%29.pdf)

Makepeace, G., Paci, P., Joshi, H., & Dolton, P. (1999). How unequally has equal pay progressed since the 1970s? *The Journal of Human Resources, 34*(3), 534–556.

Mo, L. (2010). Jusqu'à quel point les baby-boomers seront-ils plus à l'aise financièrement que leurs parents au moment de la retraite? *Cahiers Québécois de démographie, 39*(1), 27–57.

Mo, L., & Légaré, J. (2007). Revenu, logement et protection en matière de pensions durant le cycle de vie de différentes générations: jusqu'à quel point les premiers boomers québécois se préparent-ils mieux à la retraite que leurs parents? In H. Gauthier (Ed.), *Vie des générations et personnes âgées: aujourd'hui et demain* (Vol. 2, pp. 289–321). Québec: Institut de la statistique du Québec. http://www.stat.gouv.qc.ca/publications/conditions/pdf2007/generation_vol2_chap13.pdf

OECD. (2008). *Growing unequal? Income distribution and poverty in OECD countries*. Paris: OECD. www.oecd.org/els/social/inequality

OECD. (2009). What are equivalence scales? *OECD manuals, sources and methods*. Paris: OECD. http://www.oecd.org/dataoecd/61/52/35411111.pdf

Silvera, R. (1996). Les discriminations salariales entre hommes et femmes, "toutes choses inégales par ailleurs". *Economies et Societes, 30*(11–12), 199–216.

Statistics Canada. *Population, urban and rural, by province and territory (Canada)*. http://www40.statcan.gc.ca/l01/cst01/demo62a-eng.htm

Stier, H., & Mandel, H. (2009). Inequality in the family: The institutional aspects of women's earning contribution. *Social Science Research, 38*(3), 594–608.

The Conference Board, Total Economy Database. http://www.conference-board.org/data/economydatabase/

Yamada, A. (2002). *The evolving retirement income package: Trends in adequacy and equality in nine OECD countries* (OECD, Labour Market and Social Policy Occasional Paper, No. 63). Paris: OECD.

Chapter 5
Income and Poverty Among Older Koreans: Relative Contributions of and Relationship Between Public and Family Transfers

Jinkook Lee and Drystan Phillips

5.1 Introduction

The elderly population of the Republic of Korea (hereafter Korea) is growing rapidly: the share of persons aged 65 and over will increase from about 3% in the 1970s, to 11% today (out of about 49 million people, in total), to about 33% in the 2040s, and those aged 80 and over will pass from virtually none in the 1970s, to 2% today, to perhaps 10% in 2040 (KOSIS http://www.kosis.kr/eng). Sharply decreasing fertility, from nearly five children per woman in 1970 to just over one today, and increasing life expectancy, from just over 60 years in the early 1970s to 80 years today, are contributing to this change (KNSO 2009).

Economic well-being often declines for people at older ages. Withdrawal from the labour force and deteriorating health contribute to a greater risk of poverty. The risk of elderly poverty varies greatly across countries, particularly by the generosity of public transfers (Zaidi et al. 2006). Public transfers consist of two major components: public pensions, to which individuals contribute during their working age, and welfare programmes, which tend to have eligibility restrictions such as means-testing or age.

Almost all public pension programmes have a redistributive component distinguishing them from private savings. Unlike those in developed countries which provide old-age income security, public pension benefits in most developing countries seldom provide adequate income support. Welfare programmes in most developing countries are also quite limited. Korea has had remarkable economic growth in the past four decades, and it has moved from being a developing to a

J. Lee (✉)
Labor & Population, RAND Corporation, 1776 Main St., Santa Monica, CA 90407-2139, USA
e-mail: jinkook@rand.org

D. Phillips
Labor & Population, RAND Corporation, 1200 South Hayes Street,
Arlington, VA 22202-5050, USA
e-mail: dphillip@rand.org

G. De Santis (ed.), *The Family, the Market or the State?: Intergenerational Support Under Pressure in Ageing Societies*, International Studies in Population 10,
DOI 10.1007/978-94-007-4339-7_5, © Springer Science+Business Media Dordrecht 2012

developed country. Despite the country's rapid economic growth, however, the economic well-being of the Korean elderly remains at great risk. The poverty rate of Koreans 60 and older in 2000 was 32%,[1] three times that of the non-elderly (Park et al. 2003): a high level partly caused by an immature pension programme and limited government welfare spending.

Private transfers play an important role in many developing countries, including Korea, where public transfers are inadequate, and traditional family solidarity is deeply rooted in the society. Yet Korean societal values have shifted with industrialisation and urbanisation. The erosion of traditional Confucian values has adversely influenced the economic well-being of the Korean elderly in two ways: decreasing levels of multigenerational co-residence where children provide old-age support (Sung 1995; Levande et al. 2000) and reduced financial assistance from children (Kwon 2001).

Korean elderly face rapidly declining family support but slowly increasing public support. The adverse consequences of this shift are evident in high suicide rates among the elderly. Korean suicide rates (per 100,000 persons) are 97.3 for those aged 75 and older and 59.8 for those aged 65–74, while the rate for the general population is 21.9 (WHO 2009). Among those 75 and older, Korean suicide rates are 14 times those in the United Kingdom (6.8) and five times those in the United States (16.8).

In this chapter, we examine the economic well-being of Korean elderly. We first provide background on public and private transfers in Korea and the relationship between them. We then examine several measures of income and poverty for community-residing adults at least 65 years of age using the Korean Longitudinal Study of Aging (KLoSA) organised by the Korea Labor Institute (KLI). We then examine sources of income for the elderly, paying particular attention to living arrangements and sharing of economic resources with co-resident adult children. We investigate the contributions of public and private transfers to old-age income security by examining the relative contributions of public and family transfers to household income for the elderly. This is a particularly critical issue for policy reforms currently under consideration.

5.2 Public Transfers in Korea

Korea first introduced a public pension scheme in 1960 with the implementation of the Government Employees Pension. This programme expanded to include the Military Personnel Pension in 1963, the Private School Teacher's Pension in 1975, and the Specially Designated Post Office Personnel Pension in 1992. The National Pension Scheme (NPS), enacted with the National Pension Act in 1988,

[1] And also in 2006 (Lee and Lee 2009).

extended compulsory coverage over time to workplaces with ten or more employees in 1988, workplaces with five or more employees in 1992, rural workplaces with fewer than five employees, farmers, and fishermen in 1995, and the urban self-employed and urban workplaces with fewer than five workers in 1999, finally becoming a universal scheme for the public in 2006 (NPS 2010).

The scheme is not pay-as-you-go: it is funded through contributions. The initial contribution rate was set at 3% in 1988 in order to give the system popularity and stability, but it was increased to 6% in 1993 and to 9% in 1998. For average earners with 40 years of contributions, the income replacement rate was initially set at 60%, but fiscal problems reduced this to 50% in 2008, with further reductions of 0.5% each year, down to 40% by 2028.

At least 20 years of contributions are required to be eligible, and, therefore, only a few elderly are current beneficiaries of the NPS. The age for pension eligibility was 60 years in 2008, but this is increasing by 1 year each calendar year until it will reach 65 in 2013.[2] An age-eligible person with more than 10 but fewer than 20 years of contributions may receive a reduced old-age pension, while an early old-age pension is available at a reduced rate for persons reaching age 55 (with 55-year-old persons receiving 70% of benefits and a 6% increase in benefits for each year one waits after age 55 to retire). For this early stage of the NPS, a special old-age pension programme was developed for those who only contributed to the scheme between 5 and 10 years.

As of 2010, 19.1 million persons were enrolled in the NPS, and 2.3 million received old-age pension benefits (NPS 2010). The NPS also provides survivor benefits, annuities for disabled persons, and death benefits (one-time payments to defray funeral expenses). Divorced persons who were married at least 5 years during a spouse's insured period may be granted half-pension based on the marriage period once they reach age 60 (if their former spouse is already an old-age pensioner), even after remarriage.

The National Basic Livelihood Security System (NBLSS), which is comparable to Supplemental Security Income in the United States, provides welfare benefits to the poor. Eligibility is based on means-testing and kinship: the NBLSS offers welfare benefits to those who do not have any relatives (defined as parents, spouses, children and their spouses, and siblings) legally responsible for, and capable of, supporting them. Such eligibility criteria assume that informal support mechanisms will otherwise provide full old-age income support.

In an effort to reduce elderly poverty and in implicit recognition of the weakening of kinship support networks, in January 2008, the Korean government introduced a means-tested income support programme for the elderly (aged 65 and older), the Basic Old Age Support Pension (BOASP). Under the BOASP, about 60% of the elderly received 5% of the mean NPS benefit. This support is currently about 90,000 Korean won for individuals (equivalent to $90 US) per month and

[2] A special-occupation employee, such as a miner or a fisherman, is eligible for a pension between ages 55 and 60.

Table 5.1 Public transfers in OECD countries: per cent of GDP spent on old-age support

	Year				
Country	1990	1995	2000	2005	2007
Australia	3.31	3.85	4.74	4.30	4.31
Austria	8.94	10.04	10.44	10.84	10.74
Belgium	6.53	7.01	6.91	7.15	7.08
Canada	3.83	4.24	3.86	3.78	3.80
Chile	7.36	6.08	6.59	5.16	4.49
Czech Republic	5.24	5.86	7.07	6.86	6.91
Denmark	7.35	8.36	7.06	7.26	7.28
Finland	7.03	8.53	7.52	8.50	8.40
France	9.21	10.60	10.50	10.86	11.06
Germany	9.40	7.98	8.78	9.23	8.65
Greece	9.33	9.16	10.10	10.99	10.02
Iceland	3.42	3.69	3.49	3.79	2.30
Ireland	3.24	2.88	2.58	2.88	3.11
Italy	8.27	9.35	11.18	11.56	11.74
Japan	4.09	5.31	6.93	8.62	8.79
Korea	*0.61*	*1.06*	*1.24*	*1.43*	*1.61*
Luxembourg	7.62	8.24	6.94	5.20	4.85
Mexico	0.39	0.57	0.59	0.93	1.15
Netherlands	6.34	5.54	5.27	5.54	5.26
New Zealand	7.15	5.53	4.84	4.14	4.18
Norway	7.10	7.06	6.53	6.34	6.22
Poland	4.06	7.57	8.51	9.28	8.72
Portugal	4.05	6.03	6.65	8.88	9.23
Spain	7.22	8.29	8.25	7.95	6.54
Sweden	8.55	9.83	9.08	9.44	8.98
Switzerland	5.48	6.56	6.48	6.65	6.30
United Kingdom	4.85	5.49	5.48	5.94	5.77
United States	5.17	5.37	5.08	5.25	5.30
OECD – total	5.91	6.39	6.46	6.66	6.45

Source: OECD (2010)

144,000 Korean won for couples. The BOASP programme expanded its coverage to 70% of the elderly based on means-testing of income and assets in 2009. BOASP means-testing does not consider private transfers. Unlike the NBLSS, it lacks kinship-based eligibility criteria. But the legislation about these matters is far from settled, and the frequent debates in the Korean Congress over the BOASP, the NPS, and the NBLSS could lead to either expansion or reduction of each of these schemes – especially the BOASP.

The Korean government's spending for old-age support is far lower than that in other developed countries. Table 5.1 shows public transfers, including both public pension and welfare programmes, for old-age support across all OECD countries from 1990 to 2007, as a percentage of GDP. The Korean government spent only 0.61% of GDP on public transfers for old-age support in 1990, about one-tenth the OECD average (5.9%). Since then, pubic transfers for the elderly have increased

Table 5.2 Poverty rates for population and the elderly in selected countries in recent years

	Poverty rate	
	Population[a]	65 and over[b]
Austria	13	9
Belgium	15	17
Denmark	12	6
France	13	11
Germany	13	9
Greece	21	24
Italy	20	15
Korea	15	32
Mexico	14	28
Netherlands	10	2
Spain	20	29
Sweden	12	8
United Kingdom	19	14
United States	10	25

Relative poverty rate based on 50% of equivalised median income

[a]All statistics are for 2006. Sources: US Census, Eurostat, Korea Statistical Office, and IndexMundi for Mexico (http://www.indexmundi.com/)

[b]All statistics are for 2000 except for Korea (2005). Sources: Förster and Mira D'Ercole (2005), OECD (2008), Smeeding (2005) for Belgium, 2007 Survey of Income and Living Conditions for Spain carried out by the Spanish National Institute of Statistics, and KLoSA for Korea, in 2006

only modestly. In 2007, the Korean government spent 1.6% of GDP on old-age support, one-fourth of the OECD average (6.5%).

Reflecting such cross-country variations in public transfers, poverty rates among the elderly also vary by country. Table 5.2 shows cross-country differences in poverty rates for the population and the elderly in the early 2000s, where poverty is defined as having <50% of equivalised median income. Cross-country variations in poverty rates are much more pronounced among the elderly than the general population. For the total population, poverty rates range only from 10% (the Netherlands) to 21% (Greece); for the elderly population, they range from 2% (the Netherlands) to 32% (Korea). This table suggests that growing old in Korea bears much greater economic risk than in any other developed country.

5.3 Private (Family) Transfers in Korea

The erosion of traditional Confucian values has accelerated in the past five decades, beginning with the Korean War of 1950, the famine that accompanied it, and the drive for industrialisation and economic growth. Traditionally, the family played a key role in supporting elders, with children, especially the eldest son, taking care of their parents (Sung 2000). In fact, the idea of preparing in advance for one's own retirement is a relatively new concept in Korea, given the tradition of children supporting their parents as well as historically short life spans (Kim and Choe 1992; Sung 1995).

As Confucian values have waned, clear signs of diminishing willingness to care for older parents have emerged. These signs have included declines in multi-generational co-residence (Sung 1995; Levande et al. 2000) and familial support (Kwon 2001). In 1980, 76% of Koreans aged 60 or older reported family transfers as their main source of income; this proportion dropped to 57% in 1995 and 31% in 2003 (Kim 2007). At the same time, the proportion of Korean elderly who named public transfers as their main source of income increased from 2.0% in 1980 to 6.6% in 1995 to 25.6% in 2003.

5.4 The Relationship Between Public and Private Transfers

Theoretically, the linkage between public and private transfers depends on the motives for private transfers, among which altruism and exchange are those most commonly cited. Becker (1974) describes private transfers as altruistic behaviour by which donors compensate recipients for disparities in earnings. Altruistic households could go so far as to offset any changes in public transfers with private transfers (Barro 1974). Conversely, exchange theory views private transfers as strategic (Bernheim et al. 1985) and posits that donors obtain utilities not only from their and recipients' consumption but also from any services resulted from transfers (e.g. child care, visits). Under exchange theory, dollar-to-dollar transfers (often referred to as Ricardian equivalence, see Feldstein 1988) will not hold.

Empirical evidence suggests a limited link between public and private transfers: an increase in public transfers reduces only slightly the frequency and amount of familial transfers (Altonji and Villanueva 2003). This is not necessarily inconsistent with altruism: since parents and children cannot observe each other's endogenous level of labour market effort and income (Feldstein 1988; McGarry 2000), the limited link can be explained by imperfect information or information asymmetry rather than transfer motive.

The goal of this chapter, however, is not to examine the underlying motives of transfers. Instead, we examine the strength of the relationship between public and private transfers using panel data to illuminate whether and how sensitive private transfers are to changes in a recipient's income. We will consider potential strategic components of transfers, such as services that can trigger transfers to parents (i.e. care for grandchildren), in models of private transfers. There have been a few empirical studies on crowding-out effects, but not much is known about these in Korea. Because Korea is still in cultural transition and continuing reform efforts on public transfers, it is important to understand how private transfers will change as public transfers do so.

5.5 Data and Variables

We use data from the 2006 and 2008 waves of the Korean Longitudinal Study on Aging (KLoSA), a large-scale, longitudinal survey of the South Korean population ages 45 and older residing in the community. The baseline survey instrument was modelled after the Health and Retirement Survey and included detailed questions on income and assets, demographics, living arrangements, health, and labour force participation (Lee 2010).

The baseline data were collected from August to December of 2006. A stratified multistage probability sample was drawn from the 2005 Korean Census. The first stage of sampling consisted of census enumeration districts stratified by geographic location and characteristics of the enumeration districts (i.e. rural/urban and housing type). In the second sampling stage, households were sampled within the sampled enumeration districts. A total of 10,254 respondents completed the interview in the first wave.

The second, longitudinal wave of data was collected from July to November of 2008. Of the original cohort of 10,254 respondents, 187 were known to have died between waves, and an additional 1,379 did not complete the interview for other reasons. As a result, wave two of the study consisted of 8,688 individuals, almost 85% of the original group. No new households or respondents were introduced in this second wave.

We examine income and poverty of adults aged 65 or older using the most recent version of KLoSA (2008) and compare the findings with 2006. In the baseline study, 4,155 respondents were 65 or older. Of these, 3,501 were re-interviewed in 2008. Among those who were of age 63–64 in 2006 ($N = 610$), 534 respondents were re-interviewed in 2008.

The basic variables that we use are the following:

Poverty: We employ a relative measure of poverty, defining it as being below 50% of the median household income, as originally suggested by Fuchs (1969) and employed by numerous researchers (Iceland 2005). To account for variation in the economic needs of households of different sizes, as well as economies of scale, we used a single parameter equivalence scale with 0.5 equivalence elasticity (Burkhauser and Smeeding 1996). But we also examine the sensitivity of outcomes by using an alternative: the OECD equivalence scale that gives different weights for additional adults (0.7) and children (0.5).

Income: KLoSA contains detailed information about different types of income that are components of aggregate income. All income values were after-tax income received in the year prior to the survey (i.e. 2005 and 2007). Under the study design, each respondent was asked detailed questions about his or her personal income. In this study, we examine income at the family and household levels.

Total family income is the sum of the respondent's and spouse's income; total household income is the sum of all household members' income. By examining income at both family and household levels, we can evaluate the economic dependence of the elderly on their children (if they co-reside).

For the 4,035 individuals at least 65 years of age in the 2008 interview, we were able to compute total family income for 3,868 by summing their itemised income. We were unable to sum family income for 161 individuals who reported being married but whose spouse was not surveyed. We also were unable to examine income portfolios for 6 other individuals due to missing values of itemised income questions. Total household income was available for 4,020 individuals out of the 4,035 and unreported for the remaining 15.

Among the types of personal income data in the survey are (1) earnings: wage or salary income, income from self-employment, income from a side job; (2) asset income: rental income from primary residence and other properties, interests/dividends, and other investment income; (3) public pension income: occupational pension income for government workers, military personnel, railroad workers, private teachers, and postal workers and income from the NPS; (4) public welfare transfers: income from government programmes, including income from the NBLSS, income from unemployment insurance, workers' compensation, veterans' benefits, other welfare benefits; and (5) private transfers: the total amount of financial help received. We defined financial help as giving money, helping to pay bills, or covering specific types of costs, excluding shared housing and food from the definition. Private transfers include all transfers from family and friends and (6) other incomes such as alimony, loyalties, etc.

We created a set of binary variables indicating whether a respondent or spouse received income from each source and a set of continuous variables, indicating the share of each source of family income. The share of income refers to the total amount of income the elderly respondent and spouse received from a particular source divided by total household income.

In estimating private transfers, we included pre-private transfer income as the determinant of the amount of private transfer. We defined pre-private transfer income as a continuous variable of total family income, excluding private transfers.

Because private transfers are influenced by donors' economic resources and service from parents to children, we include the following two binary variables. First, because KLoSA does not collect information about income for respondents' children, we included a binary variable of the children's home ownership to represent children's economic resources (base: none of the children owns a home). Second, we employ a binary variable indicating whether a respondent or spouse of a respondent provided care for grandchildren.

Control Variables: We controlled for several time-varying characteristics of respondents: total family net worth, living arrangements, urban/rural residence, and health status. Total family net worth is the sum of the total financial and non-financial wealth of a respondent and spouse less their debts. We categorised living arrangements as living alone, living with a spouse (base), living with adult children (with or without a spouse), and living with others. We used a binary variable to indicate whether a respondent resides in an urban or rural area and a categorical variable of self-reported health status ranging from very poor to poor, fair, good, and very good health. We also controlled for respondents' demographic characteristics such as age, gender, and education.

5.6 Models and Research Questions

We first report the poverty status of the Korean elderly by key socio-demographic characteristics, using the 2008 wave, with two equivalence scales. Since age, gender, living arrangements, urban/rural residence, health status, and education are known risk factors of poverty, we report the poverty rate (i.e. the percentage of the poor) for each sub-population. To account for design effects due to the sampling design, descriptive statistics are weighted, and the standard errors are produced in accordance with the sampling design.

Using both waves of data, we then look into changes in poverty rates. We decompose such changes, first by looking into the changes in the sample, separately for those who dropped out after the first interview and those who remained keeping their socio-demographic characteristics under control.

Second, we investigate the relative contribution of public and private transfers to old-age income security by examining respondents' income portfolios. In describing income portfolios of the elderly, we present first the sources of household income, indicating the proportion of elderly households receiving income from particular income sources (e.g. public transfers), and second, the share of total household income from each family income source. We again look into the changes in income portfolios over time, specifically focusing on public and private transfers.

Finally, we examine the relationship between public and private transfers by investigating the amounts of private transfers received in relation to families' pre-transfer incomes using two waves of data available. Based on the exchange model of transfer, the amount of private transfer received by the *i*th individual at time t ($t = 0, 1$), $PrivT_{t,i}$, is modelled as a function of respondents' $Pre\text{-}transfer\ income_{t,i}$; the economic status of children who are primary providers for the elderly, $Child\_ES_{t,i}$; care of grandchildren as service to children, $Care\_G_{t,i}$; and other time-varying ($X_{t,i}$) and time-invariant (Z_i) control variables:

1. $E(PrivT_{t,i}) = \alpha + \beta_0 t + \beta_1 Pre - transfer\ income_{t,i} + \beta_2 Child\_ES_{t,i} + \beta_3 Care\_G_{t,i} + \beta_4 X_{t,i} + \beta_5 Z_i$

In the above model, α is an intercept. β_1 is the effect of pre-transfer income. β_2 is the effect of children's socioeconomic status. β_3 is the effect of parents' service to children. The time effect $\beta_0 t$ is used to account for the natural growth trend. The following time-varying control variables are included in $X_{t,i}$: the respondent's total family net worth, living arrangements, urban/rural residence, and health status. The time-invariant variables (Z_i) include demographic information. Also included in Z_i is a dummy variable for the individual-level (fixed) effect.

Given that only two waves of data are available, the mean difference or, equivalently, the first-order difference is an efficient and consistent approach to fitting the panel data model (Greene 2003; Yang and Tsiatis 2001). The first-order difference approach also adds additional benefits when there are measurement errors in the covariates (Liker et al. 1985). After taking first-order difference, the model (hereafter referred to as the first-difference model) becomes

2. $E\left(\Delta PrivT_{t,i}\right) = \beta_0 + \beta_1\,\Delta Pre - transfer\ income_{t,i} + \beta_2\,\Delta Child\_ES_{t,i} + \beta_3\,\Delta Care\_G_{t,i} + \beta_4\,\Delta X_{t,i}$

where the intercept β_0 results from the time effect. All financial variables are in the log scale before differencing. In fitting the first-difference model, we have also adjusted for the survey design information, including the clusters, strata, and longitudinal sampling weights.

At first glance, the time-invariant covariates Z_i should not appear in the first-difference model (2) because $\Delta Z_i = 0$. Nevertheless, this omission is valid under the assumption that the same time effect is shared among all individuals in the population, whereas some subgroups, e.g. female and male, may instead have distinct growth trends. This heterogeneity in time effect can be parameterised by the interaction term between Z_i and time t in (1). Note that the interaction tZ_i is time varying by itself, and $\Delta(tZ_i) = Z_i$. This leads to the appearance of Z_i in the first-difference model, where we also control for gender, education, and age.

5.7 Results

5.7.1 Poverty

First, we examine poverty rates of the Korean elderly aged 65 and older in 2008 using cross-sectional weights to obtain national representation (Table 5.3). We estimate the poverty rate to be 26% using both the OECD equivalence scale and the single equivalence scale with elasticity = 0.5. This is significantly lower than the 32% rate we estimated from the 2006 KLoSA using the same single equivalence scale (Lee and Lee 2009).

Regardless of the equivalence scale used, poverty is higher among people aged 75 and older than it is among those aged 65–74 and higher among elderly women than among elderly men. Living arrangements also influence poverty, with poverty highest among those who live alone. Poverty rates by living arrangements are sensitive to the equivalence scale used. Under the OECD equivalence scale (applying different weights for additional adults and children), elderly couples had the lowest poverty rates; under a 0.5 single equivalence scale, elderly couples living with children had the lowest poverty rates. Because living arrangements are associated with urban or rural residence, poverty rates by residence are also sensitive to the equivalence scale. There was no significant urban/rural difference in poverty rates when the OECD scale was used, but rural poverty was higher when the single equivalence scale was used. Self-reported health status shows a close association with poverty: older people with poor health are more likely to be in poverty. The number of children showed a strong non-linear association with poverty status. Two-thirds of the elderly without a living child were in poverty, while about one-fourth of the elderly with two to four children were poor.

Using both 2006 and 2008 data, we look further into what has contributed to the reduction of poverty rates from 32% to 26%. First, we look at sample differences

Table 5.3 Sample characteristics and poverty rates in Korea in 2008

		Sample characteristics		Poverty rate	
		Unweighted N	Weighted* (%)	OECD equivalence scale	0.5 single equivalence scale
All		4,020	100	26.16	26.99
Age	65–74	2,498	65.74	23.27	23.95
	75+	1,522	34.26	31.72	32.83
Sex	Men	1,679	40.59	19.53	23.60
	Women	2,336	59.41	30.66	29.30
Education	No school	1,350	32.96	36.10	32.64
	Elementary school	1,429	35.85	25.54	26.70
	Middle school	489	12.14	21.03	19.64
	High school	490	12.59	13.68	16.41
	Some college or more	262	6.46	12.96	15.84
Living arrangement	Living alone	655	16.33	44.92	44.92
	Living with spouse	1,801	44.91	18.75	31.87
	Living with children	1,350	33.31	25.47	13.07
	Living with others	214	5.44	35.35	18.17
Urban/rural residence	Urban	2,786	67.97	26.46	25.92
	Rural	1,234	32.03	25.54	29.26
Self-reported health	Very good	44	1.18	16.85	17.94
	Good	662	16.87	15.21	17.51
	Fair	1,550	38.08	22.72	22.00
	Bad	1,401	34.77	31.57	32.63
	Very bad	363	9.11	41.41	45.07
Number of children	None	72	1.66	67.73	65.81
	1	191	6.04	35.57	32.14
	2	529	13.86	24.62	23.96
	3	987	24.85	22.52	23.57
	4	934	23.27	26.18	25.18
	5	690	16.68	23.01	28.98
	6+	613	14.65	29.62	30.31

Source: Own elaborations on KLoSA data
*2008 cross-sectional weights have been used

caused by attrition and respondents (i.e. those who were 63 or 64 in 2006) entering the sample. Second, among those who were in the sample in both years, we compare the changes in poverty rates across socio-demographic characteristics.

Table 5.4 presents the sample characteristics by interview status in 2006 and 2008. Compared with those who participated in both interviews, those who dropped out in 2008 were older, less likely to live alone with their spouse and more likely to live with their children, more likely to reside in urban areas, more likely to report very poor health, and more likely to have only one living child and less likely to have five children. New entrants to the sample in 2008 were not only younger but

Table 5.4 Sample characteristics in 2006 depending on re-interview status in 2008

	All Rs interviewed in 2006		Re-interviewed in 2008		Dropped out in 2008			Newly entered in the sample in 2008		
	Mean	SE	Mean	SE	Mean	SE		Mean	SE	
Age	73.03	0.12	72.77	0.12	74.46	0.33	***	63.52	0.02	***
Gender										
% Female	59.58	0.63	59.81	0.70	58.32	1.78		53.25	2.14	**
Education										
% No school	37.38	0.99	37.54	1.05	36.50	2.14		16.60	1.67	***
% Elementary school	34.73	0.88	35.13	0.95	32.53	2.01		38.62	2.32	
% Middle school	10.73	0.51	10.55	0.55	11.73	1.41		17.99	1.72	***
% High school	11.34	0.56	11.06	0.58	12.87	1.46		18.09	1.77	***
% Some college or more	5.81	0.41	5.71	0.45	6.38	0.99		8.70	1.27	**
Living arrangement										
% Living alone	15.21	0.67	15.43	0.72	14.01	1.57		7.99	1.21	***
% Living with spouse only	41.86	1.07	42.91	1.17	36.02	2.39	*	51.42	2.41	**
% Living with children	39.24	1.09	37.93	1.16	46.53	2.46	**	37.43	2.37	
% Living with others	3.69	0.39	3.73	0.43	3.45	0.84		3.15	0.96	
Urban/rural										
% Rural	33.69	1.09	36.07	1.18	20.42	1.72	***	27.24	2.21	***
Self-reported health										
% Good or very good	19.29	0.76	19.12	0.84	20.23	1.69		31.73	2.24	***
% Fair	31.28	0.87	32.01	0.96	27.21	1.90	*	35.02	2.24	
% Poor	37.22	0.90	37.83	0.98	33.80	2.19		27.60	2.06	***
% Very poor	12.21	0.68	11.03	0.67	18.76	1.72	***	5.65	1.01	***
Number of children										
% No children	1.89	0.24	1.66	0.23	3.17	0.91		1.51	0.54	
1	4.97	0.40	4.56	0.43	7.27	1.09	*	6.87	1.25	
2	11.52	0.62	11.37	0.68	12.36	1.56		22.45	2.04	***
3	22.30	0.82	22.06	0.88	23.63	1.88		34.82	2.29	***
4	23.45	0.82	23.61	0.90	22.57	1.87		20.85	1.92	
5	18.36	0.79	18.54	0.85	17.37	1.78		9.76	1.58	***
6+	17.50	0.81	18.19	0.88	13.64	1.59	**	3.74	0.90	***
Poverty rates	31.42	1.03	30.85	1.11	34.62	2.24		25.57	2.23	*

Source: See Table 5.3
All monetary values are in 2008 KW (Korean won). 2006 cross-sectional weights have been used
*, **, *** represent a statistically significant difference at 5%, 1%, and 0.1% from individuals re-interviewed in 2008

included a greater portion of men than the older cohorts who were re-interviewed. The new entrants were also more educated, less likely to live alone and more likely to live with a spouse, more likely to live in an urban area, healthier, and more likely to have two or three children but less likely to have five or more children than those who were re-interviewed. Nevertheless, the difference in poverty rates for the new entrants and the older cohorts was only marginally significant ($p < .10$) and,

Table 5.5 Poverty rates in 2006 and 2008 by socio-demographic characteristics

	Poverty rates				
	2006 (%)	2008 (%)	Test stat	*p*-value	*
All	30.39	26.52	−3.12	0.002	**
Age in 2008					
Age 65–74	28.72	23.36	−3.70	0.000	***
Age 75+	33.58	32.54	−0.59	0.558	
Gender					
Male	28.13	23.13	−3.32	0.001	**
Female	31.91	28.95	−2.21	0.027	*
Education					
No school	38.00	35.91	−1.05	0.295	
Elementary school	28.89	26.30	−1.52	0.130	
Middle school	26.24	19.38	−2.34	0.019	*
High school	24.66	16.01	−2.97	0.003	**
Some college or more	20.14	15.45	−1.38	0.167	
Living arrangement					
Living alone	46.34	44.50	−0.62	0.536	
Living with spouse	35.06	31.37	−1.92	0.055	
Living with children	18.46	12.68	−3.62	0.000	***
Living with others	38.88	17.69	−3.49	0.001	**
Urban/rural					
Urban	30.91	25.44	−3.85	0.000	***
Rural	29.29	28.83	−0.19	0.851	
Self-reported health					
Good or very good	21.84	17.51	−2.00	0.046	*
Fair	26.90	21.47	−2.87	0.004	**
Poor	35.68	32.07	−1.69	0.091	*
Very poor	41.85	45.34	0.96	0.339	
Number of children					
None	23.76	64.29	5.49	0.000	***
1	32.57	30.51	−0.42	0.678	
2	30.90	23.57	−2.47	0.014	*
3	26.03	23.01	−1.48	0.140	
4	33.23	25.08	−3.23	0.001	**
5	32.01	28.69	−1.26	0.207	
6+	31.14	29.68	−0.49	0.622	

Source: See Table 5.3
We used longitudinal weights, accounted for sampling design
*, **, *** represent a statistically significant difference at 5%, 1%, and 0.1%

hence, does not explain the significant reduction in poverty rates (poverty rates are based on the single equivalence scale).

Next, we examine changes in poverty rates by socio-demographic characteristics (Table 5.5). To account for attrition bias, we use longitudinal weights in our analyses. Overall, poverty among the elderly (i.e. age 65 and older) diminished from 30.4% to 26.5%. This decrease was not uniform: it was concentrated among those aged 65–74, with middle-school or high-school educations, living with

Table 5.6 Household portfolio: source of income by family income and living arrangement

		All		Live alone		Live with spouse		Live with children		Other	
Income sources		%	SE	%	SE	%	SE	%	SE	%	SE
Low income		($N = 1{,}278$)		($N = 263$)		($N = 242$)		($N = 676$)		($N = 97$)	
Family income	Earnings	5.07	0.87	5.22	1.64	12.15	3.05	2.76	0.91	2.93	1.78
	Assets	5.66	0.85	4.95	1.34	8.45	2.58	5.56	1.07	1.59	1.14
	Pensions	8.45	1.09	6.96	1.70	9.32	2.58	8.32	1.36	11.00	6.94
	Welfare transfers	57.29	2.11	67.19	3.28	55.17	5.23	55.24	2.66	50.73	6.89
	Private transfers	59.06	1.97	60.40	3.25	59.36	4.50	58.24	2.45	60.21	6.35
	Others	0.16	0.11	0.77	0.56	0.00	0.00	0.00	0.00	0.00	0.00
Other HH members' income		58.30	1.83	NA		NA		95.17	1.18	97.42	1.48
Middle income		($N = 1{,}267$)		($N = 277$)		($N = 634$)		($N = 302$)		($N = 54$)	
Family income	Earnings	41.82	2.04	33.99	3.34	47.08	3.04	39.71	3.62	32.56	8.34
	Assets	21.93	1.74	17.70	2.45	23.33	2.74	24.20	3.00	14.53	5.64
	Pensions	34.36	1.94	26.83	2.93	39.23	2.92	32.89	3.43	24.52	7.71
	Welfare transfers	56.60	2.12	52.86	3.31	60.33	3.00	54.03	3.78	46.99	9.89
	Private transfers	83.48	1.49	89.04	2.10	83.60	2.24	78.37	2.97	82.71	6.34
	Others	1.69	0.51	1.12	0.67	2.66	0.96	0.54	0.39	0.00	0.00
Other HH members' income		24.07	1.66	NA		NA		85.44	2.52	75.82	7.03
High income		($N = 1{,}271$)		($N = 93$)		($N = 904$)		($N = 311$)		($N = 47$)	
Family income	Earnings	62.51	1.94	47.89	5.96	61.65	2.51	67.21	3.53	73.60	8.44
	Assets	41.06	2.32	46.32	5.90	40.59	2.93	41.20	3.89	38.17	8.95
	Pensions	47.85	1.99	38.44	5.83	50.26	2.53	43.76	3.68	51.24	9.70
	Welfare transfers	46.20	2.35	40.20	5.45	48.05	2.96	44.68	3.62	35.40	8.90
	Private transfers	77.85	1.83	80.89	4.51	81.07	2.22	70.85	3.78	62.84	9.68
	Others	3.88	0.97	12.12	4.34	2.88	0.89	3.07	1.53	11.40	6.26
Other HH members' income		17.40	1.44	NA		NA		60.63	3.77	63.24	8.39

Source: See Table 5.3
We used longitudinal weights, accounted for sampling design

children and others, living in urban areas, having two or four living children, or being in very good, good, or fair health. Quite startlingly, the poverty rate has more than doubled for the elderly without any living children. Although the sample size for the childless elderly is small ($N = 72$); this evidence suggests that childless elderly are the most economically vulnerable group. Poverty rates for other groups did not change significantly.

5.7.2 Household Income Portfolios

Table 5.6 presents sources of household income by family income and living arrangements. Family income only accounts for respondent and spouse incomes.

Table 5.7 Source of income by family income: comparison of 2006 and 2008

Income sources		2006 %	2006 SE	2008 %	2008 SE	*t*-test	*p*-value	*
Low income								
Family income	Earnings	2.89	0.61	5.07	0.87	2.21	0.027	*
	Assets	8.71	1.09	5.66	0.85	−2.34	0.020	*
	Pensions	6.52	0.99	8.45	1.09	1.50	0.134	
	Welfare transfers	34.49	2.18	57.29	2.11	10.32	0.000	***
	Private transfers	54.69	2.00	59.06	1.97	1.68	0.093	
	Others	0.23	0.13	0.16	0.11	−0.42	0.677	
Other HH members' income		52.00	1.88	58.30	1.83	2.85	0.005	**
Middle income								
Family income	Earnings	35.43	2.09	41.82	2.04	2.98	0.003	**
	Assets	20.49	1.73	21.93	1.74	0.64	0.522	
	Pensions	27.25	1.76	34.36	1.94	3.57	0.000	***
	Welfare transfers	44.04	2.26	56.60	2.12	5.56	0.000	***
	Private transfers	73.28	1.77	83.48	1.49	4.62	0.000	***
	Others	0.82	0.33	1.69	0.51	1.43	0.152	
Other HH members' income		21.38	1.78	24.07	1.66	1.42	0.156	
High income								
Family income	Earnings	66.69	1.88	62.51	1.94	−2.57	0.010	*
	Assets	41.92	2.21	41.06	2.32	−0.31	0.759	
	Pensions	42.43	2.06	47.85	1.99	2.98	0.003	**
	Welfare transfers	31.06	2.17	46.20	2.35	6.97	0.000	***
	Private transfers	70.16	2.04	77.85	1.83	3.24	0.001	**
	Others	3.80	0.75	3.88	0.97	0.07	0.945	
Other HH members' income		13.33	1.32	17.40	1.44	2.26	0.024	*

Source: See Table 5.3
Used longitudinal weights, accounted for sampling design
*, **, *** represent statistical significance at 5%, 1%, and 0.1%

Not surprisingly, more than 95% of those who are at the bottom third of family income and who live with children have income from other household members, indicating their dependence on their children. The proportion of those receiving income from children or other household members decreases as income level increases. Conversely, the proportion of families receiving income from earnings, assets, and pensions increases with income level. The proportion of families receiving income from welfare transfer decreases as income level increases but, surprisingly, at a modest rate. Among low-income families, 57% of families received welfare transfers, which is not significantly different from the proportion of middle-income families receiving such transfers. Even among families with high income, 43% received welfare transfers. The per cent of families receiving income from private transfers is noticeably less for low-income individuals than for middle- and high-income individuals.

Table 5.7 further compares reported household-income portfolios in 2006 and 2008. The percentage of low-income individuals receiving income from other household members increased significantly from 52% to 58%. In 2006, the percentage of individuals receiving welfare transfers was highest for the middle-income group, but by 2008, the proportion of low-income individuals receiving such transfers had grown fastest and was the largest among the three income groups. The percentage of individuals receiving income from private transfers increased significantly for each income bracket, with the largest increase, from 73% to 83%, in the middle-income bracket. Significantly more low- and middle-income individuals reported income from earnings in 2008 while significantly fewer high-income individuals reported income from earnings. The percentage of individuals receiving income from pensions also increased significantly for middle- and high-income individuals. These shifts in the sources of household income are informative on changing income streams but best understood by examining the shares of income that each component contributes to total household income.

Table 5.8 presents shares of income by source. Low-income elderly individuals living with their children received 91% of their household income from their children. Those not co-residing with children, especially those living either alone or with a spouse, also depended on family members, with about half of their household income from private transfers, a lower share than reported in 2006 (Lee and Lee 2009). In 2006, 65–70% of income from low- and middle-income families' household incomes was from private transfers. Dependence on welfare transfers increased from 2006 to 2008. Among low-income elderly living alone or living with a spouse, less than one-fifth of income came from welfare transfers in 2006; by 2008, one-fourth to one-third did. Among low-income individuals, those living with children or other persons received a lower share of income from public welfare transfers than did low-income individuals living alone or only with their spouse.

Table 5.9 compares mean shares of income by source in 2006 and 2008. Income composition shifted between 2006 and 2008 in several ways. Low-income individuals received a significantly smaller share of their income from assets and private transfers in 2008 than in 2006; conversely, they also received a significantly larger share of income from earnings and welfare transfers. Middle-income individuals received a significantly smaller share of their income from welfare transfers in 2008 than in 2006; conversely, they received a significantly larger share of their income from earnings and private transfers. The decrease in welfare transfers for middle-income individuals was the largest shift of any one component of household income in any of the income brackets. Welfare transfers accounted for more than 10% of middle-income individuals' income in 2006 and <2% in 2008. High-income individuals received a significantly smaller share of their income from earnings in 2008 than in 2006; conversely, they received a significantly larger share of their income from pensions, private transfers, and other household members' income. Several of these shifts suggest that government welfare transfers may significantly affect private transfers, particularly for low- and middle-income individuals.

Table 5.8 Household income portfolio: share of income by family income and living arrangement

Income sources		All %	All SE	Live alone %	Live alone SE	Live with spouse %	Live with spouse SE	Live with children %	Live with children SE	Other %	Other SE
Low income											
Family income	Earnings	3.45	0.76	4.21	1.26	11.81	3.62	0.81	0.37	0.88	0.74
	Assets	1.41	0.35	2.30	0.71	4.81	1.75	0.18	0.04	0.03	0.02
	Pensions	3.65	0.60	6.07	1.56	8.79	2.37	1.34	0.44	2.00	1.66
	Welfare transfers	12.15	1.17	33.07	3.06	27.28	4.29	1.33	0.56	1.12	0.34
	Private transfers	22.79	1.39	53.33	3.13	49.87	4.25	5.57	0.76	5.25	1.39
	Others	0.09	0.06	0.46	0.33	0.00	0.00	0.00	0.00	0.00	0.00
Other HH members' income		57.42	1.77	NA		NA		91.06	1.12	90.72	2.54
Total		*100.96*		*99.45*		*102.55*		*100.28*		*100.00*	
Middle income											
Family income	Earnings	26.92	1.49	22.09	2.49	34.18	2.33	17.99	2.04	17.75	5.11
	Assets	7.13	0.74	7.75	1.38	8.18	1.18	5.17	1.13	2.97	1.57
	Pensions	11.11	0.84	9.37	1.23	14.60	1.40	6.47	1.15	5.68	2.58
	Welfare transfers	1.81	0.32	1.31	0.43	2.43	0.58	1.07	0.39	1.40	0.57
	Private transfers	36.96	1.44	58.56	2.73	39.70	2.13	14.52	1.58	22.54	4.87
	Others	0.58	0.22	0.56	0.35	0.90	0.41	0.03	0.03	0.00	0.00
Other HH members' income		15.49	1.20	NA		NA		54.75	2.41	49.68	8.04
Total		*100.00*		*99.64*		*100.00*		*100.00*		*100.00*	
High income											
Family income	Earnings	44.94	1.68	37.22	5.16	46.74	2.15	42.51	2.89	44.52	6.59
	Assets	13.54	1.07	13.16	3.42	15.29	1.46	9.80	1.56	8.96	3.46
	Pensions	15.76	1.08	16.71	3.40	17.21	1.45	12.20	1.66	12.56	4.54
	Welfare transfers	2.47	0.46	2.79	1.59	2.36	0.57	2.97	1.02	0.27	0.19
	Private transfers	15.72	0.99	24.82	3.54	17.53	1.34	9.13	1.29	11.21	3.26
	Others	1.22	0.34	5.29	1.85	0.87	0.30	0.84	0.47	2.21	1.70
Other HH members' income		6.35	0.65	NA		NA		22.55	2.03	20.27	4.20
Total		*100.00*		*100.00*		*100.00*		*100.00*		*100.00*	

Source: See Table 5.3
Used longitudinal weights, accounted for sampling design
Individuals with 0 total household income excluded from calculations ($N = 48$)
Not all totals account for exactly 100% of income due to weighting and excluded individuals

5.7.3 *Crowding-Out Private Transfers?*

A possible crowding-out effect of public transfers on private transfers is suggested both in the baseline analysis of KLoSA data (Lee and Lee 2009) and our descriptive longitudinal analysis. Table 5.10 presents the results of two first-difference models. Model 1 does not control for any time-invariant variables. Model 2 includes the time-invariant characteristics: gender, education, and age. In both models, an increase in pre-private transfer income is associated with an increase in private transfers. A 1% change in pre-private transfer income is estimated to increase private transfers by 0.07%. Several time-variant variables were associated with

Table 5.9 Mean income share by family income: comparing 2006 and 2008 income portfolios

Income sources		2006 %	2006 SE	2008 %	2008 SE	*t*-stat	*p*-value	*
Low income								
Family income	Earnings	1.80	0.45	3.45	0.76	2.07	0.039	*
	Assets	3.40	0.64	1.41	0.35	−2.70	0.007	**
	Pensions	3.42	0.77	3.65	0.60	0.25	0.800	
	Welfare transfers	7.82	0.84	12.15	1.17	3.34	0.001	**
	Private transfers	28.17	1.58	22.79	1.39	−3.06	0.002	**
	Others	0.11	0.08	0.09	0.06	−0.17	0.866	
Other HH members' income		55.29	1.94	57.42	1.77	1.00	0.319	
Total		*100.00*		*100.96*				
Middle income								
Family income	Earnings	23.42	1.66	26.92	1.49	2.11	0.035	*
	Assets	6.98	0.77	7.13	0.74	0.17	0.868	
	Pensions	10.41	0.88	11.11	0.84	0.67	0.502	
	Welfare transfers	12.93	1.05	1.81	0.32	−10.65	0.000	***
	Private transfers	31.34	1.42	36.96	1.44	3.52	0.000	***
	Others	0.24	0.11	0.58	0.22	1.40	0.162	
Other HH members' income		14.68	1.43	15.49	1.20	0.61	0.545	
Total		*100.00*		*100.00*				
High income								
Family income	Earnings	49.56	1.78	44.94	1.68	−3.05	0.002	**
	Assets	14.90	1.19	13.54	1.07	−1.12	0.262	
	Pensions	13.17	1.04	15.76	1.08	3.20	0.001	**
	Welfare transfers	3.21	0.52	2.47	0.46	−1.54	0.124	
	Private transfers	13.67	0.98	15.72	0.99	1.85	0.065	
	Others	0.71	0.21	1.22	0.34	1.22	0.336	
Other HH members' income		4.78	0.60	6.35	0.65	1.92	0.055	
Total		*100.00*		*100.00*				

Source: See Table 5.3
Used longitudinal weights, accounted for sampling design
Individuals with 0 total household income excluded from calculations ($N = 48$)
Not all totals account for exactly 100% of income due to weighting and excluded individuals
*, **, *** represent statistical significance at 5%, 1%, and 0.1%

changes in private transfers. For example, transitions between living arrangements were estimated to have significant effects on the change in private transfers. Individuals who went from living with a spouse to living with children experienced a decrease in private transfers compared with those living with a spouse in both time periods. Individuals who went from living with children to living with others received more private transfers. Individuals whose health improved between 2006 and 2008 saw a decrease in private transfers. Individuals whose children acquired a house between 2006 and 2008 received more private transfers. On the other hand, caring for grandchildren was not significantly associated with the changes in private transfer amounts. None of the time-invariant characteristics had a significant effect on changes in private transfers.

Table 5.10 First-difference model

	Model 1			Model 2		
	Coefficient	*t*		Coefficient	*t*	
log(2008 pre-private) – log (2006 pre-private)	0.069	2.29	*	0.065	2.17	*
log(2008 net worth) – log (2006 net worth)	0.065	0.99		0.057	0.86	
Living arrangement Δ (base: spouse-spouse)						
Alone-alone	0.103	0.56		0.131	0.68	
Alone-spouse	0.000			0.000		
Alone-children	−0.567	−0.97		−0.500	−0.89	
Alone-others	−1.029	−1.97	*	−0.939	−1.86	
Spouse-alone	0.256	0.39		0.236	0.36	
Spouse-children	−0.728	−2.00	*	−0.727	−2.00	*
Spouse-other	−0.546	−0.75		−0.529	−0.73	
Children-alone	0.702	1.40		0.710	1.41	
Children-spouse	−0.254	−0.74		−0.258	−0.74	
Children-children	−0.346	−2.10	*	−0.282	−1.63	
Children-other	1.046	2.70	**	1.105	2.82	**
Other-alone	1.355	2.64	**	1.330	2.41	*
Other-spouse	0.171	0.17		0.244	0.24	
Other-children	0.533	0.58		0.664	0.72	
Other-other	0.020	0.03		0.057	0.09	
Rural Δ (base: urban-urban)						
Urban-rural	0.927	0.97		0.983	1.06	
Rural-urban	−0.181	−0.52		−0.169	−0.46	
Rural-rural	−0.311	−1.70		−0.355	−1.93	
Health Δ (base: not poor-not poor)						
Not poor-poor	−0.125	−0.71		−0.091	−0.51	
Poor-not poor	−0.499	−2.80	**	−0.497	−2.74	**
Poor-poor	−0.262	−1.82		−0.253	−1.60	
Children own house Δ (base: own-own)						
Don't own-don't own	0.363	2.16	*	0.287	1.63	
Don't own-own	0.688	2.37	*	0.646	2.21	*
Own-don't own	0.363	0.52		0.295	0.42	
Cared for grandchildren Δ (base: no-no)						
No-yes	−0.237	−0.35		−0.263	−0.39	
Yes-no	−0.094	−0.38		−0.155	−0.63	
Yes-yes	−0.655	−1.38		−0.729	−1.54	
Gender (base: male)						
Female				−0.088	−0.86	
Education (base: no education)						
Elementary school				−0.190	−1.31	
Middle school				−0.089	−0.41	
High school				−0.371	−1.63	
Some college or more				−0.329	−1.18	
Age in 2006				0.150	0.93	
(Age in 2006)^2				−0.001	−1.10	
R^2	0.036		0.041			

Source: See Table 5.3

*, **, *** represent statistical significance at 5%, 1%, and 0.1%

5.8 Discussion

While we found that overall poverty decreased for elderly individuals in Korea between 2006 and 2008, it did not do so for all individuals. In particular, individuals who were older, childless, less educated, living alone, living in a rural area, or in poor health did not see their poverty rate decrease or not significantly. Although the global financial crisis of 2008 hit the Korean economy by drying up domestic and international liquidity and reducing demand for Korea's exports, Korea was the first OECD country to escape the negative growth (Yoon 2011). As most Koreans retire earlier than age 65 (Lee and Smith 2009), the impact of the global financial crisis on the economic security of Korea's elderly is expected to be limited.

For individuals in the lowest-income bracket, welfare transfers increased both as a source of income and as a share of total household income. Also for low-income individuals, private transfers increased as a source of household income but decreased as a share of total household income. This suggests that a greater proportion of elderly receive private transfers, but that the relative contribution of private transfers to elderly household income has diminished. Taken together, these findings suggest that both public and private transfers make significant contributions to the financial well-being of the elderly, and that the increase in welfare transfers for low-income individuals was coupled with decreased family support.

Middle-income elderly saw large reductions in welfare transfers but increases in private transfers. Private transfers increased both as a source and a share of household income for middle-income individuals. Public pensions also increased as a source of income, but their share remains unchanged. As public pensions mature, we anticipate their continued growth as a share of household income.

High-income elderly also experienced increases in private transfers and pension income. Public pension income increased both as a source and share of income for the high-income elderly.

Our results do not suggest a crowding-out effect of increases in pre-transfer income on private transfers but instead that increases in pre-transfer income have a positive impact on private transfers. That is, as the elderly receive more income from other sources, they also receive more money from their family members. Our analysis also suggests that private transfers increase as children's economic status does but that such transfers are not affected by changes in the amount of service an elderly parent provides for their grandchildren. These findings suggest that children provide for their elderly parents, not in response to the services provided to them but, instead, to the extent of their ability to provide for their elderly parents.

5.9 Conclusion

The economic well-being of the Korean elderly depends on public and private transfers. We examined the economic well-being of the elderly and their reliance on public and private transfers in several ways. First, we estimated poverty status based on equivalised household income. We then examined household income portfolios, disaggregating household incomes for respondents, spouses, and co-residing household members. We then broke down the elderly's family income by source: earnings, asset income, public pension income, welfare transfer income, private transfer income, and other sources of income.

We found that 26% of the Korean elderly (i.e. individuals aged 65 or older) lived in poverty in 2008. Compared with other OECD countries, the poverty risk is substantially higher for the Korean elderly. We found a significant decrease in the elderly poverty rate between 2006 and 2008, from 32% to 26%. But poverty reduction has not benefited individuals who were older, less educated, childless, living alone, living in a rural area, or in poor health.

Household income portfolio analyses illuminate the economic dependence of the elderly through co-residence. Low-income elderly who co-reside receive more than 90% of their income from the children or the other household members with whom they co-reside. Most low-income elderly living alone or only with a spouse receive welfare or private transfer income. Welfare transfers account for no more than a third of income for low-income elderly, while private transfers accounted for about half. Nevertheless, welfare transfers grew as a proportion of income for low-income elderly between 2006 and 2008, while private transfers decreased. This suggests the BOASP has helped reduce poverty among the elderly.

We also observed a slight increase in public pension income, especially among high-income elderly. As the public pension programme matures, we anticipate its growth as a share of income for the elderly.

Our analyses of the relationship between elderly respondents' family income before private transfers and the private transfers they received suggest that crowding-out is not a real concern in increasing welfare transfers for the low-income elderly. Using the first-difference model, we found a positive relationship between changes in income for the elderly and changes in private transfers received, specifically that a 1% increase in elderly family income (through an increase in public transfers) will increase private transfer income by 0.07%. Such a positive relationship between public and private transfers is noteworthy – in a country where elderly poverty is still prevalent, public transfers do not have any crowding-out of private transfers: instead, they contribute positively to alleviating elderly poverty. We also find that changes in children's economic status influences changes in private transfer income, suggesting that if public transfer programmes influence children's income (e.g. increased tax burden), this will negatively influence the elderly's private transfer income. Further analyses with more detailed data on children's income are needed to estimate the aggregate effects.

Acknowledgements This project is funded by National Institute on Aging, National Institutes of Health: P01 AG022481 International Comparisons of Well-Being, Health and Retirement and R01 AG030153 Integrating Informaiton about Aging Surveys.

References

Altonji, J. G., & Villanueva, E. (2003). *The marginal propensity to spend on adult children* (Working Paper 9811). Cambridge: National Bureau of Economic Research.

Barro, R. J. (1974). Are government bonds net wealth? *Journal of Political Economy, 82*(6), 1095–1117.

Becker, G. S. (1974). A theory of social interactions. *Journal of Political Economy, 82*(6), 1063–1093.

Bernheim, B. D., Shleifer, A., & Summers, L. H. (1985). The strategic bequest motive. *Journal of Political Economy, 93*(6), 1045–1076.

Burkhauser, R., & Smeeding, T. M. (1996). Relative inequality and poverty in Germany and the U.S. using alternative equivalence scales. *Review of Income and Wealth, 42*, 381–400.

Feldstein, M. (1988). The effects of fiscal policies when incomes are uncertain: A contradiction to Ricardian equivalence. *American Economic Review, 78*(1), 14–23.

Förster, M. F., & Mira D'Ercole, M. (2005). *Income distribution and poverty in OECD countries in the second half of the 1990s* (OECD Social, Employment and Migration Working Paper, No. 77). Paris: OECD Directorate for Employment, Labour, and Social Affairs.

Fuchs, V. (1969). Comment on measuring the size of the low-income population. In L. Stoltow (Ed.), *Six papers on the size distribution of wealth and income* (pp. 198–202). New York: National Bureau of Economic Research.

Greene, W. H. (2003). *Econometric analysis* (5th ed.). Singapore: Pearson Education.

Iceland, J. (2005). Measuring poverty: Theoretical and empirical considerations. *Measurement, 3*, 199–235.

Kim, H. (2007). *Intergenerational transfers and old-age income security in Korea*, Monograph. Seoul: Korea Development Institute.

Kim, I. K., & Choe, E. H. (1992). Support exchange patterns of the elderly in the Republic of Korea. *Asia-Pacific Population Journal, 3*, 89–104.

KLoSA, Korean Longitudinal Study on Aging. (2008). Korea Labor Institute.

KNSO, Korea National Statistical Office. (2009). *Korea statistical information service*. Retrieved on March 13, 2009, from http://www.kosis.kr/

Kwon, S. (2001). Economic crisis and social policy reform in Korea. *International Journal of Social Welfare, 10*, 97–106.

Lee, J. (2010). Data set for pension and health: Data collection and sharing for policy design. *International Social Security Review, 63*(3–4), 197–222.

Lee, J., & Lee, Y. (2009). Old-age income security and private transfers in Korea. *Journal of Population Aging and Social Policy, 21*(4), 393–407.

Lee, J., & Smith, J. P. (2009). Work, retirement, and depression. *Journal of Population and Aging, 2*, 57–71.

Levande, D. I., Herrick, J. M., & Sung, K. (2000). Eldercare in the United States and South Korea: Balancing family and community support. *Journal of Family Issues, 21*, 632–651.

Liker, J. K., Augustyniak, S., & Duncan, G. J. (1985). Panel data and models of change: A comparison of first difference and conventional two-wave models. *Social Science Research, 14*, 80–101.

McGarry, K. (2000). *Testing parental altruism: Implications of a dynamic model* (Working Paper). Los Angeles: Department of Economics, University of California.

NPS, National Pension Service. (2010). Retrieved on December 12, 2010, from http://www.nps.or.kr/jsppage/etc/data/data01_01.jsp

OECD, Organization for Economic Co-operation and Development. (2008). *Growing unequal? Income distribution and poverty in OECD countries*. Paris: OECD.

OECD, Organization for Economic Co-operation and Development. (2010). *OECD-StatExtracts*. Retrieved on December 10, 2010, from http://stats.oecd.org/Index.aspx

Park, N. H., Yeo, Y. J., Kim, K. Y., Lim, W. S., Song, Y. K., & Park, S. Y. (2003). *The status of poverty policy and development: Focus on income security* (Research Report 2003–11). Seoul: Korea Institute of Health and Social Affairs.

Smeeding, T. (2005). *Poor people in rich nations: The United States in comparative perspective* (Working Paper 419). Luxembourg: Income Studies.

Sung, K. (1995). Measures and dimensions of filial piety in Korea. *The Gerontologist, 35*, 240–247.

Sung, K. (2000). Respect for elders: Myths and realities in East Asia. *Journal of Aging and Identity, 5*, 197–205.

WHO, World Health Organization. (2009). *World Health Organization InfoBase*. Retrieved on April 11, 2009, from http://apps.who.int/infobase

Yang, L., & Tsiatis, A. A. (2001). Efficiency study of estimators for a treatment effect in a pretest-posttest trial. *The American Statistician, 55*, 314–321.

Yoon, D. R. (2011). The Korean economic adjustment to the world financial crisis. *Asian Economic Papers, 10*(1), 106–127. doi:10.1162/ASEP_a_00058.

Zaidi, A., Grech, A. G., & Fuchs, M. (2006). *Pension policy in EU25 and its possible impact on elderly poverty* (Working Paper Centre for Analysis of Social Exclusion, CASE/116). London: London School of Economics.

Chapter 6
Heterogeneous Elderly Parents and Intergenerational Transfers in Japan

Taizo Motonishi

6.1 Introduction

This study aims to evaluate the impact of intergenerational transfers on the budgetary constraints of adult children in Japan by estimating the economic burden or benefit represented by their elderly parents, whose socioeconomic heterogeneity is kept into account. In Japan, adult children are generally expected to care for their elderly parents, by providing money or nursing care. On the other hand, it is also common for adult children to receive money from their parents as bequests or transfers and, notably, on special occasions, e.g. when they buy their homes. Thus, the existence of elderly parents is expected to have mixed effects on the budgets of their adult children.

Horioka (2009) shows that about 60% of the people in Japan are willing to give at least 10% of their income to their parents. This share is about the same as in the USA. However, <20% of the Japanese population is willing to leave a bequest to their adult children, which is much lower than the comparable figure in the USA (%). These figures suggest that differences exist between these countries with regard to the values of parent–child transfers and that elderly parents may be a larger economic burden on their adult children in Japan than in the USA.

In Japan, most studies about intergenerational transfers focus only on the behaviours of the 'average household', but the reasons behind intergenerational transfers may differ according to the type of family and its economic situation. For example, some intergenerational transfers are interpreted as welfare payments, and others could be construed as compensation for nursing services (see also Lee and Phillips, this volume). Therefore, the amount and direction of intergenerational transfers may vary with income, as well as with kinship and family structures.

T. Motonishi (✉)
Faculty of Economics, Kansai University, 3-3-35, Yamate-cho, Suita-shi, Osaka 564-8680, Japan
e-mail: tmoto@kansai-u.ac.ip

G. De Santis (ed.), *The Family, the Market or the State?: Intergenerational Support Under Pressure in Ageing Societies*, International Studies in Population 10,
DOI 10.1007/978-94-007-4339-7_6,

This possible differential effect is precisely the focus of this paper, which indeed suggests that the economic effects caused by the presence of elderly parents in the household do depend on their socioeconomic type. At one extreme, we find low-income elderly parents of husbands, who appear to have the strongest negative effect on the standards of living of their adult children's families. At the other extreme, there are high-income elderly parents of wives, whose effect appears to be positive.

Although the difference accruing from elderly parents' income levels is easy to accept, the difference between husbands' and wives' parents may require a few words of explanation. In Japan, the responsibility for looking after elderly parents generally rests more on sons than on daughters. Moreover, husbands are the main income earners in most families in Japan, and husbands usually carry on the family name. These factors may underpin the differential effects of the responsibilities placed on sons (and their families) as compared to daughters (and their families).

The heterogeneous effects of elderly parents on their adult children's budgets suggest that the common assumption of 'representative' elderly parents may oversimplify a complex reality. An adult family having the husband's low-income elderly parents has to earn 12% more than the reference, one-generation family, in order to maintain the same living standard. In contrast, a middle-aged family having the wife's high-income elderly parents can maintain the family's living standard with 24% less income. These results provide a backdrop for conventional wisdom about the economic relationship between adult children and their elderly parents in Japan.

6.2 Estimation Framework of Intergenerational Transfers

This chapter deals with intergenerational transfers in Japan, but it does not attempt to estimate their amount directly. What it tries to do, instead, is to estimate the economic burden that derives from maintaining elderly parents. This burden falls on the shoulders of adult children and has two peculiarities that are worth noticing: it includes implicit transfers (when adult children and elderly parents co-reside), and it may be negative, if the presence of well-off elderly parents proves to be an economic advantage, for instance, because they contribute to expenses or because the prospects of some substantial bequests reduces the need to save.

Defining exactly what is meant by 'transfers' is a challenging task. Some types of transfers are indeed not properly transfers: rather, they can be interpreted as payments for goods or services. For example, affluent elderly parents might provide financial support to their adult children in exchange for nursing care. More generally, since all voluntary transfers are made to acquire satisfaction, it is not totally clear how much of (implicit) payment for current or future services is embedded in them.

Other kinds of transfers can be labelled as 'involuntary', because they are imposed by a set of social norms. For example, Japanese society would not allow middle-aged children to abandon their elderly parents in distress. In this case, middle-aged children may feel forced to provide support for their elderly parents, which is something that they would rather not do, if they were free to choose. Of course, the two aspects may well coexist, since social obligations and exchanges of money versus services are not mutually exclusive.

The distinction between voluntary and involuntary transfers affects the feeling of satisfaction that accompanies each of them and normally escapes empirical observation. But some of the material consequences of this complex web of exchanges may be observed, and, within limits, it is possible to assess whether the presence of elderly parents is neutral, favourable, or unfavourable on the living standards of middle-aged children.

Living standard is in general difficult to measure, and even when a whole set of empirical indicators exists, it is not totally clear how to synthesise them into a single dimension. A possible solution is to apply the Engel method, i.e. using the share of food expenditure out of total expenditure as an inverse indicator of the living standard: the higher this share, the lower the standard of living of the household. This method has several advantages: it is well established (it was proposed by Engel at the end of the nineteenth century), is easy to apply, and has been widely used, for instance, in the analysis of the cost of children or, more generally, of any extra member in the household. Although, to the best of my knowledge, it has never been used for the type of application I am proposing here – the study of how costly (or advantageous) it is to co-reside with one's aged parents.[1]

Microeconomists do not trust this method for two main reasons: it derives not from theoretical considerations but merely from observations of empirical regularities, and it does not allow for trade-off between goods, consistent with some utility theory, whereby less food can be compensated for by, say, more heating at home, and ultimately grant the same level of satisfaction: see, e.g. Browning (1992) or van de Ven (2004). The latter property matters especially when there are repeated observations over time (as in this case: see Sect. 6.4), and relative prices change appreciably (but not in this case: see Sect. 6.4). But the more general question remains: can one simple variable, food share, be considered a reliable indicator of such a complex concept as a 'family standard of living'? In the following, I will assume that the answer is positive, but, of course other, more refined analyses will have to confirm or rebut my conclusions, which I am merely offering as tentative, here.

As for the microfoundation of the Engel curves, 'much progress has been made in reconciling functional specifications with standard assumptions about utility maximization' (Chai and Moneta 2010: 237): for instance, the necessary conditions for their use for the calculation of equivalence scales are discussed by Perali (2002).

In this chapter, I will try to construct an equivalence scale, based on food share (dependent variable) and a set of independent variables describing household

[1] Of course, there are several indirect estimates of other types of cost: Keefe et al. (this volume), for instance, estimate the time that adult children dedicate to assist their aged relatives.

characteristics, among which a few concentrate specifically on the presence of, separately, his and her aged parents and their economic status. As mentioned, this approach is very similar to that used for the estimation of child costs but with at least one noteworthy difference: the number of children is endogenous, because parents can choose how many to have as well as how much to spend on each of them, and this complicates considerably the rationale behind the estimation of equivalence scales.[2]

Parents, instead, are not chosen, but co-residence with them is subject to choice. And since the decision of adult children and their elderly parents to live together can be highly endogenous, I use instrumental variable estimation, in order, at least in part, to alleviate the problem.

Some studies have proposed totally different approaches to the estimation of the living standards of households. One possibility is to ask people about happiness through surveys (e.g. Kahneman and Krueger 2006 or Stewart 2009). Surveys are good at illuminating factors that are difficult to observe but, as Steckel (2008) points out, 'nagging questions remain about whether people's evaluations of what they report as their "happiness" mean the same thing in one country or era as another'. Steckel himself suggests, as an alternative, biological measures like life expectancy or stature, which, however, are not perfect: they suffer from possible contamination from genetic factors and low sensitivity when living standards are high.

My research can also be interpreted as a contribution to the thorny issue of how to estimate the degree of intergenerational altruism, the research on which has thus far produced mixed and sometimes contradictory results (see, e.g. Hayashi 1995; Cigno and Rosati 1997; Horioka 2009, and also Lee and Phillips, this volume). An altruism model predicts that a decrease in parents' income by one dollar combined with an increase in the child's income by one dollar will reduce the transfer from parents to child by one dollar, i.e. intergenerational transfer through taxes or pension systems is fully cancelled by private transfers. Altonji et al. (1997) show that the rate of cancellation by private transfers is in fact much lower, only about 13%, which is a far cry from altruistic behaviour. Yamada (2006) compares two types of selfish hypotheses and finds support for the exchange motive by analysing co-residence, distance between residences, and frequency of contact. Overall, existing studies are negative about the existence of intergenerational altruism.

6.3 Social Security Reforms in Japan

What happens at the micro-level depends, among other things, on the macro-context: how well off are the adults and the old in Japan, how secure do they feel about their likely future socioeconomic standing, etc. Although Japan is a rich

[2] There are, of course, several attempts at circumventing these difficulties: Motonishi (2009), for instance, uses twin data to control for endogeneity in the number of children.

country, Tachibanaki (2006) points out that Japan's poverty rate is one of the highest among advanced countries and that inequality has increased significantly since the 1980s. He also argues that older people are those most significantly affected by poverty. Intergenerational conflicts of interest have intensified in Japan in recent years due to the difficulties of the existing pension system,[3] aggravated by very low fertility rates. Although there have been repeated attempts at reforming the social security system in Japan, no consensus has been reached yet as to where the system should head. Let me give a brief summary of recent reforms in the social security system in Japan.

A series of policy changes in the Japanese social security system has been implemented over several decades. In 1954, the Japanese public pension system for employees was completely revised.[4] In 1961, a universal public pension system covering all citizens was introduced. The benefit levels have been raised since then until the 1985 Reform, which, for the first time, introduced a reduction of benefits. In the 1994 and 2000 Reforms, pension eligibility age was raised in steps from 60 to 65. More recently, in 2004, a large-scale reform was introduced. Although the reform includes both increased pension premiums and decreased pension benefits depending on macroeconomic conditions, the policy change was interpreted by many as a guarantee that future pension benefits will continue to exist and was considered to be a senior-friendly policy decision. Even before the introduction of this pension reform, the rate of return for the public pensions of middle-aged people was expected to be negative, and it will worsen in the future. All residents in Japan over 20 years of age are obliged to join the public pension system and to contribute to it, but opinion polls show that many middle-aged people are, understandably, not satisfied with the current pension system and would rather opt out of it.

Tachibanaki (2006) points out that before the introduction of the pension system in Japan, there were two important sources of income of retired people: economic support from their adult children and self-support. He also argues that although the pension system in Japan is now very effective in reducing the number of poor elderly, 'there is a non-negligible portion of older people whose public pension benefits are considerably low or who receive no public pension benefits, for various reasons' (p. 22).

Health-care expenses are covered in part by insurance and in part by the beneficiaries themselves. Things are getting worse in this domain too, because the self-pay ratio has gradually increased for the aged in recent years, at different speeds, depending on age and income. In 1973, the government implemented free medical care for people over 70, but a small amount of copayment was reintroduced

[3] The main pillar of the pension system in Japan is pay-as-you-go. De Santis, in this volume, argues that it is possible to set up a pay-as-you-go pension system of the *AIPS* type ('almost ideal pension system,' or AIPS), which would solve several problems. Even in this case, however, twists in the age structure of the population create tensions, because they push contribution rate upwards. All the more so in Japan, where *AIPS* is not applied.

[4] For more about public pension reforms in Japan, see Oshio et al. (2011).

in 1983 and has since been gradually increased. In 2001, the self-pay ratio was set at 10%, and in 2006, the government formulated a plan to raise the self-pay ratio for people aged 70–75 from 10% to 20%, but the implementation of the policy is temporarily suspended, due to the strong opposition of the elderly.

In 2000, a public nursing-care insurance system was introduced. Under this system, elderly people can receive home-care services by paying 10% of the cost. The other 90% is funded by premiums and taxes paid by Japanese residents who are over 40 years of age. The system is now widely accepted and is considered indispensable for supporting the old. As expected, however, the financial condition of the nursing-care insurance is worsening. The premium for nursing-care insurance has been gradually raised since its introduction, and future increases in premiums and self-pay ratios are expected.

It is highly possible that the Japanese government will have to continue reforms of the social security system in the face of Japan's rapid ageing. In 2010, people aged 65 or over accounted for more than 23% of the population (16% in Europe); in 2050, the ratio is expected to rise to almost 40% (27% in Europe).[5]

6.4 Model and Data

The baseline regression equation of this study is as follows:

$$E_i = a_0 + a_1 \ln X_i + a_2 \ln N_i + h_1 H_{1i} + h_2 H_{2i} + h_3 H_{3i} + w_1 W_{1i} + w_2 W_{2i} + w_3 W_{3i} \tag{6.1}$$

The Engel curve is of the Working–Leser type (linear in the logarithm of expenditure). For each household i containing an adult child,

E is Engel's indicator of the standard of living, i.e. the food share

X is total expenditure of which the natural logarithm is considered

N is the size of the family, excluding the (female) respondent and excluding the elderly parents

The other variables are dummies for the presence of elderly individuals in the households, who can be parents either of the husband (H), or of the wife (W), or of both. Each of these are classified into three income classes: 0–5, 5–10, and 10+ (in million Yens per year),[6] collapsing the seven originally provided in the questionnaire.

[5] National Institute of Population and Social Security Research 'Population Statistics of Japan 2011'.

[6] The average household income in the sample period was 5.98 million Yen (Comprehensive Survey of Living Conditions of the People on Health and Welfare). In thousand Euros per year, the three classes are, respectively, 0–45, 45–90, and 90+. The average inflation rate in the sample period was 1.18% (1998–2006, GDP deflator). Under this near-zero inflation rate, the constant nominal threshold incomes should not pose a serious threat to our regression analysis.

Six dummy variables are created according to the six categories: husband's or wife's parents, with high, middle, or low income. But these dummies are then further manipulated, in order to take into account the number of adult siblings (of the husband or the wife) who share the responsibility for their elderly parents. In this exploratory analysis, I simply divided the dummy variables by the number of adult children of the elderly. For example, if a middle-aged husband has high-income elderly parents and he also has two brothers, the variable for the high-income husband's elderly parents is equal to one-third.

There are two other characteristics that we should take into account in our analysis. First, whether elderly parents are widowed or not should be considered. It is difficult, however, to introduce a defensible way to adjust the six variables introduced above to reflect this characteristic. Therefore, our regression is performed twice: first using the entire sample and later excluding households with single elderly parents.

Second, I also distinguish between elderly parents who co-reside with their adult children and those who do not: in practice, the original six 'dummies' are increased to 12 by introducing the characteristic of co-resident or not. It should be noted, however, that the decision of elderly parents and their middle-aged children to live together or not can be highly endogenous. Although our regression analyses provide a partial remedy for this, by using instrumental variables, the estimation results should not be interpreted as conclusive.

The estimation methods used in this study are pooled OLS. Although fixed-effects and random-effects estimations are also employed, they did not lead to significant results and are not shown here. This is probably because our sample is relatively small and variability is not sufficiently high in the period examined. As expected, between-effects estimation[7] has led to point estimates similar to pooled OLS estimation but with low significance levels, and its results are not reported here.

The data we use derive from the Japanese Panel Survey of Consumers (JPSC), conducted by The Institute for Research on Household Economics, which is one of the few panel surveys of Japanese consumers that allow researchers to use their unit record data. The survey started in 1993 by asking 1,500 women, who were 24–34 years of age questions about their family structure, expenditures, income, assets, and family characteristics, including those pertaining to parents not living with them. The survey also included questions about the incomes of the respondents' and their husbands' parents, irrespective of whether they lived together or not. This survey is conducted every year for the initial cohort, and new cohorts were added in 1997 and 2003. The data used in this chapter derive from nine surveys conducted between 1998 and 2006.

Two other major consumer surveys are conducted in Japan. The National Survey of Family Income and Expenditure is conducted every 5 years by the Ministry of

[7] Between-effects estimation is equivalent to OLS by using average values over the sample period.

Internal Affairs and Communications and has a sample of about 56,000 families. The Family Income and Expenditure Survey is conducted every month by the Ministry of Internal Affairs and Communications on about 7,000 households. The biggest advantage of the JPSC survey over these alternative surveys is that it includes questions about the incomes of elderly parents and about the number of siblings of the husband and wife, which are crucial to our empirical analyses. Moreover, the JPSC data have a panel structure, while the two major surveys are merely repeated cross sections of observations.

Our dependent variable, food share, is calculated for each entire family, including elderly parents, if present. Some elderly parents, however, keep their own budget separate from that of their co-residing middle-aged children. In this case, the food share of the elderly parents' budget is not taken into account. Although possible barter transactions between the two budgets (e.g. middle-aged children pay for the food of the household and elderly parents pay for the house rent) may distort the food share of middle-aged children, we assume that this type of transaction is not significant.

Unmarried respondents were dropped from the sample so as to focus on the behaviour of married people. Some observations were considered unreliable and dropped from the sample: for instance, families with very low or very high food shares (outside the two standard deviations range), with very young husbands (younger than 17 years old), or with no reported monthly expenditures.

The JPSC data are, obviously, not perfect. Apparently, some respondents have trouble in answering detailed questions about their consumption behaviour. Moreover, middle-aged children may not be fully aware of their elderly parents' income, but since we work with very large income classes, approximate answers can be equally satisfactory for our purpose. But there are also indications that the quality of the JPSC data is not bad, overall. The yearly attrition rate is relatively low (<5% on average), and the mere fact of asking the same questions over the years induces respondents to collect information and be more aware of the topic. It is probably not by chance that the JPSC data are widely used in several academic papers.[8] Finally, as described below, our estimation results show that the difference in elderly parents' income leads to estimate coefficients that are significantly different, which would not occur if respondents were answering randomly about their elderly parents' income.

Table 6.1 shows the basic statistics of the JPSC sample. In the Family Income and Expenditure Survey, which is more comprehensive than JPSC, the average family size was 3.16, and the average age of household heads was 55.2 for households of two or more persons in 2006. Because of the selection criterion (presence of at least a woman aged 24–34 in the first wave), the JPSC sample is biased towards larger families (4.36) and younger household heads (38.0). Figure 6.1 shows the share of elderly parents with low-, middle-, and high-income levels. Most elderly parents (about 70%) belong to the low-income group.

[8] For a list of papers, please see http://www.kakeiken.or.jp/jp/jpsc/bibliography/

Table 6.1 Basic statistics

Average family size (including elderly parents, if present)	4.36
Average age of husband	38.0
Average age of wife	35.4
Average yearly income of husband	5.11 million yens (≈46,000 Euros)
Average yearly income of wife	0.99 million yens (≈9,000 Euros)
Share of families living with husband's parents	0.25
Share of families living with wife's parents	0.09
Average number of siblings of husband	2.70
Average number of siblings of wife	2.52
Number of households	10,555

Source: Own elaborations on JPSC data (1998–2006)

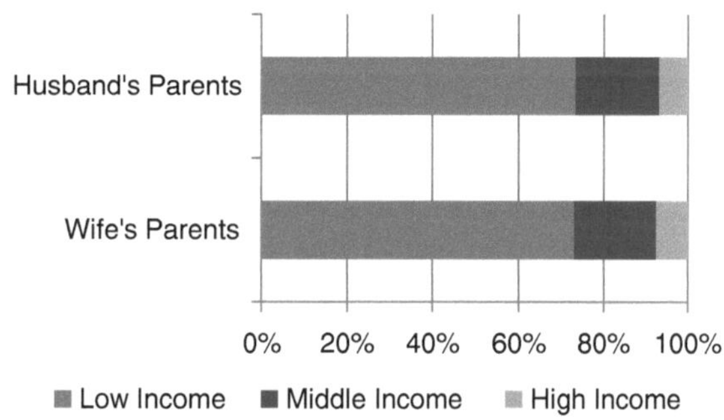

Fig. 6.1 Income distribution of parents

6.5 Regression Results

Table 6.2 shows the estimation results. A negative (positive) coefficient indicates a decrease (an increase) in food share and a benefit (cost) to the budget of middle-aged children. Insignificant coefficients indicate that the variable is neutral to the budget. This is typically the case of those elderly parents with intermediate income, whose cost and benefit to their adult children's budget are balanced. Columns 5–8 show the estimation results for the limited sample in which households having single ageing parents are excluded. This is necessary to avoid lumping widowed and non-widowed elderly parents together. There are three sets of elderly parent variables according to different degrees of categorisation. Columns 1 and 5 are for the simplest husband or wife categorisation. Columns 2 and 6 use six categories for elderly parents, distinguishing between three income categories. Columns 3, 4, 7, and 8 use 12 categories, which incorporate whether the elderly parents co-reside with their middle-aged children or not.

The estimation method is pooled OLS except for columns 4 and 8, in which instrumental variable estimation is used to cope with the possible endogeneity problem, implicit in the decision of elderly parents and their middle-aged children

Table 6.2 The effects of elderly parents on their middle-aged children's budget

			1	2	3	4	5	6	7	8
			All sample				Single elderly parents excluded			
Dependent variable food share (%)			OLS	OLS	OLS	IV	OLS	OLS	OLS	IV
Log expenditure			−9.076***	−9.199***	−9.296***	−9.451***	−8.998***	−9.111***	−9.212***	−8.803***
			(0.315)	(0.315)	(0.315)	(0.402)	(0.407)	(0.407)	(0.407)	(0.553)
Log family Zize			4.872***	4.343***	4.109***	3.809***	4.196***	3.633***	3.505***	3.413***
			(0.526)	(0.530)	(0.533)	(0.721)	(0.674)	(0.680)	(0.687)	(1.014)
Hub's parents	Low income	Co-residing	0.250	0.894	3.658***	4.139***	1.664*	2.270**	4.515***	5.330**
					(0.948)	(1.345)			(1.310)	(2.092)
		Not co-residing		(0.754)	−0.080	1.523		(1.035)	2.090*	4.193***
					(0.800)	(1.125)			(1.090)	(1.615)
	Middle income	Co-residing		−1.420	−0.012	3.287		0.372	1.641	11.175
					(1.841)	(7.169)			(2.080)	(9.940)
		Not co-residing	(0.739)	(1.010)	−1.748	−3.413	(1.009)	(1.261)	0.470	−0.122
					(1.072)	(2.411)			(1.337)	(3.041)
	High income	Co-residing		−0.978	−2.429	−7.445		−0.049	−2.495	−12.339
					(2.701)	(6.528)			(3.183)	(7.670)
		Not co-residing		(1.486)	−0.627	4.895		(1.756)	0.933	8.603*
					(1.661)	(3.784)			(1.927)	(4.506)
Wife's parents	Low income	Co-residing	−1.240	−0.250	2.039**	3.842**	−0.608	0.402	5.177***	10.210***
					(1.028)	(1.524)			(1.503)	(2.635)
		Not co-residing		(0.778)	−0.856	−0.823		(1.064)	−0.095	−0.161
					(0.835)	(1.175)			(1.121)	(1.646)
	Middle income	Co-residing		−3.725***	−3.570	−22.330***		−2.161*	−4.208	−50.571**
					(2.474)	(9.761)			(3.150)	(20.291)
		Not co-residing	(0.763)	(1.010)	−3.853***	−7.427***	(1.036)	(1.304)	−2.516*	−3.917
					(1.050)	(2.312)			(1.346)	(3.084)
	High income	Co-residing		−5.713***	−5.457	−7.877		−4.486***	−4.434	−4.195
					(3.561)	(6.754)			(3.639)	(7.155)
		Not co-residing		(1.371)	−5.824***	−7.269**		(1.600)	−5.076***	−8.464**
					(1.440)	(3.123)			(1.690)	(3.676)
Adjusted R2			0.101	0.107	0.109	0.109	0.097	0.102	0.105	0.062
Number of observations			7,471	7,471	7,471	4,396	4,581	4,581	4,581	2,560

***$p<0.01$; **$p<0.05$; *$p<0.1$

on whether to co-reside.[9] As instruments, for the 12 parent variables, I used not only one- but also two- and three-period lagged variables (situation of children and parents 1, 2, and 3 years before the current survey) in order to reinforce my conclusions and minimise the effects of random errors: the IV estimation results shown in columns 4 and 8 are those obtained with two-period lag variables as instruments (the others, not reported here, are similar). The estimated coefficients are not significantly different from OLS estimates, except for low- and middle-income, co-residing wife's parents. Since there are not many cases of middle-aged children living with the wife's parents, it is plausible that these anomalous estimates depend on the small number of observations, coupled with other problems with our data (e.g. multicollinearity of the 12 parental variables).

The coefficients of expenditure and family size variables are estimated with correct signs and are significant for all regressions. In contrast to this, some parent variables are not significant. There are several reasons for this. First, burdensome and beneficial effects of elderly parents on their middle-aged children's budgets may balance and level out. Second, in the larger categorisation estimates, some significant estimates, appearing with more detailed categorisation, are diluted and tend to vanish. Third, smaller categorisation may lead to insignificant results because there are too few observations, especially for high-income parents.

It is important to note the discrepancies in the estimated coefficients of parent variables in different categories. First, having higher-income elderly parents is generally not burdensome and can even be beneficial to the budgets of their adult children. This is fairly reasonable because high-income elderly parents tend to be financially independent and may give support to their adult children through voluntary transfers and/or bequests.

Second, there are significant differences between the husband's and wife's parents. Column 6 of Table 6.2 shows that while low-income husband's parents are financially burdensome for their adult children, low-income wife's parents are not. The same regression shows that while high-income wife's parents are financially beneficial for their adult children, high-income husband's parents are not. The difference between the husband's parents and wife's parents is interesting and, to the best of my knowledge, new to the study of intergenerational transfers. We will elaborate on the background of this important result in the next section.

Third, not surprisingly, the effects of elderly parents on adult children's household budgets depend on whether the children live with their parents or not. Poor elderly parents become a burden to their adult children, especially when they live in the same house. As for the beneficial effects of rich elderly parents (of wives), the effects of living together is ambiguous. This may be a consequence of the endogeneity problem mentioned before that not even our IV estimation solves

[9] For instance, if it is predominantly the most needy parents, those who cannot afford to live alone, who co-resided with their adult children, the effect of co-residence will appear to be (negative), whereas it is in fact due to the self-selection of the most needy into this (co-residing) category.

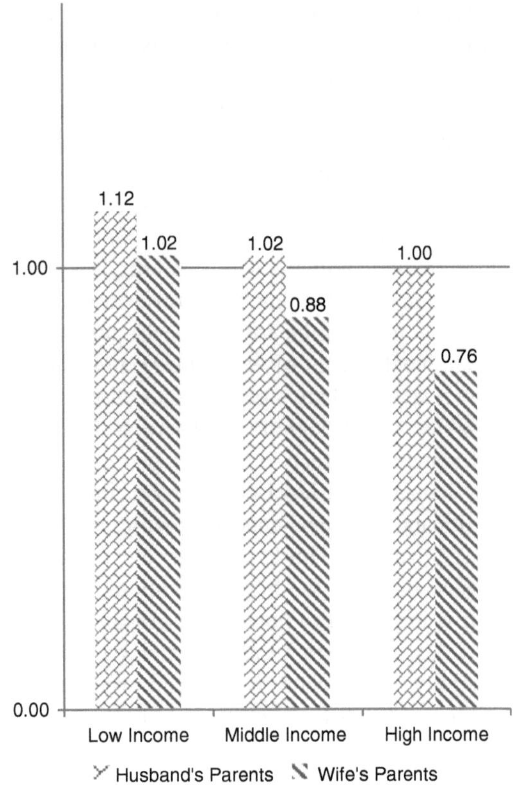

Fig. 6.2 Equivalence scales for old parents by income class

completely. However, the results in columns 3, 4, 7, and 8 on the difference between co-residing and non-co-residing parents are suggestive of the importance of this characteristic.

Using the point estimates of our regression, we can evaluate the quantitative effects of elderly parents on their adult children's budgets. Figures 6.2 and 6.3 show the equivalence scales of having elderly parents, which were calculated using columns 6 and 8 of Table 6.2. The ratio of the estimated coefficients of husband's low-income parents (2.270 in column 6) and of log expenditure (−9.111) shows the financial impact of having husband's low-income parents on the household budget. By assuming that the husband has one sibling to support his elderly parents together, we can obtain an equivalence scale for the elderly parents. The equivalence scales show the relative income needed to maintain the family's standard of living with elderly parents compared to a reference family, who is comparable but has no elderly parents. Figure 6.2 shows that middle-aged parents living with the husband's low-income elderly parents have to earn 12% more to maintain the family's living standard than when they do not support the husband's elderly parents.

Fig. 6.3 Equivalence scales for co-residing old parents by income class

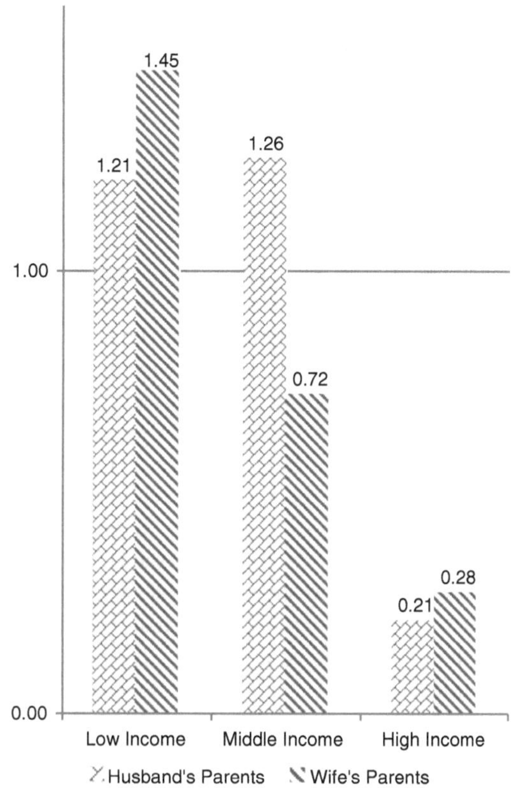

In contrast, middle-aged parents living with the wife's high-income elderly parents can maintain the family's living standard with 24% less income than when they do not support the wife's elderly parents.

Figure 6.3 shows equivalence scales for co-residing elderly parents calculated from the point estimates in column 8 of Table 6.2. The difference depending on income categories is larger in Fig. 6.3 than in Fig. 6.2. This can be interpreted as the result of the close relationship between co-residing elderly parents and their middle-aged children, although, noted earlier, this result should be interpreted cautiously because of the possible bias induced by endogeneity.

6.6 Discussion

The regression results suggest differences in the relationships between elderly parents and their adult children. Whereas low-income elderly parents are financially dependent on their sons' families, high-income elderly parents tend to support their daughters' families. It is apparent that these differences spring from voluntary transfers because the effects of involuntary transfers on adult children's budgets do not depend on the conditions of their elderly parents.

Why do high-income elderly parents support their daughters? Several possible reasons should be considered. First, couples in Japan have to choose a single family name when they get married. More than 90% of couples choose the husband's family name. Moreover, husbands are the main earners in most families. In our sample period, the average income of husbands was about five times as much as that of wives. For these reasons, sons tend to feel more responsible for looking after their parents than do daughters. By the same token, it is likely that sons decline financial support from their wealthy parents. When adult sons live with their parents, sons may insist on covering the expenditures of their elderly parents. For these reasons, elderly parents may become economic burdens on the families of sons.

In contrast, the family names of married daughters usually differ from those of their elderly parents, and married daughters do not normally earn high incomes. Therefore, it is possible that such daughters do not feel as financially responsible for looking after their elderly parents as do sons. From the parents' perspective, it may be much easier to give financial support to their daughters than to their sons. Sons may feel more disgraced than daughters by offers of financial support made by their own parents, given that sons are expected to be the main earners in most families.

Our regression results also suggest that the impact of elderly parents on the budgets of their adult children is greater for extended families, with more generations living together, than for nuclear families. Although the cause-and-effect connection is not totally clear, with our data, the correlation is clear. When adult children live with their elderly parents, the boundaries between the budgets of the two families (adult children and elderly parents) tend to merge. Moreover, the decision to live together is a manifestation of financial support to, and from, the elderly parents. Therefore, we would expect to find greater financial help within extended families than between nuclear families.

From the point of view of elderly parents, living as part of an extended family can be different if it is their son's or their daughter's family. In 2002, 28% of the families in the sample lived with the husbands' elderly parents and only 9% lived with the wives' elderly parents. The decision of married adult children to live with the wife's parents is somewhat exceptional and usually based on the desire of the wife's parents. Some of those elderly parents who do not have sons may be concerned about the extinction of their family names and about having no one to support them when they get very old. It is possible that these elderly parents may ask their sons-in-law to carry their family name, to cohabitate with them, and even to be adopted by them in exchange for financial support.

Although the analysis in this chapter does not directly address the budgets of elderly parents, it does suggest that financial support provided and received by children varies greatly depending on the sex of the child, income levels of elderly parents, and family type (nuclear or extended).

6.7 Conclusion

Focusing on differences in kinship structures, this analysis of the budgets of adult children reveals a difference in transfers. While low-income elderly parents impose a strain on their sons' budgets, significant transfers are made from elderly parents to their daughters' budgets. These transfers tend to be larger in the (relatively rare) case of cohabitation. The results suggest the importance of incorporating kinship structures into the analysis of intergenerational transfers.

Although the analyses of this paper are focused only on Japanese intergenerational transfers, similar analyses in other countries are also of interest. The key to this type of analysis is the availability of income data of elderly parents of adult children. It is highly possible that results will differ from country to country depending on kinship traditions.

Acknowledgements Financial support from Kansai University's Overseas Research Program and a Grant-in-Aid for Young Scientists were also instrumental in the completion of this project.

References

Altonji, J. G., Hayashi, F., & Kotlikoff, L. J. (1997). Parental altruism and inter vivos transfers: Theory and evidence. *Journal of Political Economy, 105*, 1121–1166.
Browning, M. (1992). Children and household economic behavior. *Journal of Economic Literature, 30*, 1434–1475.
Chai, A., & Moneta, A. (2010). Retrospectives: Engel curves. *The Journal of Economic Perspectives, 24*, 225–240.
Cigno, A., & Rosati, F. C. (1997). Rise and fall of the Japanese saving rate: The role of social security and intra-family transfers. *Japan and the World Economy, 9*, 81–92.
Hayashi, F. (1995). Is the Japanese extended family altruistically linked? A test based on Engel curves. *Journal of Political Economy, 103*, 661–674.
Horioka, C. Y. (2009). *Bequest motives and parent-child relations in the United States, Japan, and China*. Paper presented at Department of Economics, University of Auckland, Auckland.
Kahneman, D., & Krueger, A. B. (2006). Developments in the measurement of subjective well-being. *The Journal of Economic Perspectives, 20*, 3–24.
Motonishi, T. (2009). *The cost of children in Japan and South Korea*. Presented at Crawford School of Economics and Government, Australian National University, Mimeo.
Oshio, T., Oishi, A. S., & Shimizutani, S. (2011). Social security reforms and labour force participation of the elderly in Japan. *The Japanese Economic Review, 62*, 248–271.
Perali, F. (2002). Some curiosities about the Engel method to estimate equivalence scales. *Economics Bulletin, 4*, 1–7.
Steckel, R. H. (2008). Biological measures of the standard of living. *The Journal of Economic Perspectives, 22*, 129–152.
Stewart, M. B. (2009). The estimation of pensioner equivalence scales using subjective data. *Review of Income and Wealth, 55*, 907–929.
Tachibanaki, T. (2006). Inequality and poverty in Japan. *The Japanese Economic Review, 57*, 1–27.
van de Ven, J. (2004). *Demand based equivalence scale estimates for Australia and the UK* (NIESR Discussion Paper No. 228). http://www.niesr.ac.uk/pubs/searchmaster.php?typeofpub=4
Yamada, K. (2006). Intra-family transfers in Japan: Intergenerational co-residence, distance, and contact. *Applied Economics, 38*, 1839–1861.

Part III
Time Is on Whose Side? Mutual Support and Exchanges Between Generations

Introduction to Part III

Time Is on Whose Side? Mutual Support and Exchanges Between Generations

Living is not only a matter of material resources. Health is important, and those who suffer from some physical or mental impediment typically need assistance. Who are the main providers?

The chapter by Janice Keefe and colleagues reminds us that the title of this book might as well have been longer: 'The family, the market, the state, or the voluntary sector?' Indeed, in today's Canada, informal care provided by neighbourhood volunteers, in a sort of local mutual assistance, is more important than customarily imagined. And it will need to become even more important in the future, as family structures get thinner (eroded by divorce and cohabitation), children rarer and possibly living far away, and the elderly grow in number and age and therefore, probably, also in needs.

Beyond material help, psychological support, too, is worth considering. Will the elderly of tomorrow be neglected, or even abandoned, or will they have close relations and contacts with their children? Are there regional differences in this respect? And, if yes, what do they depend on? The idea of analysing contacts between generations is not new (see, e.g. Tomassini et al. 2008), nor is the finding that in Mediterranean countries adult children tend to live close to their elderly parents (see, e.g. Tomassini et al. 2003). But Valeria Bordone introduces two new elements in the debate: (a) she underlines the importance of norms, rather than culture, and suggests a way to measure their force, and (b) she tries a three-level analysis (country-elderly relative-adult children) which shows that the context (i.e. norms) matters at least as much as personal traits in determining the frequency of adult-elderly contacts.

Finally, Maria Letizia Tanturri brings us back to the beginning. Ageing occurs, in large part, because fertility is low, and one of the reasons why it is low, she suggests, is that children are very expensive, perhaps not so much in terms of money, but surely in terms of time, at least in Italy. Italian women do not participate very much in the labour market (their employment rate at ages 15–64 is <50% – very low by European standards), but their workload is high, higher than men's, for instance. When a child arrives, the workload increases for both partners, but mothers work much more indoors (and less for the market), while fathers intensify their labour market activity.

Tanturri, with her data, cannot investigate the causes of this complex mechanism (culture? lack of alternatives for child care? other?), but the consequences are clear enough: if children cost so much, either other activities must be foregone (work, care of the elderly, or leisure), or fertility reduced, or both. With low fertility, populations age. And with ageing, the difficulties of intergenerational support increase. Vicious circles can be broken, however, and identifying their mechanisms is, by necessity, the first step.

References

Tomassini, C., Wolf, D., & Rosina, A. (2003). Parental housing assistance and parent-child proximity in Italy. *Journal of Marriage and the Family, 65*, 700–715.

Tomassini, C., Grundy, E., & Kalogirou, S. (2008). Potential family support for older people 2000–2030. In J. Gaymu, P. Festy, M. Poulain & G. Beets, (Eds.), *Future elderly living conditions in Europe* (pp. 71–98) (Les cahiers de l'INED, no. 162). Paris: INED.

Chapter 7
Intergenerational Support to Older Canadians by Their Adult Children: Implications for the Future

Janice A. Keefe, Jacques Légaré, Patrick Charbonneau, and Yann Décarie

7.1 Introduction

Population ageing throughout the developed world has created an appetite for dialogue on the complementary role of the family, the marketplace, the voluntary sector, and the state in the care of older people who need assistance. Contributions from family members have been expected by the state in the past, but extension of life expectancy and changing birth patterns result in an eventual decline in the structural possibility that adult children will continue to provide assistance at the current rate. Smaller family sizes coupled with potential decreased accessibility of family members because of increased mobility, increased labour force participation of women, and changing expectations for care in families experiencing divorce and remarriage all point to the need to rely on non-familial systems of care. Policy shifts to community care with its attempt to reduce institutionalisation, together with the higher incidence of certain illnesses and diseases in the context of population ageing, suggest an increasing demand for care, yet question the availability and capacity of the informal network of family and friends. Who will care for the increasing number of older people and ensure their well-being remains central to policy decisions?

J.A. Keefe (✉)
Department of Family Studies and Gerontology, Mount Saint Vincent University, 166 Bedford Highway, Halifax, NS B4E 3J1, Canada
e-mail: janice.keefe@msvu.ca

J. Légaré • P. Charbonneau
Département de Démographie, Université de Montréal, C.P. 6128, succursale Centre-ville, Montréal, QC H3C 3J7, Canada
e-mail: jacques.legare@umontreal.ca

Y. Décarie
Programme de Démographie, Institut National de la Recherche Scientifique, 385, rue Sherbrooke Est, Montréal, QC H2X 1E3, Canada

G. De Santis (ed.), *The Family, the Market or the State?: Intergenerational Support Under Pressure in Ageing Societies*, International Studies in Population 10,
DOI 10.1007/978-94-007-4339-7_7,

The metaphor of the welfare diamond was first developed by Pijl (1994) to identify the relationships among four sectors of society that provide for an individual's well-being: the state, the voluntary sector, the marketplace, and the family, the latter the most important. The objective of this chapter is to assess the implications of changing demographic structures on the distributions of responsibility across these four sectors. Specifically, we describe the current contributions of adult children compared to other members of the social network of older Canadians in need of assistance, and we use a micro-simulation model to project the potential availability of these resources in the future. The effects of these demographic changes will be discussed in terms of their implications for an increased role of the state, the voluntary sector, and the marketplace.

7.2 Literature Review

The share of Canada's older population is projected to increase from 14% in 2010 to 23% in 2031, using a medium-growth scenario (Statistics Canada 2010). Higher fertility patterns of post World War II resulted in a baby boom occurring in several European countries (Lanzieri 2011), as well as many Western countries including Canada. In comparison to European countries though, population ageing is accelerated in Canada by even higher post-war fertility (Gaymu et al. 2010), and, like other countries (Hoffmann and Rodrigues 2010), Canada worries about the need for, and availability of, long-term care for its elderly. Within community-based care, two types of care networks typically provide support for older individuals. The informal care network relies on a range of human resources, including family, friends, and neighbours, while the formal care network delivers care either as employees of the state, the marketplace, or volunteers with community-based agencies. Most of these formal workers are paraprofessionals often referred to as home or personal support workers. Formal supports are more likely to provide assistance with personal care, nursing, and specialised treatment, whereas family members are more likely to assist with ADLs such as meal preparation, running errands, finances, and moving about the home (Fournier-Savard et al. 2010).

In most countries, older people rely on the informal much more than on the formal network, (Pickard et al. 2000; Huber et al. 2009; Johnson et al. 2007). Within the informal network, immediate family, defined as spouses, if available, and adult children, comprise the majority of care and assistance that is needed by individuals with health limitations. Typically, this care is unpaid and predominantly provided by women (Cranswick and Dosman 2008; Hoffmann and Rodrigues 2010). The central role of the spouse in the provision of support is indisputable. Older people who need assistance are mostly to receive it from their spouses when they are available (Keating et al. 2003; Pickard et al. 2000).

Projections of the future need of care, in Canada and elsewhere (Pickard et al. 2000), indicate that more elderly people are likely to receive informal care than normally believed, because the decline in mortality reduces the number of widows and increases the number of elderly women with partners. This will likely increase the importance of 'spouse carers', although reliance on these carers should be cautioned since spouses are also likely to be elderly and potentially in poor health (Gaymu et al. 2010; Pickard et al. 2000). The implications on admissions to residential, nursing, and hospital care for the future elderly people are, therefore, far from clear, and the financial consequences might be important (Pickard et al. 2000).

Adult children continue to provide a significant amount of support to ageing parents. Indeed, many countries rely on these unpaid contributions to enable social policies that promote care of older persons in their own homes (Chan Cheung Ming et al. 2007; de Vaus et al. 2003; Tarricone and Tsouros 2008), and Canada is no exception, although it lags behind most industrialised countries in terms of policy for caregivers of older persons (Keefe and Rajnovich 2007).

Projections of intergenerational support must consider demographic changes in family composition over time, since the outcomes will vary based on the place in the life cycle of different elderly cohorts in the future. The boomer generation has had fewer children than their parents' generation; it stands to reason then that they will have fewer adult children available to care for them. However, this generation will not reach age 75+—the threshold for increased need—until 2021 (Carrière et al. 2007). Their elderly parents in the short term may therefore be in a better position in terms of informal care options.

It is not easy to assess the economic value of the contributions that informal caregivers are currently making (family sector) or the costs of the alternative, formal care that should be provided, should informal care become less available. But it is certainly high: Hollander et al. (2009), for instance, report that the market value of Canada's informal caregivers' contribution was between 24 and 31 billion Canadian dollars in 2007, accounting for 1.6–2.0% of Canadian GDP.

7.3 Relationship Between Formal and Informal Care

Researchers examining the relationship between informal and formal care have proposed several models of the effect of introducing formal care. Neither the substitution model, where formal care displaces the care provided by informal care, nor the compensation model, where formal care only comes into play when informal care is exhausted, has strong empirical supportive evidence (Dykstra 2010). The 'complementary model', where formal care is used to supplement informal care when the needs of the older person exceed the resources of the informal care system, is probably the one that best fits both the European (Dykstra 2010) and the Canadian case (Ward-Griffin and Marshall 2003).

Formal support to older persons in the community may come from the voluntary/social economy sector, be purchased privately in the marketplace, or be subsidised through government home care programmes. It is estimated that 25–30% of the hours of home support received by older persons in need of assistance in Canada was provided by the formal care network (Keefe et al. 2011; Lafrenière et al. 2003), not all of them from state-subsidised services. Indeed, other Canadian research suggests that expansion in government-subsidised services is not always proportional with increases in care need (Wilkins 2006).

The recent Canadian data suggest that the costs of home care policies, promoting acute care substitution, may continue to increase. For example, Wilkins (2006) reports that the number of people needing personal care services almost doubled between 1994/1995 and 2003, but the *proportion* of people who received assistance from government-subsidised home care programmes decreased from 46% to 35%. Recipients, on average, were getting younger (by almost 3 years), spent fewer days in hospital, and were more often receiving nursing and personal care (52%, up from 39% in 1994/1995). While more people needed help in 2003 than in 1994/1995, 'a smaller share of individuals received care'. Wilkins' findings suggests that some of the burden of care is shifting from governments to private home care agencies—or to family members and friends for needs that require less specialised services, such as housework. Similar findings have been reported in the province of British Columbia, where the likelihood of receiving home support declined between 1991 and 2000, despite an increase in total hours reported annually. Data from the British Columbia study also showed an increase in receipt of home nursing during the period studied (Brackley and Penning 2009).

Not surprisingly, the availability of informal support reduces the cost associated with long-term care of older adults, although this effect varies across countries and time. Indeed, informal care is an effective substitute for long-term care only as long as the needs of the elderly are low and do not require special skills (Yoo et al. 2005).

Our previous work has focused on projecting the proportion of assistance that will need to come from formal and informal sources of support (Carrière et al. 2007), where 'informal' means, broadly, help provided by spouses, children, siblings, friends, and neighbours. More recently, we have extended our research to assess the *amount* of assistance from informal and formal sources of support to meet the demands of an ageing population.

In this chapter, we focus our research question on the part of assistance provided by adult children to older parents (aged 65 and over) living in the community. Among the Canadian population aged 65 and over, 6% live in special care facilities such as nursing homes, residences for senior citizens, and chronic and long-term care facilities (Statistics Canada 2011a). Women, especially those 75 and over, are more likely than men to live in a special care facility. According to the 2006 Census, 299,375 Canadians live in a special care facility. The vast majority of them (92%) are 65 years old and over (Fig. 7.1).

This chapter first presents evidence of the changing networks of family structure in Canada and projects its likely evolution in the coming decades. Second, we disaggregate the help coming from the informal network to understand what amount is provided by children. From these data, we consider implications for the future demand for support from other sectors of society—the state, the market, and the community—and policy options that will need to be developed.

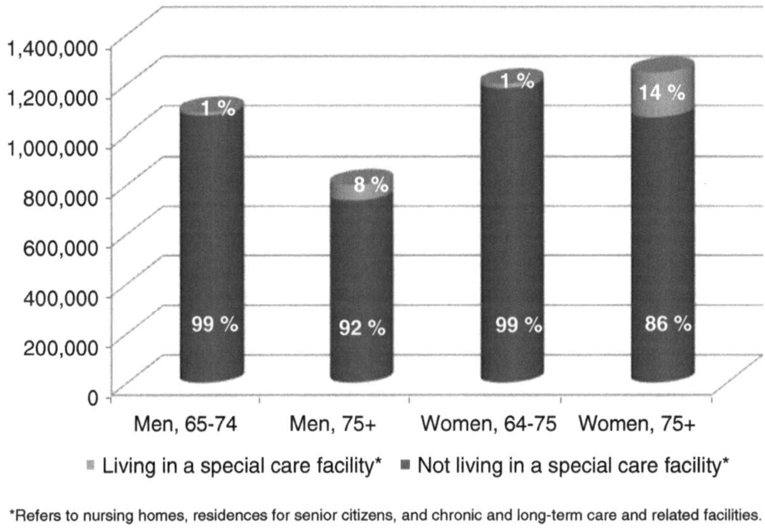

Fig. 7.1 Population of elderly Canadians according to the dwelling type, by age and sex, in 2006 (Source: Statistics Canada, 2006 census)

7.4 Methodology

Statistics Canada's LifePaths micro-simulation model is used to project differing family compositions between 2001 and 2031. LifePaths is a dynamic micro-simulation model representative of individual behaviour and used to project future scenarios, ranging from kinship networks to urban traffic flow (Statistics Canada 2011b). A great advantage is its ability to answer questions by taking into account a large number of data based on individual life histories and applying them to a population. All micro-simulation models make projections, not predictions. A limitation is the inherent assumption that social and economic factors will remain constant. For example, micro-simulations do not take into account changes in cultural norms or behaviours around caregiving that may occur with future cohorts of older people, changes in long-term care policies introduced by the state, or model significant economic events that impact on individuals' and states' resources.

For this analysis, a series of overlapping cohorts was created, within which each individual can be in one of several possible states at the beginning of a period (e.g. by age, sex, and marital status) and, from there, can transit to several other states, simultaneously keeping into account the chances of survival, marriage, divorce, etc. Canadian death, marriage, and divorce rates observed since the end of the nineteenth century were extended with the assumption that women's life expectancy will increase, but less rapidly than men's. The presence of a surviving child was also micro-simulated using the LifePaths model. Four types of family networks are projected: (1) with spouse/partner and at least one surviving child; (2) with spouse/partner, no surviving children; (3) without spouse/partner, at least one surviving child; and (4) neither spouse/partner nor children.

Within these groups, we are interested in understanding the amount of support that is provided by children. Secondary data analyses of the 2002 General Social Survey were conducted to determine the effects of socio-demographic characteristics on the probability that an older person, with different levels of disability, receives assistance from adult children. On this basis, the amount of hours per week received by Canadians aged 65 and over because of a long-term health problem or chronic illness was calculated from seven activities of daily living: (1) personal care, (2) house cleaning, (3) meal preparation, (4) grocery shopping, (5) transportation, (6) banking/bill paying, and (7) household maintenance/outside work. Respondents were included if they received help with at least one of the first four activities. Not included in these hours are those for temporarily difficult times such as an acute illness or injury from an accident, as both the number of hours of need and the pressure on the caregiver are less than for those with long-term health problems. Also, temporary health problems have more impact on the population in the labour force and not on the population aged 65 and over.

Among those who received assistance, we calculated the amount of this assistance received from spouses, children (including children-in-law and stepchildren), and other informal sources (including all other family relationships, friends, and neighbours) as well as the amount received from formal sources (including government, non-government, and voluntary agencies). The amount of assistance is stated in terms of hours per week. In total, 3,826 cases were included. In 723 of these, the aggregate data on hours of support was not available and was imputed, differentiating formal and informal hours. The multiple imputation method was based on the following variables: disability, age, sex, and marital status. In situations where there was more than one informal source of support providing the imputed number of hours, such imputations were calculated proportional to the average proportions observed in the sample, case by case.

7.5 Findings

7.5.1 Projections of Family Composition

Projections of the number of surviving children among differing cohorts of older women in Canada reveal that among younger cohorts of older people (65–74), the declining proportion of women with surviving children is most evident (Fig. 7.2). In the short term, however, the effects of the baby boom population predominate. The age group 65–74, who by 2011 are the first wave of baby boomers, are less likely to have children and, therefore, exhibit an increased proportion without surviving children over time.

Among those aged 85 and older, there is a steady decline in the proportion without surviving children between 2001 and 2026. These are the parents of baby boomers; they are the ones who, for the next 15 years, will have increased 'potential help' to receive from their children.

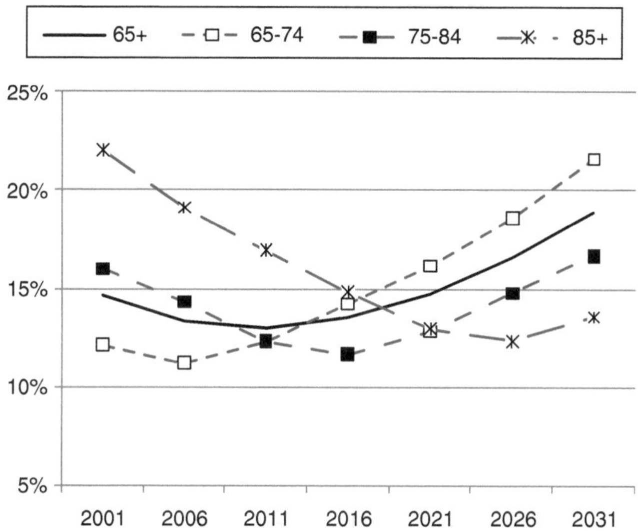

Fig. 7.2 Proportion of Canadian women aged 65 years and older, living in private households, without surviving children, by age group between 2001 and 2031 (Source: Keefe et al. 2008c)

Four configurations describing the family networks of older people are derived and projected to 2031: with and without spouse and with and without children (Fig. 7.3). The first 15 years from 2001 to 2016 will see a steady increase in the number of elderly people needing assistance, of all family forms and at all ages, and an acceleration thereafter, which, in general, will be stronger for older people without surviving children, particularly among those aged 65–74. In this age group, those with neither spouses nor surviving children increase from 7% of families in 2001 to 13% in 2031. Among those aged 85 and older, however, the highest rate of increase will be in the family configuration with surviving children (either with spouse or without).

As Fig. 7.4 indicates, among older men, the greatest change will be for those with neither spouse nor surviving children. Among women, on the other hand, the most significant change will be in the number of those with a spouse but no surviving children, who will be more than three times as numerous as they are today, increasing from 4% to 6% of all families. In the future, who will replace the care that is currently provided by adult children?

7.5.2 *Amount of Assistance from Informal and Formal Sources*

The proportion of the use of formal services will in all likelihood eventually increase, driven by the reduced capacity of the informal support system (Carrière et al. 2007). In 2002, some 12.5 million hours of assistance with activities of daily

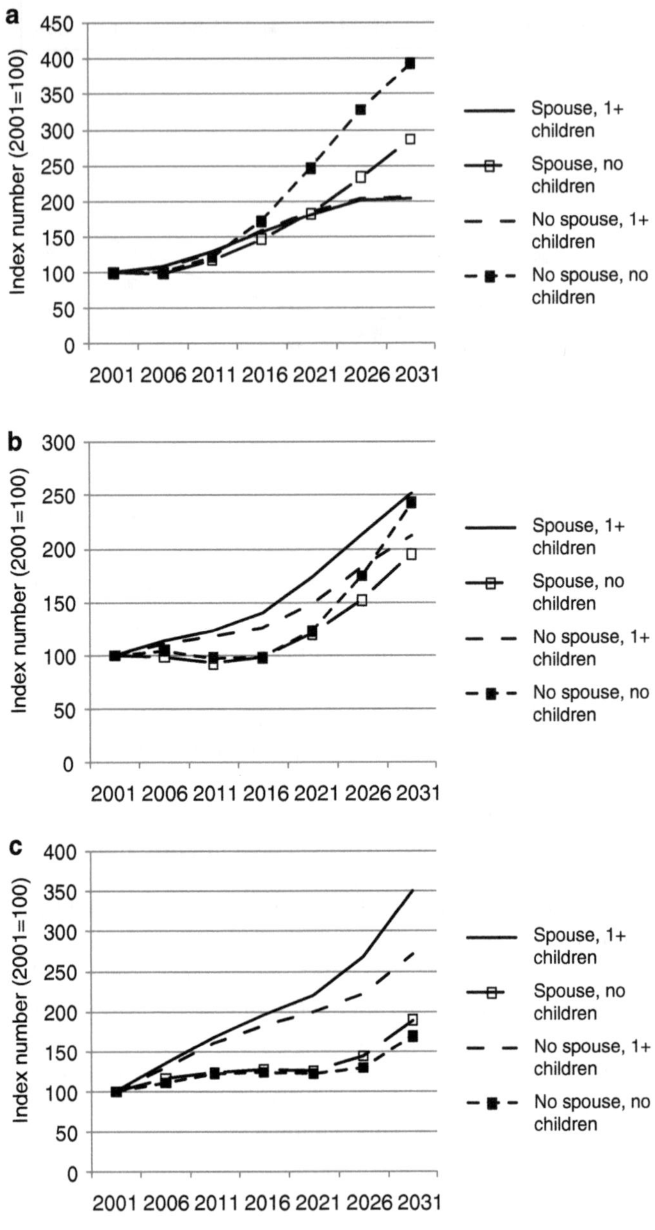

Fig. 7.3 Population increase between 2001 and 2031 of older Canadians living in private households, who need assistance according to different family compositions. (**a**) 65–74 years, (**b**) 75–84 years, (**c**) 85 years and older (Source: Keefe et al. 2008c)

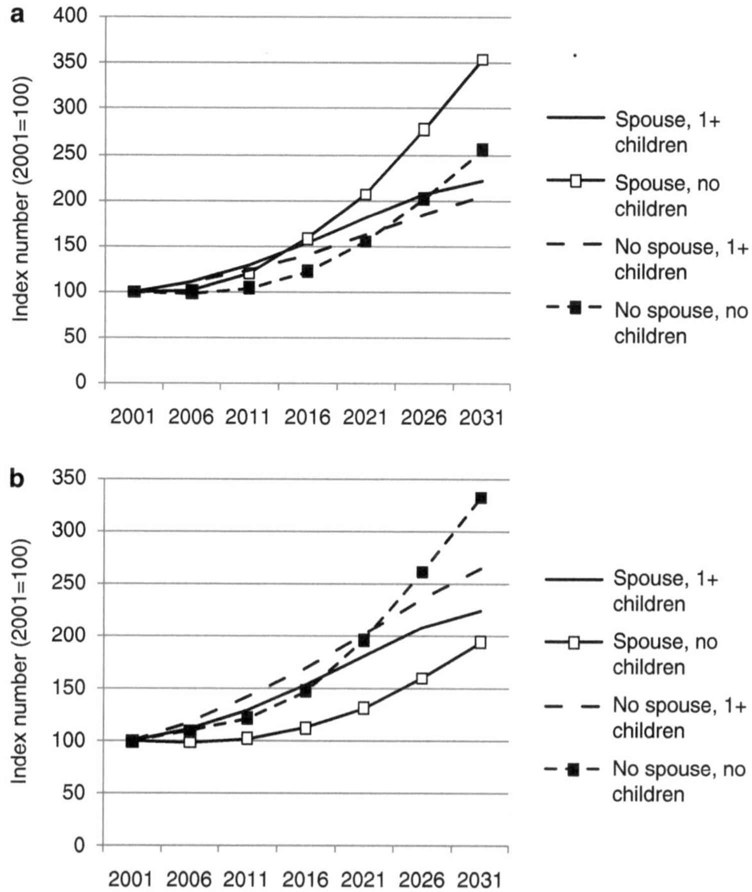

Fig. 7.4 Population increase between 2001 and 2031 of older Canadians aged 65 years and over living in private households, who need assistance according to different family compositions. (**a**) Women, (**b**) Men (Source: Keefe et al. 2008c)

living were provided weekly to older Canadians with long-term chronic illness or disability, and children were the main providers, accounting for about a third of this. Less than a quarter of this assistance was provided by formal sources (Fig. 7.5).

The importance of the contributions by adult children is still greater among women aged 75 and older (Table 7.1).

Older women living in the community receive almost twice as much long-term assistance as do men, and the contribution from adult children is particularly noteworthy, close to 50% of the total and, in absolute terms, close to some 1.2 million hours of assistance per week. Among older age groups, a lower proportion of assistance is received from a spouse either because he/she is absent or because he/she is in turn old and frail. The proportion of support from other

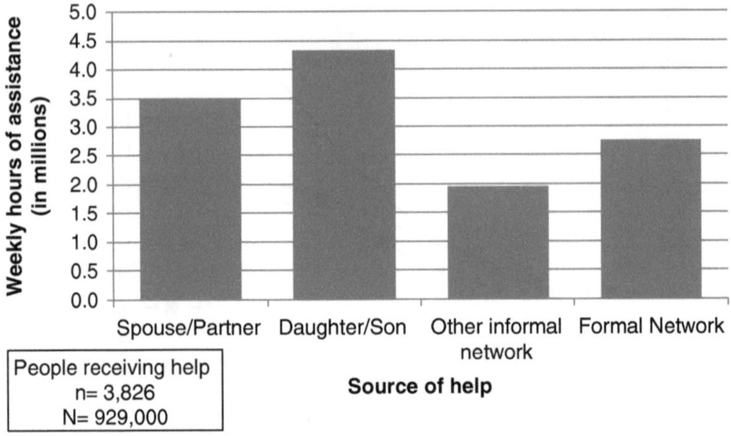

Fig. 7.5 Total number of weekly hours of assistance received by older Canadians aged 65 years and over living in private households who need assistance, by source of help, in 2002 (Source: Statistics Canada 2002, General Social Survey, cycle 16, unpublished data)

informal sources remains relatively constant across age groups. Among women, it is only among those 85 and older that a significant proportion (a third) of assistance is provided by the formal network.

Table 7.2 presents the average amount of assistance by type of family composition. When no spouse is present, it is the children who step in and provide most of the help. This finding is particularly remarkable when one considers that in Canada most older parents do not co-reside with their children and many live at a distance. For example, Vézina and Turcotte (2010) show that only 13% of adult child caregivers aged 45 or older co-reside with their assisted parent, and 22% of these caregivers live more than 1 h away from their parents. It appears that children play a complementary role as a caregiver when spouses are present and are a substitute when a spouse is not present.

Among those who have neither a spouse nor surviving children, other informal support networks (such as other family, friends, and neighbours) are very important and provide the highest proportion of assistance (44%). Interestingly, assistance from daughter/son relationships continues to be there because included in this relationship category are daughters-in-law and sons-in-law. While they provide on average only 2.2 h per week, they comprise almost 19% of the assistance received.

This critical role of family and children stands out when one considers the role of the formal network providers—that is, marketplace providers or state-run services. Among families with both spouses and children, 15% of care is formal. When one of these caregiver types is absent (either spouse but no children or children but no spouse), about one-quarter of the total weekly amount of care is provided by formal supports. And when both are absent (neither spouses nor surviving children), formal support provides fully 37% of the assistance received by older people in the community.

Table 7.1 Weekly hours of assistance received by older Canadians (65+ years) living in private households, who need assistance, by source of help, sex, and age group, in 2002

		Men				Women			
		65–74	75–84	85+	Total	65–74	75–84	85+	Total
Source of help		%	%	%	%	%	%	%	%
Spouse/partner		59.7	46.4	28.5	46.7	29.5	21.0	4.0	17.2
Daughter/son		14.3	17.8	37.3	21.1	33.3	44.2	45.7	42.1
Other informal		11.0	12.2	11.5	11.6	21.3	16.4	17.3	17.9
Formal network		15.0	23.7	22.7	20.5	15.9	18.4	33.0	22.8
Total	(%)	100	100	100	100	100	100	100	100
	In thousands	1,489	1,939	1,035	4,463	1,928	3,356	2,745	8,029
People receiving help	*n*	335	532	230	1,097	717	1,370	642	2,729
	N	113,000	141,000	59,000	313,000	195,000	279,000	142,000	616,000

Source: General Social Survey, cycle 16, 2002 unpublished data

Table 7.2 Average number of weekly hours of assistance received by older Canadians (65+ years), living in private households, who need assistance, by source of help and family composition, in 2002

		Family composition							
		Spouse and at least one child		Spouse, no children[a]		No spouse, at least one child		Neither spouse nor children[a]	
Source of help		%	*AVG*	%	*AVG*	%	*AVG*	%	*AVG*
Spouse/partner		58.0	*7.9*	55.1	*7.9*	0.0	*0.0*	0.0	*0.0*
Daughter/son		16.9	*2.3*	17.6	*2.5*	56.0	*7.6*	18.6	*2.2*
Other informal		7.9	*1.1*	3.2	*0.5*	19.5	*2.6*	44.6	*5.4*
Formal network		17.2	*2.3*	24.0	*3.5*	24.3	*3.3*	36.7	*4.4*
Total	(%)	100	*13.6*	100	*14.4*	100	*13.5*	100	*12.0*
	In thousands	5,662		318		5,617		895	
People receiving help	*n*	1,216		63		2,155		392	
	N	416,000		22,000		417,000		75,000	

Source: General Social Survey, cycle 16, 2002, unpublished data

[a]May include daughters-in-law and sons-in-law

7.6 Discussion

As we look to the future, attention will need to be given to the implications of lower fertility patterns and its outcome of fewer adult children as sources of support, the increase of life expectancy and its outcome of increasing numbers of very old couples, and the ways in which our current patterns of assistance cannot be assumed to continue. The implications of our projected results on patterns of assistance from informal and formal sources will be discussed. Children, spouses, extended family, neighbours, and friends are discussed first, followed by formal care systems available from the marketplace, the state, and the voluntary sector (the welfare diamond approach, once again). Policies can, and probably must, be developed across multiple sectors to address the challenges of the older population in need having less available children to provide care.

Lower fertility among baby boomers translates into reduced availability of adult children to care for this cohort when they need support and eventually will lead to a greater reliance on other sources of support. Our projections indicate that in 2011, women aged 65 and older will have a decreased likelihood of having a child. For those aged 85 and older, this projected decline will not occur until 2026. Because children are an important contributor to both the source and amount of assistance to older parents, especially when a spouse/partner is not present, not having them available has significant implications. Among those without a spouse, the average amount of support per week given by adult children was almost equal to that of a spouse/partner in family formations where they were available.

The proportion of older persons who have a spouse in their family network is projected to increase. For example, the proportion of older women who have a spouse/partner but no children is projected to be 3.5 times more likely in 2031 than in 2001. For men, this family formation is expected to double in the same time period. Extrapolating from our descriptive analysis of the source and amount of assistance, spouses, if available, are most likely to provide care and provide the greatest amount of care. Increases in the availability of a spouse who survives into old age may help to address some of the future caregiving needs, but such increases in life expectancy may well result in two frail people, both in need of care.

In situations where there is neither spouse nor children, more distant relatives and friends and neighbours appear to emerge as a significant contributor to the care provided in the community. Of course, since this research is limited to those who are old and sick, but live in private households (not in special care facilities), it suffers from a selection bias: those who keep on living in the community in these cases are highly likely to have neighbours and other relatives available and willing to provide care.

A 2011 OECD report 'Help wanted? Providing and paying for long term care' highlights the need to pay more attention to the needs of family carers, since as we have shown in this chapter, 80% of the help given to persons in need is provided by family/friends in almost every age group. Policies that pay attention to carers may occur in multiple policy domains of labour, income security, health, and continuing care. They may include the development of employment policies that enable more choice and flexibility, cash support policies to mitigate against the financial consequences of caregiving, and home care policies involving supportive services that go beyond respite care.

In Canada, one option is the expansion of family policy to include the range of informal supports that exist outside the immediate family composition. Recent changes to the Canadian National Employment Insurance Compassionate Care programme exemplify this approach. Eligibility for employment insurance to care for a dying relative was initially restricted to spouse, children, and parents but later expanded to include all family relationships, as well as 'family-like' relationships (Keefe 2011; Service Canada 2011). And, as we have seen, the role of such supports becomes crucial in situations where spouses and children are not available.

Another option is financial support policies. Carer allowances that provide cash to caregivers are rare in Canada, except for the province of Nova Scotia, but are available in some English-speaking countries (Australia, Ireland, New Zealand, and the United Kingdom) (OECD 2011) and a number of European countries (Keefe et al. 2008b; Keefe 2011).

Implications of the decreased availability of adult children in the longer term coupled with decreased access to adult children because of increased mobility and labour force participation of women point to the need to rely on non-familial systems of care. These sources of care include formal care systems available from the marketplace and the state, as well as through the voluntary sector.

Formal sources of assistance become increasingly prevalent as the family network of the older person in need of care shrinks. Formal network providers comprise the smallest proportion and lowest average hours of support when both spouses and children are present and the highest when they are absent. Thus, among family compositions that have neither a spouse nor an adult child, formal providers are most critical. Among men and among persons aged 65–74, this family composition is projected to increase by 350% and 400%, respectively. Consequently, the demand for these formal supports will likely also increase, particularly for men. Among women, the family composition that is increasing the most in the future is that with a spouse but no adult children. This family composition has a medium amount of involvement from formal services. On a positive note, the analysis demonstrated that among those who are 85 and older, the family composition of having a spouse and a child is projected to increase by 350%, suggesting that for many in this group, access to informal caregivers may mitigate the need for assistance from the formal network. Consequently, it is men who may be an increasing proportion of consumers of formal sources of support in the coming years.

These findings are consistent with research in other countries. Johnson et al. (2007), using the DYNASIM3 model in the United States, have projected an increasing need for care among the elderly population in the future, with an increasing share of this needing to come from the formal network. A study of European countries notes that 'family care may well reach its limits in the coming decades as family patterns become more "vertical"' (Lanzieri 2011). Policies can, and probably must, be developed across multiple sectors to address the challenges of the older population in need and with less available children to provide care. It is assessing the implications of our findings in each of these policy areas to which we now turn.

The cost of formal home care services in Canada continues to increase despite limits being placed on the scope of services that are available under the publically funded system of home care. For example, the total public home care spending per capita rose from CDN $55 in 1994–1995 to $94 in 2002–2003 (inflation adjusted) (Canadian Institute for Health Information [CIHI] 2007). That is much more than the rate at which health expenditure grew over the same period. As a result, the share of home care spending in health expenditures in Canada increased from 3.1% in 1994–1995 to 4.2% in 2003–2004 (CIHI 2007, p. 10). Despite these increases in spending, analysis of the types of support being covered within the long-term care system suggests that state funding is not keeping up with the demand for supportive services. There is indeed an increase in home health usage but a decline in the *proportion* of home care users from government-subsidised programmes. Emphasis on nursing care rather than supportive care from government subsidies may be a result of the government's expectation that these non-nursing supports can be provided by family and friends or that the individual can afford to purchase such services privately from the marketplace. This downloading of responsibility to family and friends may work in the short term and for some people with resources; however, our results demonstrate that projected changing family compositions in the longer term call into question assumptions that adult children are available to provide this care. Consequently, alternative approaches to home support services will need to be enhanced.

Caregivers are not official clients of the home care system and are generally not entitled to services in their own right—they receive services such as respite education and information indirectly through the care receiver (Keefe et al. 2008a).

Some jurisdictions, such as England, have had a legislated right for caregivers to be assessed by a professional (separately from their care recipients) for over a decade (Keefe 2011). Assessment of caregiver needs implies the opportunity to meet these needs with an array of services and programmes. Enhancement of home care policies that increase respite services and educational support for caregivers is needed; however, given the projected increase in the demand for existing supports as implied by our projections and current economic challenges, these changes may again be relegated to the sidelines.

Another option to increasing supports for older persons in need of assistance is to enhance the voluntary sector. Volunteering is distinct from informal support in that it is defined as 'doing activities without pay on behalf of a group or organization' (Hall et al. 2009, p. 49). A recent report of the National Seniors Council (2010) on volunteerism suggested a number of initiatives to promote the role of the volunteer and prepare for the increased need for supportive services to an ageing population. Proposed initiatives included tax credits for volunteers in recognition of expenses associated with their activity and working with private sector partners to provide incentives to promote volunteerism in their communities. Coordination of volunteers at municipal and provincial levels was also proposed as an approach to help not-for-profit agencies adapt to the needs of an ageing population. Yet, such approaches assume a cadre of available volunteers willing and able to take up additional roles of unpaid labour in an era of projected decline in the supply of workers to meet economic demands. Attempts to further develop this sector are commendable but not a panacea for addressing care needs among elderly Canadians.

Finally, the marketplace has a role in the development of opportunities and services to meet the care needs of older persons with long-term health problems. Delivery of quality front-line services to older persons in need of support to remain in their private households requires investment: in infrastructure (to meet the organisation of care), in human resources training, and in recruitment and retention (to ensure there will be a workforce available to deliver the human services). The OECD report on long-term care (2011) suggests that the increasing demand on this sector and the need for an adequate supply of workers is a 'manageable challenge' if multiple strategies are used. These strategies include improving recruitment efforts by, among other things, hiring of migrant workers, increasing retention by improving pay and working conditions, and increasing worker productivity. Such strategies also come with a financial cost. Many countries will not be able to meet this extra financial burden, and yet the alternative of institutional care costs even more.

This research is based on results of a micro-simulation exercise using Statistics Canada's LifePaths model. While this model is known for its sophistication, it cannot take into account changes in cultural norms or behaviours around caregiving, new policies, or economic events. Consequently, the implications of the findings are subject to social and economic factors remaining constant. These assumptions are particularly problematic when it comes to the 'boomer' cohort who have had somewhat different pathways throughout their lives than previous or subsequent cohorts leading to potentially different behavioural patterns in later life.

Nevertheless, micro-simulation is a logical tool for analysing intergenerational support due to its emphasis on 'linked lives' (Spielauer 2011). Future research in this area needs to analyse the effects of a change in policies or changing behaviours on the projections of sources of support in the future. For example, scenarios of increased consumer purchase of services by the boomers could be modelled as could the effect of having greater access to subsidised government supports. In Canada, as in other developed nations, population ageing calls in to question the availability of support systems to help sustain older persons in need of assistance in the community and outside of expensive nursing homes. Changes in family formation likely projected to occur in the coming decades call for governments to expand policies in all sectors of the welfare state to enhance contributions from family, voluntary, and marketplace sectors.

Acknowledgements This research is supported by the Canadian Institutes of Health Research (#81108).

References

Brackley, M. E., & Penning, M. J. (2009). Home care utilization within the year of death. Trends, predictors and changes in access equity during a period of health policy reform in British Columbia, Canada. *Health & Social Care in the Community, 17*(3), 283–294.

Canadian Institute for Health Information. (2007). *Public-sector expenditures and utilization of home care services in Canada: Exploring the data.* Ottawa: CIHI.

Carrière, Y., Keefe, J., Légaré, J., Lin, X., & Rowe, G. (2007). Population ageing and immediate family composition: Implications for future home care services. *Genus, LXIIII*(1–2), 11–31.

Chan Cheung Ming, A., Cheng, S. T., & Phillips, D. (2007). The aging of Asia: Policy lessons, challenges. *Global Asia, 2*(2).

Cranswick, K., & Dosman, D. (2008). Eldercare: What we know today. In *Canadian social trends* (Catalogue no. 11–008-X: 48–56). Ottawa: Statistics Canada.

de Vaus, D., Gray, M., & Stanton, D. (2003, October). Measuring the value of unpaid household, caring and voluntary work of older Australians. In *Australian institute of family studies* (Research Paper No. 34). Melbourne: AIFS.

Dykstra, P. (2010). *Intergenerational family relationships in ageing societies.* New York/Geneva: United Nations Economic Commission for Europe, United Nations.

Fournier-Savard, P., Mongeon, C., & Crompton, S. (2010). Help with activities of daily living for people with a disability. Living with a disability series. In *Canadian social trends* (Catalogue no. 11–008-X). Ottawa: Statistics Canada.

Gaymu, J., Busque, M. A., Légaré, J., Décarie, Y., Vézina, S., & Keefe, J. (2010). What will the family composition of older persons be like tomorrow? A comparison of Canada and France. *Canadian Journal on Aging, 29*(1), 57–71.

Hall, M., Lasby, D., Ayer, S., & Gibbons, W. D. (2009). *Caring Canadians, involved Canadians: Highlights from the 2007 Canada survey of giving, volunteering and participating* (Catalogue no. 71–542-XIE). Ottawa: Statistics Canada.

Hoffmann, F., & Rodrigues, R. (2010, April). Informal carers: Who takes care of them? In *Policy brief.* Vienna: European Centre for Social Welfare Policy and Research.

Hollander, M. J., Liu, G., & Chappell, N. (2009). Who cares and how much? The imputed economic contribution to the Canadian healthcare system of middle-aged and older unpaid caregivers providing care to the elderly. *Healthcare Quarterly, 12*(2), 42–49.

Huber, M., Rodrigues, R., Hoffmann, F., Gastor, K., & Marin, B. (2009). *Facts and figures on long-term care. Europe and North America*. Vienna: European Centre for Social Welfare Policy and Research.

Johnson, R. W., Toohey, D., & Weiner, J. M. (2007). *Meeting the long-term care needs of the baby boomers: How changing families will affect paid helpers and institutions*. Washington, DC: The Urban Institute.

Keating, N., Otfinowski, P., Wenger, G. C., Fast, J., & Derksen, L. (2003). Understanding the caring capacity of informal networks of frail seniors: A case for care networks. *Ageing and Society, 23*(1), 115–127.

Keefe, J. (2011). Supporting caregivers and caregiving in an aging Canada. *IRPP Study No. 23*.

Keefe, J., & Rajnovich, B. (2007). To pay or not to pay: Examining underlying principles in the debate on financial support for family caregivers. *Canadian Journal on Aging, 26*, S77–S89.

Keefe, J., Fancey, P., Guberman, N., Barylak, L., & Nahmiash, D. (2008a). Caregivers' aspirations, realities, and expectations: The care tool. *Journal of Applied Gerontology, 27*(3), 286–308.

Keefe, J., Glendinning, C., & Fancey, P. (2008b). Financial payments for family carers: Policy approaches and debates. In J. Philips & A. Martin-Matthews (Eds.), *Ageing and caring at the intersection of work and home life: Blurring the boundaries*. New York: Lawrence Erlbaum Associates.

Keefe, J., Vézina, S., Busque, M. A., Décarie, Y., Charbonneau, P., & Légaré, J. (2008, December). *Planning for Canadian human resources needs in chronic home care: Policy implications of projected needs 2006–2031*. Paper presented at the 4th annual symposium of the population, work and family policy research collaboration, Gatineau.

Keefe, J., Vézina, S., Décarie, Y., & Légaré, J. (2011, April). *Projecting human resources needs to deliver chronic home care in Canada: Changes in the organization of care*. Paper presented at the European conference on ageing, Bologna.

Lafrenière, S., Carrière, Y., Martel, L., & Bélanger, A. (2003). Dependent seniors at home – Formal and informal help. *Health Reports, 14*(4), 31–40.

Lanzieri, G. (2011). *The greying of the baby boomers: A century-long view of ageing in European populations* (Eurostat European Commission Catalogue no. KS-SF-11–023-EN-N) (ISBN 1977–0316).

National Seniors Council. (2010). *Report of the National Seniors Council on volunteering among seniors and positive and active aging*. Retrieved from http://www.seniorscouncil.gc.ca/eng/research_publications/volunteering/page00.shtml

OECD – Organization for Economic Cooperation and Development. (2011). *Help wanted? Providing and paying for long-term care*. Paris: OECD.

Pickard, L., Wittenberg, R., Comas-Herrera, A., Davis, B., & Darton, R. (2000). Relying on informal care in the new century? Informal care for elderly people in England to 2031. *Ageing and Society, 20*, 745–772.

Pijl, M. (1994). When private care goes public: An analysis of concepts and principles concerning payments for care. In A. Adalbert, M. A. Pijl, & C. Ungerson (Eds.), *Payments for care: A comparative overview*. Vienna: European Centre for Social Welfare Policy and Research.

Service Canada. (2011). *Employment Insurance (EI,) compassionate care benefits*. Ottawa: Service Canada. Retrieved October 21, 2011, from http://www.servicecanada.gc.ca/eng/ei/types/compassionate_care.shtml

Spielauer, M. (2011). What is social science microsimulation? *Social Science Computer Review, 29*(1), 9–20.

Statistics Canada. (2010). *Population projections for Canada, provinces and territories: 2009–2036* (Catalogue No. 91–520-X).

Statistics Canada. (2011a). *Table 380–0030. Gross domestic product (GDP) and gross national product (GNP) at market prices and net national income at basic prices*. Ottowa: CANSIM, Statistics Canada.

Statistics Canada. (2011b). *The LifePaths microsimulation model: An overview*. Retrieved October 20, 2011, from http://www.statcan.gc.ca/microsimulation/lifepaths/overview-vuedensemble-eng.htm
Tarricone, R., & Tsouros, A. (Eds.). (2008). *Home care in Europe: The solid facts*. Copenhagen: World Health Organisation.
Vézina, M., & Turcotte, M. (2010). Caring for a parent who lives far away: The consequences. In *Canadian social trends* (Catalogue No. 11–008-X) Ottawa: Statistics Canada.
Ward-Griffin, C., & Marshall, V. (2003). Reconceptualizing the relationship between public and private eldercare. *Journal of Aging Studies, 17*, 189–208.
Wilkins, K. (2006). Government subsidized home care. *Health Reports, 17*(4), 39–42.
Yoo, B. K., Bhattacharya, J., McDonald, K. M., & Garber, A. M. (2005). Impacts of informal caregiver availability on long-term care expenditures in OECD countries. *Health Services Research, 39*(6), 1971–1992.

Chapter 8
Social Norms and Intergenerational Relationships

Valeria Bordone

8.1 Introduction

Traditional expectations about family responsibilities in industrialised societies have changed in the past 50 years, in part because of increased longevity and decreased fertility, but also because of a rising diversity in family forms, norms, and behaviours (Cherlin and Furstenberg 1986).

Social policy on public care or pension policy implications is mainly concerned about cohort relationships; this work instead focuses on the coexistence of, and the interaction between, members of the same family belonging to different generations located in a system of ranked descent.

Intergenerational relationships between parents and children demand time: at younger ages, parental time is used to care for the child – in a decreasing amount as the child grows into an adult (Chap. 9 by Tanturri, in this volume); when parents age, it is (in general) the adult child that offers elderly care. This mechanism is delicate, however: its working depends on several preconditions, among which the willingness and the availability of adult children living close by. In the future, other, more costly forms of support, such as formal care, are likely to be increasingly needed (Chap. 7 by Keefe et al., in this volume).

The study of intergenerational relationships was developed first in the USA (e.g. Sussman and Burchinal 1962) and then in Europe (e.g. Pitrou 1977; Willmott and Young 1957/1986). Over the past two decades, the research in this field has evolved considerably, drawing largely from 'social network theories' (e.g. Antonucci and Akiyama 1987). In particular, the focus has more and more shifted towards the relationship between elderly parents and adult children. Older people tend to

V. Bordone (✉)
Wittgenstein Centre for Demography and Global Human Capital, Research Institute Human Capital and Development, Vienna University of Economics and Business, Nordbergstraße 15/A/6, 1090 Wien, Austria
e-mail: valeria.bordone@wu.ac.at

G. De Santis (ed.), *The Family, the Market or the State?: Intergenerational Support Under Pressure in Ageing Societies*, International Studies in Population 10,
DOI 10.1007/978-94-007-4339-7_8,

rely on a small number of long-time relationships. Spouses, children, and siblings dominate, therefore, the social network of the elderly (Connidis and Davies 1990). However, partners and siblings, generally having about the same age and lifestyle, may not be capable of providing all the necessary help (Antonucci 1990). Intergenerational relationships frequently become the first source of support in old age.

Some scholars (e.g. Popenoe 1993) fear that demographic trends, geographical mobility, and sociocultural changes may pose a threat to family support towards the elderly. Because of decreased fertility, families are becoming thinner (Bengtson 2001), with fewer horizontal ties within generations. Due to progress in life expectancy, the duration of family ties is now potentially longer. But several demographic changes of the last decades (e.g. decreasing marriage and multigenerational co-residence and increasing divorce rates, singleness, and childlessness) have, in fact, apparently weakened family ties (European Commission 1995; Kohli et al. 2005). Other significant macro societal changes are the increase in women's independence, larger participation in higher education, the declining influence of the church, and the spread of more individualistic values (Lesthaeghe and Meekers 1986). However, the lengthened duration of the parental and child role increases the importance of mutual obligations: even if in a new way, the family may thus continue to play a central role for its members (Lüscher and Schultheis 1993) by securing family support over time and across the generations (Bengtson 2001; Bengtson and Roberts 1991), following a pattern of reciprocity in the long run (Dykstra and Fokkema 2011). This holds for the whole of Europe (Blome et al. 2009; Bordone 2009; Fokkema et al. 2008; Hank 2007).

Although cross-country differences in intergenerational relationships remain evident, no previous international comparison has attempted to trace family associational solidarity directly back to cultural-contextual factors.

In this chapter, I will focus on the frequency of contacts between elderly parents and their adult children in ten European countries. Indeed, child-parent contact is a prerequisite for support. Frequent contacts make children and parents more aware of each other's needs, which is also likely to stimulate other forms of intergenerational support. Of course, there is also a question of the quality of the parent-child relation (Silverstein and Bengtson 1997). But, when contacts are frequent, the perceived quality of the relationships is generally better (Kalmijn and Dykstra 2006) and support higher (Silverstein et al. 1995).

In agreement with Saraceno (2008: 10), 'the focus on solidarity and support, whatever definition is used, [...] has the merit of documenting how intergenerational relations within families also maintain an important solidaristic role in increasingly individualised and welfare-state societies'.

The remainder of this chapter is structured as follows. First (Sect. 8.2), I provide a review of the existing literature. Moreover, in a field calling for theories, I propose a conceptual framework which encompasses the role of micro- and macro-levels in shaping individual behaviours of solidarity. Based on the theoretical background derived from the disciplines of economics and sociology, I formulate the specific hypotheses to be tested in this study. The next section (Sect. 8.3) is dedicated to the data used in the empirical analyses (from the Survey of Health, Ageing and

Retirement in Europe) and the methodological approach adopted. After reporting the results from both descriptive and multilevel ordered logistic analyses (Sect. 8.4), I discuss them in the concluding section (Sect. 8.5).

8.2 Background: A Theoretical Framework for Intergenerational Solidarity

The research on intergenerational relationships has developed in several fields (sociology, demography, anthropology, and so forth), each with its own definition of 'support': see, for example, Cobb (1976), Cohen and Syme (1985), House (1981), and Weiss (1974). Still, the 'gold standard' model for assessing intergenerational relationships between parents and children (Silverstein et al. 2010: 1007) is that suggested by Bengtson (Bengtson 2001; Bengtson and Roberts 1991). This comprehensive paradigm describes sentiments, behaviours, attitudes, values, and structural arrangements in parent-child relationships. In the Bengtson tradition, family relationships are distinguished along six dimensions: associational, structural, affectual, functional, normative, and consensual solidarity. This study pays attention to the dimension of associational solidarity: in particular, I concentrate on the frequency of child-parent contacts.

Before turning to the empirical application, however, let us consider the issue from a more general, theoretical point of view (for a discussion, see Hagestad and Dannefer 2001). Over the last decades, several authors have indeed expressed alarm about the 'atheoretical and descriptive' social science work on ageing (Hagestad and Dannefer 2001; Myers 1996).

Individual choices can be said to be driven by *constraints* and *benefits*, given *preferences*. The economic rationality approach, however, has often been used beyond the conventional economic sphere (e.g. Becker 1976; Green and Shapiro 1996; Swedborg 1990) to answer the new challenges of modern societies: low fertility, for example (Becker 1981; Becker and Barro 1988).

In the case of intergenerational relationships, it is perhaps preferable to use the more sociological terms 'opportunities' and 'needs'. In Szydlik's definition (2008), *opportunity structures* reflect enabling or preventing resources for social interaction. For example, a child's educational attainment increases personal aspirations in the labour market to find a good job, even if far from his or her parents. Education is therefore an opportunity that tends to weaken parent-child structural solidarity. *Need structures* may refer to health or emotional problems, or economic difficulties. Marital disruption suffered by the adult child may, for example, lead to an increase of phone calls to the mother in order to get some emotional comfort.

In order to explain the type and level of intergenerational relationships, socioeconomic and demographic characteristics of the child and the parent, as well as geographical differences, are used as covariates in the majority of the analyses. Previous studies reveal that children require help when they have their own children: they themselves become then the driving force to closeness (Malmberg and Pettersson 2007). Moreover, the presence of siblings might be crucial: Michielin and Mulder (2007) show that the presence of a sister makes it easier for an adult child to live far away from his/her parents. Concerning parental needs, separated and divorced parents typically have fewer contacts with their children, as compared to married parents. Empirical results consistently find that women are more engaged in kin-keeping roles, as mothers, daughters, or both (Gerstel and Gallagher 1993; Kaufman and Uhlenberg 1998; Nauck 2009; Rossi 1993).

However, the frequency of parent-child contacts differs not only between individuals and families but also according to the specific contextual conditions under which it takes place (Lowenstein and Ogg 2003). Comparative studies (e.g. Bordone 2009) show that both needs and opportunities of both recipients and givers exert a comparable influence on the exchange of support in northern and southern European countries. However, the diversity of intergenerational relationships from country to country remains significant within Europe (see also Hank 2007; Tomassini et al. 2004), pointing to the need of also considering contextual determinants (Bengtson 2001).

In the attempt to explain the north-south European divide in family relations, the vague concept of culture has been frequently used. For instance, Glaser and Tomassini (2000: 736) argue that 'in Italy, parent-child proximity may reflect a *cultural preference* regardless of need'; and Hank (2007: 170) suggests that '*national cultural characteristics* [...] are likely to matter' in order to explain differences within Europe. However, over time, *culture* has been interpreted in several ways by different scholars. The most common explanation at the macro-level still distinguishes on the basis of weak versus strong family ties (Reher 1998). Thus, in northern Europe, familial care is complemented to a large degree by publicly supported services. Conversely, in southern European countries, most care is provided at home and almost exclusively by family members. Obviously, this is also linked to the type of welfare state (Esping-Andersen 1990), but the correspondence is not as strict as one may at first suspect, and there are a few countries, such as the Netherlands, which are difficult to classify. It may be preferable, then, to consider a broader spectrum of macro-variables, in order to better assess their differences: Murphy (2008), for instance, proposes to consider indicators such as GDP per head, life expectancy at birth, the Human Development Index, level of corruption, and geographical factors in the analysis of kin contact.

A more comprehensive framework, of Durkheimian orientation, would distinguish three levels of analysis: the individual, the family, and the society. In general, *cultural-contextual factor structures*, with roots lying far back in history, could be identified as the institutional framework (i.e. socio-economic conditions, the tax system, the welfare system, and labour and housing markets) as well as the social norms within which intergenerational relations develop (Szydlik 2000, 2008).

Because of the political economy focus on structural factors, most cross-national comparative research on intergenerational relations that takes into account the social context in later life has centred around helping and care from a welfare production point of view (e.g. Brandt et al. 2009; Broese van Groenou et al. 2006) rather than on emotional cohesion between generations. The labour market and the educational system, housing conditions and housing policy, and the welfare regime are of substantial importance to explain country-specific (and sometimes even regional) behaviours of social support. However, these contextual factors seem to play a key role in certain forms of intergenerational solidarity, such as residential choices and therefore child-parent proximity (Mandic 2008; Saraceno and Keck 2008). 'Besides the willingness to help and emotional ties, attachment of the two generations living together reflects [...] the necessity of help and actual living conditions' (Synak 1990: 336).

In contrast to the other forms of support, contact could be seen mainly as a voluntary form of intergenerational solidarity (Heylen and Mortelmans 2009; Tomassini et al. 2004), still partly motivated by a normative obligation (Kalmijn and De Vries 2009; Rossi and Rossi 1990).

For a long time, sociologists (e.g. Durkheim 1895/1983; Merton 1968; and Parsons 1937), demographers (e.g. Lesthaeghe 1980; Oppenheim Mason 1983), and even economists (e.g. Dosi et al. 1999; Elster 1989) have viewed social norms (together with rationality) as major explanations for regularities in social behaviour. 'Norms are prescriptions or proscriptions about behaviour in the form of should and should not; [and] they are supported by consensus' (Settersten and Mayer 1997). The debated element of sanctions which enforces norms through various mechanisms of social control is not included in the definition of norm adopted in this study (for a discussion, see Gibbs 1981; Horne 2003).

Despite the calls of social scientists to study how larger social structures regulate emotional expression (Thoits 1989), researchers may have neglected the importance of social norms in the last decades (Liefbroer and Billari 2010), and little is known about the association between societal norms and intergenerational contact. It is acknowledged that the individualisation process (Lesthaeghe 1995; van de Kaa 1987) may reduce the importance of social norms in shaping choices in post-industrial societies. As a result, family relationships may be less often economically and normatively motivated and more often guided by affective and individual concerns (Beck and Beck-Gernsheim 2002; Brückner and Mayer 2005). Nevertheless, culturally prescribed notions about duties and obligations have a role in family relationships and are endorsed even by highly educated and secularised people (e.g. Billari and Liefbroer 2007; Liefbroer and Billari 2010). Recent studies document the importance of values and norms at the societal level in explaining country-specific patterns of other dimensions of intergenerational solidarity (e.g. Heylen and Mortelmans 2009 on proximity). Since 'to accept a social norm as a motivational mechanism is not to deny the importance of rational choice' (Elster 1989: 102), differences in norms can also be expected to play an important role in intergenerational contact behaviours.

Keeping the theoretical constructs of this chapter in mind, let us now try to answer the following research question: what is the role of 'norms' in the explanation of country differences in the frequency of intergenerational contact between older parents and their adult children?

Note that this study focuses on the role of macro-level traits (norms) for a micro-level action (contact) and, therefore, requires a multilevel approach. Although the nature and content of norms may have changed over time, I expect the normative contextual factors at the society level to still have a significant role in explaining between-country differences in the frequency of child-parent contacts in post-modern societies.

The literature mainly refers to the crowding-in and crowding-out hypotheses when dealing with the offer of services from the family and the state. The state might indeed displace family services ('crowding out'), stimulate family support ('crowding in'), as well as work in 'complementarity' with the other sources of support (Daatland and Lowenstein 2005; Motel-Klingebiel et al. 2005). Although this work does not speculate about the state-family divide in providing elderly care, it explores the normative beliefs about this aspect. Sociologists tend to confirm that affection and a sense of obligation provide motives to continue to give support. I expect that in societies with normative beliefs more oriented towards the family and the traditional division of roles between the family and the state, associational solidarity is higher, even in families with 'modern' values.

8.3 Data and Method

8.3.1 Data Sources, Selection of the Sample, and Construction of the Variables

My empirical analysis applies to cross-country data from the *Survey of Health, Ageing and Retirement in Europe* (SHARE). SHARE is a multidisciplinary and cross-national database of micro-data on health, socio-economic status, and social and family networks, representative of people aged 50 and over in Europe (Börsch-Supan and Jürges 2005). Up to now, SHARE counts two waves, respectively, in 2004 and 2006. A third wave collected retrospective data in 2008. For this work, I combine the respondents from the first wave (2004) and the refresher sample from the second wave (2006): each respondent is therefore interviewed only once. The sample under study includes 19,975 adult children and their respective 9,685 parents from:

1. Scandinavia (Denmark and Sweden)
2. Central Europe (Austria, Belgium, Germany, France, and the Netherlands)
3. The Mediterranean (Greece, Italy, and Spain).[1]

[1] Following the classification of welfare states, three regimes or clusters of family policy are identified (e.g. Esping-Andersen 1990; Ferrera 1996): (1) the Scandinavian social democratic countries (DK, SE), (2) the conservative countries (AU, BE, DE, FR), and (3) the familistic regimes in the Mediterranean (ES, GR, IT). The Netherlands is considered a hybrid between liberal, conservative, and social democratic, and its classification depends on the focus of study. SHARE collected data also in Ireland and Israel. However, these countries are not considered in this chapter in order to keep the focus on the three clusters mentioned above.

Contact between the adult child and the respective parent is the (ordinal) *dependent variable*, based on the question '*During the past twelve months, how often did you have contact with {child name}, either personally, by phone or mail?*' The categories of answer range between 'no contact at all' (labelled 1) and 'daily contact' (=5). In this study, I select the sample of children by considering only those who are not living together with their parents.[2]

Although SHARE interviews people aged 50 and over and their respective partners, the CAPI main questionnaire is designed in such a way that the couple's first person interviewed serves as the family respondent: he/she will also answer questions about children on behalf of the couple. In the following analyses, the information on the family refers to the parent who answered the questions about the children.

The macro-indicator used as an *independent explanatory variable* on social norms about responsibility for elderly caregiving derives from the following Eurobarometer 67.3 Survey question (European Commission 2007), '*Imagine an elderly father or mother who lives alone and can no longer manage to live without regular help because of his or her physical or mental health condition. In your opinion, what would be the best option for people in this situation?*' The possible answers are 'they should live with one of their children; one of their children should regularly visit them; public or private service providers should visit them; they should move to a nursing home'. Assigning a score to each category from 1 ('they should live with their children') to 4 ('they should move to a nursing home'), I calculate an average value for each country and use it as an explanatory macro-variable: higher values refer to less traditional norms on elderly caregiving (cf. Fig. 8.2).

In terms of *independent variables*, I distinguish between individual variables related to the child (*gender, being the youngest, marital status, education, number of siblings, having own children, age at nest-leaving*) and those related to the parent (*gender, age, marital status, education, being homeowner, depression, disability, religion*). An indicator of normative *values* within the family is then used to measure the propensity of the family towards traditional versus 'modern' values. The questions used to construct such an indicator relate to the opinion of the interviewed parent about (1) grandparents' duty ('whether or not it is grandparents' duty to help grandchildren's parents in looking after grandchildren') and elderly parents' support ('whether it is mainly the family, mainly the state, or both that should provide (2) financial support, (3) help with household chores, and (4) personal care for older people who are in need'). The scale is constructed on the basis of Cronbach's alpha (Cronbach 1951), which determines the internal consistency, or average correlation, of items in a survey instrument to gauge its reliability. The items considered have relatively high internal consistency, as the alpha coefficient for the four items, which is usually considered poor when below 0.60, is about 0.71.

---

[2] I have also controlled for the presence of at least one sibling living with the parents, and results (not shown here) do not change appreciably from those presented below.

A control for residential proximity between the elderly parent and the adult child captures, at least in part, the possible interaction between the normative and structural macro-dimensions, which is the result of a historical evolution of societies.

8.3.2 Estimation Strategy: Multilevel Regression

It is clearly unrealistic to assume that people who live in the same country can be completely independent of each other, as they are subject to a common social framework (Rabe-Hesketh and Skrondal 2005) that reverberates in their attitudes and their answers in a questionnaire. The same holds for children within the same family. Failure to explicitly account for this multilevel structure would result in biased estimates of the parameters and of their standard errors. An advantage of multilevel regression is that it allows researchers to combine predictors lying at different levels, which can act simultaneously and not necessarily in the same direction (Gelman and Hill 2007). Besides, the total variance can be subdivided between the various levels.

In this chapter, I use a three-level structure: individuals (the adult children) are clustered within their families, which are in turn clustered within countries.

While previous studies accounted for context by including country indicators in the regression models (e.g. Hank 2007; Kalmijn and De Vries 2009), I measure the effect of social norms in a multilevel analysis of child-parent associational solidarity in Europe. This type of methodological analysis has usually been used for family levels, such as grandparents, parents, and grandchildren (Geurts et al. 2009), or living parents, adult children, and the couple they are part of (Nazio and Saraceno 2008). Although the impact of the social sphere is a central topic of discussion in the field of intergenerational solidarity (as suggested by Heylen and Mortelmans 2009, or Lowenstein and Ogg 2003), the existing evidence is limited to some explorative works on the functional dimension of solidarity (see, e.g. Brandt et al. 2009).

The use of three levels (child, parent, and country) rather than two (parent and country) is quantitatively justified by the significance of the log-likelihood ratio test run on the empty models with two and three levels, respectively. The potential drawback of increased complexity is paid off by the creation of more realistic models which take into account group-level variation. The dependent variable, contact, is ordinal. Therefore, the estimates use ordered logistic models, specified as follows (Snijders and Bosker 1999):

$$y^*_{ijk} = \theta_{ijk} + \varepsilon_{ijk} \tag{8.1}$$

where y^*_{ijk} is the latent response variable ('propensity to keep in touch') for level one unit i in level two unit j in level three unit k, y_{ij} is the observed categorical variable related to y^*_{ijk}, and $\theta_{ijk} = \beta_{0jk} + \sum_{p=1}^{P} \beta_p x_{pijk}$.

In the absence of explanatory variables and random intercepts, and assuming the distribution of the error term ε_{ijk} to be logistic, the cumulative logit model can be written as

$$\log\left[\frac{P_{ijk(c)}}{1-P_{ijk(c)}}\right] = \log\left[\frac{\Pr(y_{ijk} \leq c)}{\Pr(y_{ijk} > c)}\right] = \gamma_c - \theta_{ijk},\ c = 1, \ldots C-1 \qquad (8.2)$$

with $(C - 1)$ strictly increasing model thresholds γ_c (i.e. $\gamma_1 < \gamma_2 \ldots < \gamma_{C-1}$), for category $c = 1, \ldots, C - 1$.

The observed categorical variable y is therefore related to y^* via

$$y = \begin{cases} 0 & \textit{if } y* \leq \gamma_0 \\ 1 & \textit{if } \gamma_0 < y* \leq \gamma_1, \\ r & \textit{if } \gamma_{r-1} < y* \leq \gamma_r \quad (r = 2, \ldots, c-2), \\ c-1 & \textit{if } \gamma_{c-2} < y* \end{cases} \qquad (8.3)$$

with the values for the C ordered categories defined as $0, 1, \ldots C - 1$.

Adding explanatory variables, the level 1 random intercepts model becomes

$$\log\left[\frac{\Pr(y_{ijk} \leq c | x_{ijk}, \beta_{0jk})}{1 - \Pr(y_{ijk} \leq c | x_{ijk}, \beta_{0jk})}\right] = \gamma_c - \left(\beta_{0jk} + \sum_{p=1}^{P} \beta_p x_{pijk}\right). \qquad (8.4)$$

The model can therefore be written as

$$y^*_{ijk} = \beta_0 + \sum_{p=1}^{P} \beta_p x_{pijk} + V_{00k} + U_{0jk} + R_{ijk}. \qquad (8.5)$$

The intercept is allowed to vary across countries: randomly and, by assumption, independently. Instead, the slope is not assumed to vary randomly, because the literature on intergenerational contact suggests that the micro-level indicators work in the same way on shaping the regression results in the various countries considered.[3]

The comparison between the models with and without the macro-indicator is based on changes of country-level variance, likelihood-ratio tests, and two measures

[3] The *gllamm* command in STATA with a minimum of eight integration points allows three-level models with an ordered logistic framework (Rabe-Hesketh and Skrondal 2005).

of fit: the *Akaike's Information Criterion* (AIC) and the *Bayesian Information Criterion* (BIC).[4]

Country differences in the mean level of child-parent contact may be attributable to contextual influences or to differences in the individual composition of the countries in terms of demographic and socio-economic characteristics. By adjusting for individual characteristics, I take into account (part of) the compositional differences and explain some of the country variance detected in the empty model. The proportional change in variance (PCV) calculates the percentage reduction from the estimated variance in the empty model as a result of incorporating a new factor in the model (Gelman and Hill 2007). The PCV equation is

$$\mathrm{PCV}_{\mathrm{country}} = \left(V_{\mathrm{country-empty\ model}} - V_{\mathrm{country-model}}\right) / V_{\mathrm{country-empty\ model}} \tag{8.6}$$

where $V_{\mathrm{country-empty\ model}}$ is the estimate of the initial variance at the country level before adjusting for any contextual factor in the model and $V_{\mathrm{country-model}}$ is the country-level residual variance after adjusting for covariates.

8.4 Results

8.4.1 Descriptive Findings

Descriptive results show that the highest levels of contact between children and parents are registered in southern European countries, with about 80% child-parent dyads having more than one contact per week in Greece, Italy, and Spain. Although Denmark, Sweden, and the Netherlands have the lowest percentages reporting a daily contact, in all the countries considered, more than three-fourths of the sample had at least one contact per week with parents over the 12 months preceding the interview (Fig. 8.1).

Figure 8.2 gives a descriptive overview of the highest frequency of child-parent contact in the countries under consideration here, and it also illustrates the bivariate association between the proportions of child-parent dyads having daily contact and

[4] Both the AIC (Akaike 1971, 1974) and the BIC (Schwarz 1978) are measures of the goodness of fit of an estimated model used for model selection between parametric models with different numbers of parameters. AIC and BIC are calculated as follows: $\mathrm{AIC} \equiv -2\log(L) + 2(k)$; BIC $\equiv -2\log(L) + k\log(N)$, where L is the maximum likelihood for the estimated model, k is the number of independently adjusted parameters within the model, and N is the number of data-points used in the fit. Given several competing models, AIC and BIC allow a ranking. Models with smaller deviance, AIC, and BIC should be preferred over other models. Whereas the deviance which is −2 times the log-likelihood can simply be reduced by adding a new predictor to the model, the AIC and the BIC penalise for adding new predictors to the model, with BIC being more conservative than the AIC (Gelman and Hill 2007: 524–525).

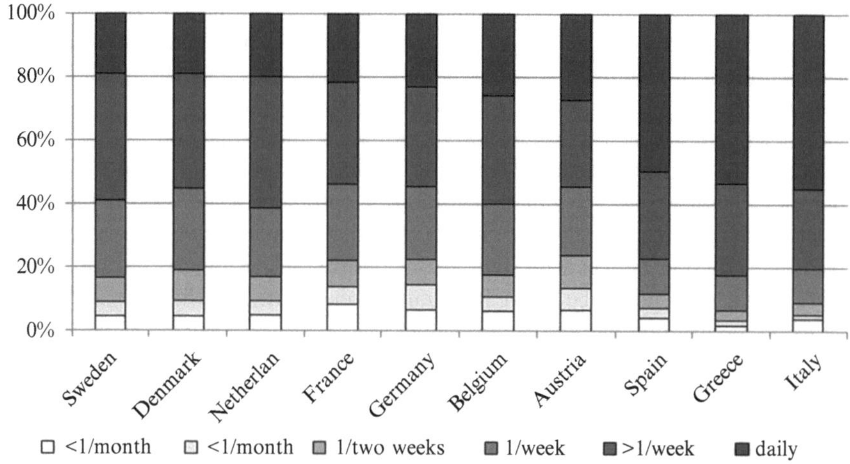

Fig. 8.1 Child-parent contact (%) during the 12 months preceding the survey interview. Note: Countries in ascending order of proportion with 'daily' frequency of contact. Parent-child couples living in the same household are not included (Source: SHARE 2004 (wave 1); 2006 (refresher sample from wave 2). Author's calculations)

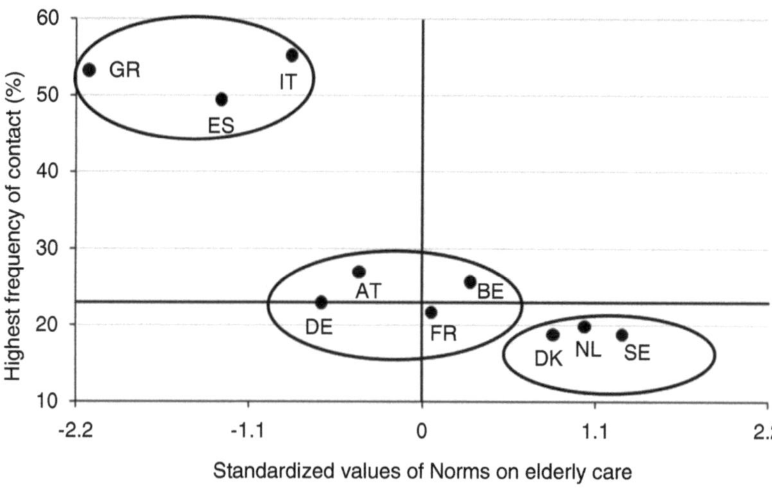

Fig. 8.2 Bivariate associations between frequency of child-parent contact and selected macro-level indicators. Note: The variable 'norms of elderly care' tends to −2 (after standardisation) if the general belief in that country is that elderly care is primarily a family responsibility; it tends to +2 (after standardisation) if it is instead felt that this is primarily a state responsibility (Source: SHARE 2004 (wave 1); 2006 (refresher sample from wave 2); Eurobarometer 2007. Author's calculations) AT = Austria; BE = Belgium; DE = Germany; DK = Denmark; ES = Spain; FR = France; GR = Greece; IT = Italy; NL = Netherlands; SE = Sweden

the macro-level indicator in the study. The scatter diagram is divided into four quadrants, which are defined by the median values of the *Y* (proportion of children with daily contact to the parent) and the centre of the standardised value of the *X* (social norms scale) variables.

During the 12 months before the interview, about 50% of the child-parent dyads in the Mediterranean countries had daily contact, but this happened to less than 20% of the children in Denmark, Sweden, and the Netherlands, with the Central European countries lying somewhere in between (20% and 30%).

Contacts are indeed fewer where 'normative modernisation' prevails (i.e. Denmark, the Netherlands, and Sweden at the bottom right) and more frequent in countries characterised by a more familistic view about responsibilities towards the elderly (i.e. Greece, Italy, and Spain). Austria, Germany, Belgium, and France are at the crossing between the two axes, confirming the hypotheses formulated above of an association between intergenerational contact behaviour and social norms on the division of elderly care labour.

8.4.2 Multivariate Results

The most relevant result of our analysis, an ordered three-level regression logistic model, is the strong correlation that emerges between the macro-indicator considered here (norms, level 3) and the probability of a higher frequency of child-parent contact (level 1; $r = -0.783$).

The first step is the empty random-intercept model with no independent variable (empty model). In a second step, the covariates relating to first and second levels (the child and the parent) are added to the model (base model). Finally, the macro-level indicator is included (macro model). Since the evidence that I find for the association between frequency of contact and the characteristics of children and parents is consistent with that of most prior research, I will not discuss in detail the odds ratios that I estimate. The results of Table 8.A.1 indicate that contacts are more frequent for women (both as adult children and elderly mothers), for middle- and high-school-educated adult children, when there is proximity, when the parental family holds more traditional and religious values, etc.

Table 8.1 shows the odds from the third-level analyses (referring to the macro-level explanatory variable), and it additionally includes model characteristics, variances, and measures of fit of all the regression models. Expectations are confirmed: individuals living in societies with more traditional social norms tend to have more frequent contact with their parents.

Not only is the macro-indicator highly statistically significant (the odds are 0.639, with a standard error of 0.050), but all the measures of fit point to an improvement in the model once norms are considered: the AIC and the BIC of the macro model are reduced as compared to the empty model and the base model once the macro-indicator is included in the analysis. The improvement of fit may appear small, but the log-likelihood test, comparing the macro model to the empty model first and to the base model afterwards, tests the null hypothesis of no significant difference between the pair of models considered. In all the cases, we can reject the null hypothesis and conclude that there is a statistically significant difference or that, in other words, the macro model provides a better fit (it has the lowest log-likelihood) than the empty model and the base model. The intra-class

Table 8.1 Analysis of contact (excluding co-residing kin) on ten countries: odds ratio and standard error of the level 3 indicator, model characteristics, variances, and measures of fit for the empty, base, and macro models

	Empty model	Base model	Macro model with Social Norms: Elderly care (Family vs. State)	
Macro-level indicator	/	/	0.639***	
			(0.050)	
Intra-class correlation countries	0.097	0.058	0.049	Model characteristics
n child-parent relationship (level 1)		19,975		
n parents (level 2)		9,685		
n countries (level 3)		10		
Level 1		$\pi^2/3$		Variances
Level 2	2.284	2.491	2.478	
	(0.151)	(0.193)	(0.189)	
Level 3	*0.600*	*0.355*	*0.299*	
	(0.085)	(0.054)	(0.032)	
AIC	58021.31	52383.09	52349.25	Measures of fit
BIC	58076.63	52620.15	52594.22	
Log-likelihood	−29003.65	−26161.54	−26143.62	
LR test, Prob > Chi2				
(Ref. empty)	/	0.000	0.000	
(Ref. base)	/	/	0.000	
PCV (ref. empty)	/	41%	50%	

Source: SHARE 2004 (wave 1); 2006 (refresher sample from wave 2); Eurobarometer 2007. Author's calculations
Multilevel ordered logistic models maintain the level 1 variance constant at $\pi^2/3$
Significance: $^{+}p < 0.10$; $^{*}p < 0.05$; $^{**}p < 0.01$; $^{***}p < 0.001$
/For the indicator: not included. For the tests: not pertinent

correlation declines from 0.1 in the empty model to 0.05 in the macro model. The inclusion of norms in the model about elderly care explains a large part of the country differences in child-parent frequency of contacts. Although the country variance attributed to compositional factors seems to be relatively small (level 3 variance in the empty model is 0.6), and there remains a little fraction of the variance still unexplained, the contextual factor selected for this work makes it possible to explain up to 50% more of the between-country variance as compared to the empty model regression. This value is the PCV (proportional change in variance) of the model including norms about family roles in the analysis of ten European countries (as compared to the empty model in the same framework).

8.5 Discussion

The study of intergenerational relationships has mostly considered the characteristics of the child and the parent. But a third level of analysis is also worth considering: the association of social norms with certain individual actions – for example, maintaining strong family ties, even in one's adult and old years. In this work, I have therefore attempted to investigate child-parent associational solidarity as a contextual phenomenon, by adapting a three-level multilevel model, where the third level is precisely an indicator of the country's norms about the 'proper' division of elderly care duties between the family and the state.

A close association between social norms and frequency of contacts between adult children and elderly parents emerges, both at the descriptive level and in the in-depth analysis: contacts are definitely more frequent where social norms are more demanding on family members. Although individual characteristics and child-parent proximity explain a large part of the phenomenon (frequency of contacts) within any given country, an important further explanation to between-country differences seems to lie in the normative context. The norm-indicator chosen in this study significantly contributes to the explanation of the north-south European divide in child-parent contact: in northern countries, it is normatively accepted that elderly care be delegated to public or private services, and it is here that contacts are rarer. Vice versa, individuals clustered in societies where it is normatively expected that the child will take care of the elderly parents in need maintain with their parents a higher frequency of contact. Since associational solidarity is the basis on which other types of support are built, this result seems to point towards an intergenerational pact in societies more normatively guided. Note, also, that individuals in 'traditional' societies tend to have higher levels of parent-child associational solidarity, even in families with 'modern' views with regard to family obligations.

These results are consistent with the possibility that state intervention crowds out relatives in intergenerational relationships, but the causal chain might also work in the opposite direction; where adult children feel fewer obligations towards their elderly parents, the state must step in and fill the void. In practice, the mechanism behind the association between social norms and intergenerational contact may well be circular: social norms and individual preferences tend to reinforce each other.

Note that most previous work in this field looks at the relation between the parent and one selected child, who usually is the one that is most frequently contacted. I, instead, examine contact behaviours for each child separately. Although this does not alter the main results in terms of individual characteristics, it allows me to draw descriptions and construct explanatory models which include the characteristics not only of the parent and one selected child but also of the various children within the family. Therefore, the impact of the macro-variable is net of the effect of the characteristics of each parent-child dyad.

This study suggests the need to take into account the social context and the effect it has on intergenerational relationships in ageing societies. In order to understand the various mechanisms at work and expand this strand of research, different sets of social norms should be widely considered as, for example, specific normative values about the division of gender roles within and outside the family. Further developments of this study would require the availability of life course data tracing beliefs over time to investigate the causal direction of the association social norms – individual behaviour. Future analyses might also consider the role played at the society level by an interaction of norms and institutional factors, such as social policies in terms of child and elderly care.

Acknowledgements This chapter uses data from SHARE release 2.3.0, as of November 13th 2009. SHARE data collection in 2004–2007 was primarily funded by the European Commission through its 5th and 6th framework programmes (project numbers QLK6-CT-2001-00360; RII-CT-2006-062193; CIT5-CT-2005-028857). Additional funding by the US National Institute on Aging (grant numbers U01 AG09740-13S2; P01 AG005842; P01 AG08291; P30 AG12815; Y1-AG-4553-01; OGHA 04-064; R21 AG025169) as well as by various national sources is gratefully acknowledged (see http://www.share-project.org for a full list of funding institutions).

Appendix

Table 8.A.1 Base model: odds ratios and respective standard errors of the control variables in the estimation of contact on ten countries (excluding child-parent co-residing). Level 1 (characteristics of the child) and level 2 (characteristics of the family)

Variable	Base model	
Gender: daughter (Ref.: son)	2.324***	Child characteristics
	(0.065)	
Age difference parent-child	0.995	
	(0.008)	
Youngest child (Ref.: other)	0.989	
	(0.032)	
Married (Ref.: not)	0.915+	
	(0.048)	
Education: middle (Ref.: low)	1.261***	
	(0.084)	
High	1.364***	
	(0.116)	
Number of siblings (Ref.: 0)	0.751***	
	(0.014)	
Own children (Ref.: not)	1.034+	
	(0.020)	
Age at nest leaving	1.066***	
	(0.009)	
Gender: female (Ref.: male)	1.560***	Parent characteristics
	(0.087)	
Age	1.033***	
	(0.009)	
Marital status: other (Ref.: married)	0.904***	
	(0.015)	
Education: middle (Ref.: low)	0.943	
	(0.063)	
High	1.013	
	(0.060)	
Homeowner (Ref.: not)	1.096	
	(0.129)	
Depressed (Ref.: not)	1.000	
	(0.000)	

(continued)

Table 8.A.1 (continued)

Variable	Base model
Physical limitations (Ref.: not)	0.977
	(0.030)
Pray: daily or more (Ref.: never)	1.267**
	(0.100)
Once or twice a week	1.099^{+}
	(0.057)
Less than once a week	1.126^{+}
	(0.077)
Other/missing	1.471***
	(0.145)
Proximity	2.244***
	(0.111)
Family values (Ref.: more traditional)	0.947***
	(0.010)

Source: SHARE 2004 (wave 1); 2006 (refresher sample from wave 2); Eurobarometer 2007. Author's calculations

Significance: $^{+}p < 0.10$; $^{*}p < 0.05$; $^{**}p < 0.01$; $^{***}p < 0.001$

References

Akaike, H. (1971). Autoregressive model fitting for control. *Annals of the Institute of Statistical Mathematics, 3*, 163–180.

Akaike, H. (1974). A new look at the statistical model identification. *IEEE Transactions on Automatic Control, AC-19*, 716–723.

Antonucci, T. C. (1990). Social supports and social relationships. In R. H. Binstock & L. K. George (Eds.), *Handbook of aging and the social sciences* (3rd ed., pp. 205–226). San Diego: Academic.

Antonucci, T., & Akiyama, H. (1987). Social networks in adult life and a preliminary examination of the convoy model. *Journal of Gerontology, 42*, 519–527.

Beck, U., & Beck-Gernsheim, E. (2002). *Individualization: Institutionalized individualism and its social and political consequences*. London: Sage.

Becker, G. (1976). *The economic approach to human behaviour*. Chicago/London: The University of Chicago Press.

Becker, G. S. (1981/1991). *A treatise on the family*. Cambridge: Harvard University Press.

Becker, G. S., & Barro, R. J. (1988). *A reformulation of the economic theory of fertility*. Chicago: University of Chicago – Population Research Center 85–11.

Bengtson, V. L. (2001). Beyond the nuclear family: The increasing importance of multigenerational bonds. *Journal of Marriage and the Family, 63*, 1–16.

Bengtson, V. L., & Roberts, R. E. L. (1991). Intergenerational solidarity in aging families: An example of formal theory construction. *Journal of Marriage and the Family, 53*, 856–870.

Billari, F. C., & Liefbroer, A. C. (2007). Should I stay or should I go? The impact of age norms on leaving home. *Demography, 44*, 181–198.

Blome, A., Keck, W., & Alber, J. (2009). *Family and the welfare state in Europe. Intergenerational relations in ageing societies*. Cheltenham/Northampton: Edward Elgar.

Bordone, V. (2009). Contact and proximity of older people to their adult children: A comparison between Italy and Sweden. *Population, Space and Place, 15*, 359–380.

Börsch-Supan, A., & Jürges, H. (2005). *Health, ageing and retirement in Europe – Methodology*. Mannheim: MEA.
Brandt, M., Haberkern, K., & Szydlik, M. (2009). Intergenerational help and care in Europe. *European Sociological Review, 25*, 585–601.
Broese van Groenou, M., Glaser, K., Tomassini, C., & Jacobs, T. (2006). Socio-economic status differences in older people's use of informal and formal help: A comparison of four European countries. *Ageing and Society, 26*, 745–766.
Brückner, H., & Mayer, K. U. (2005). De-standardization of the life course: What might it mean? And if it means anything, whether it actually took place. In R. Macmillan (Ed.), *The structure of the life course: Standardized? Individualized? Differentiated?* (Advances in life course research, Vol. 9, pp. 27–53). Amsterdam: Elsevier.
Cherlin, A. J., & Furstenberg, F. F. (1986). *The new American grandparent*. New York: Basic Books.
Cobb, S. (1976). Social support as a moderator of life stress. *Psychosomatic Medicine, 38*, 300–314.
Cohen, S., & Syme, L. S. (1985). *Social support and health*. New York: Academic.
Connidis, I., & Davies, L. (1990). Confidants and companions in later life: The place of family and friends. *Journal of Gerontology, 45*, S14–S149.
Cronbach, L. J. (1951). Coefficient alpha and the internal structure of tests. *Psychometrika, 16*, 297–334.
Daatland, S. O., & Lowenstein, A. (2005). Intergenerational solidarity and the family-welfare state balance. *European Journal of Ageing, 2*, 174–182.
Dosi, G., Marengo, L., Bassanini, A., & Valente, M. (1999). Norms as emergent properties of adaptive learning: The case of economic routines. *Journal of Evolutionary Economics, 9*, 5–26.
Durkheim, E. (1983). *Les règles de la méthode sociologique*. Paris: Quadrige/Presses Universitaires de France. (Original work published in 1895).
Dykstra, P. A., & Fokkema, T. (2011). Relationships between parents and their adult children: A west European typology of late-life families. *Ageing and Society, 31*, 545–569.
Elster, J. (1989). Social norms and economic theory. *Journal of Economic Perspectives, 3*, 99–117.
Esping-Andersen, G. (1990). *The three worlds of welfare capitalism*. Princeton: Princeton University Press.
European Commission. (1995). *The demographic situation in the European union, 1994 report*. Luxembourg: Office for Official Publications of the European Commission, DGV.
European Commission. (2007). *Eurobarometer 67.3: Health care service, Undeclared Work, EU relations with its neighbor countries, and development aid*, May-June 2007 (Computer file). Conducted by TNS OPINION & SOCIAL, Brussels, requested and coordinated by the European Commission, Directorate General Press and Communication, Opinion Polls. ZA4561 [version identification]. Cologne: GESIS.
Ferrera, M. (1996). The 'Southern' model of welfare in social Europe. *Journal of European Social Policy, 6*, 17–37.
Fokkema, T., ter Bekke, S., & Dykstra, P. A. (2008). *Solidarity between parents and their adult children in Europe* (NIDI Report No. 76). Amsterdam: KNAW Press.
Gelman, A., & Hill, J. (2007). *Data analysis using regression and multilevel/hierarchical models*. Cambridge: Cambridge University Press.
Gerstel, N., & Gallagher, S. K. (1993). Kin keeping and distress: Gender, recipients of care, and work-family conflict. *Journal of Marriage and the Family, 55*, 598–607.
Geurts, T., Poortman, A. R., van Tilburg, T., & Dykstra, P. (2009). Contact between grandchildren and their grandparents in early adulthood. *Journal of Family Issues, 30*, 1698–1713.
Gibbs, J. P. (1981). *Norms, deviance, and social control: Conceptual matters*. New York: Elsevier.
Glaser, K., & Tomassini, C. (2000). Proximity of older women to their children. A comparison of Britain and Italy. *The Gerontologist, 40*, 729–737.
Green, D. P., & Shapiro, I. (1996). *Pathologies of rational choice theory: A critique of applications in political science*. New Haven: Yale University Press.

Hagestad, G. O., & Dannefer, D. (2001). Concepts and theories of development: Beyond microfication in social science approaches. In R. H. Binstock & L. K. George (Eds.), *Handbook of aging and the social sciences* (5th ed., pp. 3–21). New York: Academic.

Hank, K. (2007). Proximity and contacts between older parents and their adult children: A European comparison. *Journal of Marriage and the Family, 69*, 157–173.

Heylen, L. & Mortelmans, D. (2009). *Explaining parent-child proximity in Eastern and Western Europe: A micro and macro perspective*. Deliverable 2.1 for the FP-7 funded project "How demographic changes shape intergenerational solidarity, well-being, and social integration: A multilinks framework". Antwerp:Universiteit Antwerpen.

Horne, C. (2003). The internal enforcement of norms. *European Sociological Review, 19*, 335–343.

House, J. S. (1981). *Work, stress and social support*. Reading: Addison Wesley.

Kalmijn, M., & De Vries, J. (2009). Change and stability in parent-child contact in five western countries. *European Journal of Population, 25*, 257–276.

Kalmijn, M., & Dykstra, P. (2006). Differentials in face-to-face contact between parents and their grown-up children. In P. Dykstra, M. Kalmijn, T. C. M. Knijn, A. E. Komter, A. C. Liefbroer, & C. H. Mulder (Eds.), *Family solidarity in the Netherlands* (pp. 63–88). Amsterdam: Dutch University Press.

Kaufman, G., & Uhlenberg, P. (1998). Effects of life course transitions on the quality of relationships between adult children and their parents. *Journal of Marriage and the Family, 60*, 924–938.

Kohli, M., Kuenemund, H., & Ludicke, J. (2005). Family structure, proximity and contact. In A. Börsch-Supan et al. (Eds.), *Health, ageing and retirement in Europe – First results from the survey of health, ageing and retirement in Europe* (pp. 164–170). Mannheim: MEA.

Lesthaeghe, R. (1980). On the social control of human reproduction. *Population and Development Review, 6*, 527–548.

Lesthaeghe, R. (1995). The second demographic transition in Western countries: An interpretation. In K. Oppenheim Mason & A. M. Jensen (Eds.), *Gender and family change in industrialized countries* (pp. 17–62). Clarendon: Oxford.

Lesthaeghe, R., & Meekers, D. (1986). Value changes and the dimensions of familialism in the European Community. *European Journal of Population, 2*, 225–268.

Liefbroer, A. C., & Billari, F. C. (2010). Bringing norms back in: A theoretical and empirical discussion of their importance for understanding demographic behavior. *Population, Space and Place, 16*, 287–305.

Lowenstein, A., & Ogg, J. (2003). *Old age and autonomy: The role of service systems and intergenerational family solidarity*. OASIS Final Report, Center for Research and Study of Aging, The University of Haifa, Israel.

Lüscher, K., & Schultheis, F. (1993). *Generationsbeziehungen in "Postmodernen" Gesellschaften*. Konstanz: Universitätsverlag Konstanz.

Malmberg, G., & Pettersson, A. (2007). Distance to elderly parents: Analyses of Swedish register data. *Demographic Research, 17*, 679–704.

Mandic, S. (2008). Home-leaving and its structural determinants in western and eastern Europe: An exploratory study. *Housing Studies, 23*, 615–636.

Merton, R. K. (1968). *Social theory and social structure*. New York: Free Press.

Michielin, F., & Mulder, C. H. (2007). Geographical distances between adult children and their parents in the Netherlands. *Demographic Research, 17*, 655–678.

Motel-Klingebiel, A., Tesch-Römer, C., & von Kondratowitz, H. J. (2005). Welfare states do not crowd out the family: Evidence for mixed responsibility from comparative analyses. *Ageing and Society, 25*, 863–882.

Murphy, M. (2008). Variations in kinship networks across geographic and social space. *Population and Development Review, 34*, 19–49.

Myers, G. C. (1996). Aging and the social sciences: Research directions and unresolved issues. In R. H. Binstock & L. K. George (Eds.), *Handbook of aging and social sciences* (4th ed., pp. 1–11). San Diego: Academic.
Nauck, B. (2009). Patterns of exchange in kinship systems in Germany, Russia, and the People's Republic of China. *Journal of Comparative Family Studies, 40*, 255–278.
Nazio, T., & Saraceno, C. (2008, April 11–12). *Does cohabitation provide weaker intergenerational bonds than marriage? A comparison between Italy and the United Kingdom.* Paper presented at the Equalsoc conference, Berlin.
Oppenheim Mason, K. (1983). Norms relating to the desire for children. In R. A. Bulatao & R. D. Lee (Eds.), *Determinants of fertility in developing countries* (Vol. 1, pp. 388–428). New York: Academic.
Parsons, T. (1937). *The structure of social action.* New York: McGraw Hill.
Pitrou, A. (1977). Le soutien familial dans la société urbaine. *Revue Française de Sociologie, 18*, 45–84.
Popenoe, D. (1993). American family decline, 1960–1990: A review and appraisal. *Journal of Marriage and the Family, 55*, 527–542.
Rabe-Hesketh, S., & Skrondal, A. (2005). *Multilevel and longitudinal modeling using stata.* College Station: Stata Press.
Reher, D. S. (1998). Family ties in Western Europe: Persistent contrasts. *Population and Development Review, 24*, 203–234.
Rossi, A. S. (1993). Intergenerational relations: Gender, norms, and behavior. In V. L. Bengtson & W. A. Achenbaum (Eds.), *The changing contract across generations* (pp. 191–211). Hawthorne: Aldine de Gruyter.
Rossi, A. S., & Rossi, P. H. (1990). *Of human bonding, parent-child relations across the life course.* New York: Aldine de Gruyter.
Saraceno, C. (2008). *Families, ageing and social policy.* Cheltenham: Edward Elgar.
Saraceno, C., & Keck, W. (2008). *The institutional framework of intergenerational family obligations in Europe: A conceptual and methodological overview.* Available online at http://www.multilinks-project.eu/info/papers. Accessed 18 June 2009.
Schwarz, G. (1978). Estimating the dimension of a model. *The Annals of Statistics, 60*, 461–464.
Settersten, R. A., Jr., & Mayer, K. U. (1997). The measurement of age, age structuring and the life course. *Annual Review of Sociology, 23*, 233–261.
Silverstein, M., & Bengtson, V. L. (1997). Intergenerational solidarity and the structure of adult child–parent relationships in American families. *The American Journal of Sociology, 103*, 429–460.
Silverstein, M., Parrott, T. M., & Bengtson, V. L. (1995). Factors that predispose middle-aged sons and daughters to provide social support to older parents. *Journal of Marriage and the Family, 57*, 465–475.
Silverstein, M., Gans, D., Lowenstein, A., Giarrusso, R., & Bengtson, V. L. (2010). Old parent – Child relationships in six developed nations: Comparisons at the intersection of affection and conflict. *Journal of Marriage and the Family, 72*, 1006–1021.
Snijders, T., & Bosker, R. (1999). *Multilevel analysis: An introduction to basic and advanced multilevel modeling.* London: Sage Publishers.
Sussman, M. B., & Burchinal, L. (1962). Kin-family networks. *Marriage and Family Living, 24*, 231–240.
Swedborg, R. (1990). *Economics and sociology.* Princeton: Princeton University Press.
Synak, B. (1990). The Polish family: Stability, change and conflict. *Journal of Aging Studies, 4*, 333–344.
Szydlik, M. (2000). *Lebenslange Solidarität? Generationenbeziehungen zwischen Erwachsenen Kindern und Eltern.* Opladen: Leske & Budrich.
Szydlik, M. (2008). Intergenerational solidarity and conflict. *Journal of Comparative Family Studies, 39*, 97–114.
Thoits, P. A. (1989). The sociology of emotions. *Annual Review of Sociology, 15*, 317–342.

Tomassini, C., Kalogirou, S., Grundy, E., Fokkema, T., Martikainen, P., Broese van Groenou, M., & Karisto, A. (2004). Contacts between older parents and their children in four European countries: Current patterns and future prospects. *European Journal of Ageing, 1*, 54–63.

van de Kaa, D. J. (1987). Europe's second demographic transition. *Population Bulletin, 42*, 1–57.

Weiss, R. S. (1974). The provisions of social relationships. In Z. Rubin (Ed.), *Doing unto others: Joining, molding, conforming, helping, loving* (pp. 17–26). Englewood Cliffs: Prentice-Hall Spectrum Books.

Willmott, P., & Young, M. (1986). *Family and kinship in East London*. London: Routledge & Kegan Paul. (Original work published in 1957).

Chapter 9
How Much Does a Child Cost Its Parents in Terms of Time in an Aged Society? An Estimate for Italy with Time Use Survey Data

Maria Letizia Tanturri

9.1 Introduction

Time is an important economic resource, which is normally exchanged between generations. Children require a large amount of parental time when they are young and are expected to give some back when they become adults and their parents grow old (see e.g. Chap. 8 by Bordone, this volume, or Chap. 7 by Keefe et al., this volume). In ageing societies, there is an intense competition of time spent for children and for elderly relatives. In southern Europe, where fertility rates have fallen dramatically in the recent past and where welfare systems are less developed, this competition is particularly severe: the so-called sandwich generations thus could be under pressure. Family support, indeed, is generally found to be more proactive in those countries, although there are signs that the southern European family may be under stress (Ogg and Renaut 2006).

The high costs of children in terms of time – and not only in terms of money – are considered an important factor associated with low fertility, which is by itself one of the factors causing population ageing. In modern societies, rearing children is a time-intensive activity, but parents' time is typically scarcer and scarcer, especially when both parents are full-time workers. Nevertheless, and perhaps surprisingly, recent studies show that parents spend more time with their children today than they did in the previous decades (Sayer et al. 2004 for the US, Gauthier et al. 2004 for selected industrialised countries). For Italy, such long time series of Time Use data do not exist, but we might similarly expect that if children are fewer, their parents want to spend much time with each of them. In such an aged society, however, this wish could be prevented by the obligations towards elderly relatives who survive until older ages.

M.L. Tanturri (✉)
Department of Statistics, University of Padua, via C. Battisti 241, 35121 Padua, Italy
e-mail: tanturri@stat.unipd.it

G. De Santis (ed.), *The Family, the Market or the State?: Intergenerational Support Under Pressure in Ageing Societies*, International Studies in Population 10,
DOI 10.1007/978-94-007-4339-7_9, © Springer Science+Business Media Dordrecht 2012

In this chapter, I concentrate on the descending flux of time from parents to young children and try to estimate the additional working time that the presence of children requires.[1] This is what I call the 'time cost of children'. In Italy, several studies have been carried out on the cost of children in monetary terms (De Santis 2004), but little is known about their cost in terms of time. Studies normally concentrate on reconciliation issues and 'opportunity costs' (see for instance: Di Pino 2004; Del Boca et al. 2005), but the effects of children may well go beyond a reduction of their parents' working time. Our hypothesis is that also (and in some cases mainly) pure leisure time and the time dedicated to personal care (e.g. sleeping, bathing) may be reduced because of child-related activities. As money is diverted into child-specific goods when a child is born into a household, parent's time is redirected towards childcare from other types of time use (Craig and Bittman 2008).

It is reasonable to expect that child cost in terms of time is high in Italy, where family ties are strong and parents invest very much in what is frequently, if perhaps misleadingly, called 'child quality' (Reher 1998; Dalla Zuanna 2001; Dalla Zuanna and Micheli 2004). Women are supposed to bear the largest part of this investment – Italy is still a deeply gendered society – which may explain in part why fertility is so low (Mencarini and Tanturri 2004; Mills et al. 2008). As far as I know, however, there are no previous studies trying to measure precisely how large is the time cost of children for their parents in Italy and what proportion of the cost is paid by the mothers.

This chapter investigates how Italian couples' time use varies, qualitatively and quantitatively, when they have children and how it changes according to the number and age of children. To this end, we will exploit the 2002–2003 Italian Time Use Survey, carried out by ISTAT. My methodology is a loose adaptation of the one normally used in microeconomics, except that here the dependent variable is time, not money. The methodology largely relies on a seminal paper by Craig and Bittman (2008) on Australia. The marginal time costs of children in Italy are assessed by comparing the daily workload (separately: childcare, total unpaid work, and total work) of couples with and without children. In the second part of the chapter, I examine how the cost of children is distributed between parents, in a gender perspective.

9.2 Background

The low Italian fertility is amply studied in demographic literature (Salvini 2004; Kohler et al. 2002). Period fertility in Italy has been below replacement since the mid-1970s and has been one of the first in the world to reach 'lowest-low' levels

[1] It would be interesting to estimate also the ascendant flux of time from the couple to their parents, but with Time Use data, we could only estimate time dedicated to care for co-residing elderly relatives. Consequently, we would sketch only a partial picture, as co-residence has been almost substituted by residential proximity nowadays in Italy.

(TFR <1.3) in the 1990s (Kohler et al. 2002). Since 2000, a small recovery has brought our TFR close to 1.4. Fertility pathways across generations reveal that the proportion of high-parity women in the cohorts born since the 1940s has fallen considerably, and the 'norm' has gradually shifted from having 'at least two children' to 'no more than two' (Santini 1995). Moreover, recent estimates for the cohorts born after 1960 show a steep increase in the proportion of women who are childless (from 14.6% for the cohort of 1960 to 22.5% for that of 1966) or have an only child (28.7% for the 1966 cohort vs. 25.7% for the 1960 cohort).

In Italy, low fertility interplays with strong family ties and values (Reher 1998; Livi Bacci 2001), with familism and high parental investments in child quality (Dalla Zuanna 2001; Dalla Zuanna and Micheli 2004), and with women's scarce labour market participation (Del Boca 2003). The increase in both direct and indirect costs of children (De Santis and Livi Bacci 2001), the difficulties in combining motherhood and labour market participation (Del Boca 1997; Del Boca et al. 2005), and the lack of gender equity in the division of domestic tasks and childcare (McDonald 2000a, b; Mencarini and Tanturri 2004; Mills et al. 2008; Anxo et al. 2011) are amongst the factors that can explain the reluctance of couples to have more offspring.

The high cost of Italian children in terms of time can be a further and quite unexplored determinant of low fertility. The time costs of children are partly endogenous and partly exogenous. On the one hand, parents choose to spend time with their children, in part, possibly, because of social pressure and expectations, in part for the high value attributed to children (Dalla Zuanna 2001). On the other hand, the lack of childcare services – especially for very young children – contributes to increasing exogenously the time that parents must dedicate to child-rearing. In addition, the scarce working opportunities of Italian women give them more free time than in other countries, some of which they spend with their children. Indeed, it is still common for young women (especially for those with lower educational levels, resident in the South of Italy, or with short-term work contracts) to permanently drop out of the labour market after childbearing (ISTAT 2007). Conversely, women participating in the labour market – subject to working-time rigidity and under the personal costs of the double burden – may be deterred from having (more) children, for fear that might compromise their job opportunities or damage their individual life (Del Boca et al. 2005). This may explain why in Italy low female employment goes hand in hand with very low fertility.

The difficulties in reconciling family and work are aggravated by the characteristics of the Italian labour market, with high rates of self-employment, high shares of people employed in small firms, a high degree of employment protection for the male breadwinner, combined with a high degree of informal flexibility mainly through the underground economy.

The familistic character of the Italian welfare regime does not help to reduce child costs in terms of time for parents in general and for mothers in particular. In Italy, as well as in other Southern European countries, families are expected to support their own members (family responsibilities and obligations extend beyond the nuclear family) with only limited help from the state. Accordingly, family policies are scarcely developed, in comparison with other EU countries. This feature is mirrored in the low share (4.7%) of social expenditure related to family and children, with respect to the average EU-27 level (8.7%; OECD 2001). Mandatory maternity leave duration is long (20 weeks) and well paid for employed mothers (at 80% of previous earnings, 100% in the public sector), but balancing child-rearing and market work is made difficult by the limited supply of public childcare for children under 3, both in terms of availability (only 15% of children attend formal childcare) and opening hours (ISTAT 2011). Grandparents are usually the main care providers when both parents work, according to a long tradition of intergenerational solidarity (ISTAT 2007). This practice is far from diminishing, but on the contrary, the households with children under 14 receiving informal childcare have increased in the last 10 years: for instance, in 2009, more than two children out of three spend a few afternoons at their grandparents' home (ISTAT 2011). However, if the grandparents are not available, or if they also need to be cared for or helped to some extent, the balance can be easily broken, given the scarcity of care facilities and work-family reconciliation policies.

As gender roles are still shaped in a traditional way, paternity leave has never been enacted. It is only since 2000 that both fathers and mothers can take parental leave for a total period of 36 weeks, at 30% of previous earnings (previously it was only mothers), and an additional month is given if the father takes at least 3 months of parental leave. But in 2004, the take-up rate of eligible mothers was 75% and that of eligible fathers only 7% (Anxo et al. 2011).

The lack of gender equity has been put forward as a possible cause for the persistence of low fertility in Italy (McDonald 2000a, b). Over the past two decades, Italian women have greatly improved their educational attainment and have accordingly raised their labour market ambitions: indeed, they work more than they did in the recent past, although their employment rate is still low by European standards (47%), and gender gaps in employment and unemployment rates remain amongst the highest in the EU-27. However, the responsibility for family care and domestic work still falls almost exclusively on women's shoulders. Italian men seem to be particularly reluctant to carry out domestic chores, even when their partners are in the labour market. In this context, childbearing tends to exacerbate an already heavily unbalanced division of household labour, and this discourages fertility (Cooke 2003; Mencarini and Tanturri 2004; Mills et al. 2008).

The experience of parenthood often implies a crystallisation or even a deterioration of the gender role set (Coltrane and Adams 2008), with an increase of women's time spent in housework and childcare as well as a decrease in their leisure time – and things are obviously worse for working mothers, who are thus subject to a 'dual burden' or 'second shift' (Crompton 2006). Craig and Mullan (2010) state that 'care responsibilities potentiate the vulnerability of gender', as the distribution of labour becomes more pronounced after children are born. A recent comparative study shows that in Italy when a child is born, men typically increase the time devoted to paid work (this effect has not been observed in countries like France, Sweden, or the USA; see Anxo et al. 2011), while women reduce it or even leave the labour market (see also: ISTAT 2007; Mencarini and Tanturri 2004). Another comparative article finds that Italian parents of children under 5 have higher, less gender-equal domestic workloads than childless couples, but the extra workload associated with the presence of children is lower than in the USA and Australia. In Italy, however, the gender division of labour is wide also amongst non-parents (Craig and Mullan 2010).

9.3 Data and Definitions

In Italy, the Time Use Survey was carried out within the Multipurpose Survey Project by the National Institute of Statistics in 2002–2003 on a sample of over 55,000 individuals (ISTAT 2005). The diary days are randomly distributed across days of the week and throughout the year. The daily diary was filled in by (or for) all the members of the household aged 3 years or over. The time diary technique, whereby individuals report their time use over 24 h, provides extremely detailed information on the activities performed during that day. The diary data are based on a grid of 10-min intervals, with a description of the main activity carried out by the respondent (in their own words), the secondary (or concurrent) activity, their location, and the presence of other persons. Besides the diary, all the data sets contain detailed information on the background and socio-economic situation of individuals and households.

From the 2003 Italian Time Use Survey, we selected a subsample of 4,827 married or cohabiting couples, where both partners are aged 20–54 years old and are either childless (20%) or with at least one child under 13 (80%). Households with other adults other than the marital or de facto couples are excluded to avoid the confounding effect of other adults able to provide childcare or domestic tasks. Similarly, complex households are eliminated from the subsample. We created family typologies, combining the number of children in a family (one, two, three, or more) with the age of the youngest child (0–2, 3–5, and 6–12 years old), so as to deal only with relatively homogeneous groups. The absolute and relative frequencies of the typologies thus created are shown in Table 9.1.

We will try to estimate the incremental time cost of children, taking into account not only the time devoted directly to childcare but the total amount of unpaid work under the hypothesis that a child also engenders an increase in the time dedicated to other mundane tasks as, for instance, meal cooking, cleaning, or tidying up (Craig 2007; Craig and Mullan 2010). In the definition of childcare, the following activities are included: interactive childcare, physical care, transport, and minding with only the children in the household. In the definition of unpaid work, we include childcare, care of other family members (e.g. the aged or disabled), housework, home maintenance, shopping, paying bills, and household management and transport related to these activities. Moreover, total work (total household production) has also been included in the analysis, given by the sum of time dedicated to both paid and unpaid work. Paid work encompasses employment-related activities, work breaks, job searches, education, and travels associated with these activities.

Table 9.1 Couple typologies in the subsample (absolute frequencies and column percentages)

Couple typologies	*N*	Percentage (%)
Childless	966	*20.0*
Youngest child 0–2		
One child	491	*10.2*
Two children	449	*9.3*
Three children	150	*3.1*
Youngest child 3–6		
One child	360	*7.5*
Two children	452	*9.4*
Three children	162	*3.4*
Youngest child 7–12		
One child	457	*9.5*
Two children	1,052	*21.8*
Three children	288	*6.0*
Total	*4,827*	*100*

Source: Italian Time Use Survey 2003 (own calculation)

The hypothesis is that couple's total work is influenced by the number and age of children. What remains after (total) work is the time dedicated to personal care, e.g. sleeping and bathing, and to (pure) leisure. Since days are made of 24 h, if a couple increases its total work by 1 h when a child arrives, the time that parents devote to self-care (sleeping for instance) or leisure (e.g. cinema) must correspondingly decline.

In the computation of the time devoted to children, we will only refer to the primary activity recorded in the diary, which of course leads to an underestimation of child costs: parents – especially mothers – very often care for their children while they are performing some other 'main' activity (Craig 2007). The consideration also of the secondary or concurrent activity would lead to a more realistic assessment of the true time costs (Folbre et al. 2005), but the large numbers of missing values in the Italian survey discourages its use. Similarly, it is not possible to use the information on the presence of other persons during the activity (other than care) to assess the time parents spend with their children (even during leisure activities, e.g. going to the swimming pool), because it is impossible to distinguish children from other young family members unequivocally.

9.4 Descriptive Findings

Descriptive statistics of the time spent in unpaid and paid work by women and men by family type is given in Tables 9.2 and 9.3. The first column for each gender shows the average daily hours spent in a certain activity calculated on the whole sample, while the second column shows the average calculated only on those doing a certain specific activity on the interview day. The third column shows, for each sex, the proportion of people performing a certain activity on the interview day.

Table 9.2 Average daily hours dedicated to unpaid work by family typologies and sex. Average calculated on the whole sample, and only on doers and percentage doers, on any given day

	Women			Men		
	Average time on the whole sample	Average time only on doers	% doers	Average time on the whole sample	Average time only on doers	% doers
Childless	4.25	4.34	96.9	1.41	2.16	74.2
1 Child, 0–2	7.29	7.30	99.9	2.07	2.23	89.2
1 Child, 3–5	7.02	7.02	99.9	1.52	2.14	83.9
1 Child, 6–12	6.14	6.16	99.3	1.48	2.11	82.3
2 Children, the youngest 0–2	8.42	8.42	100	2.30	2.51	87.7
2 Children, the youngest 3–5	7.26	7.28	99.7	2.04	2.24	86.4
2 Children, the youngest 6–12	7.13	7.15	99.5	1.54	2.28	77.1
3 Children, the youngest 0–2	9.36	9.36	100	2.23	2.44	86.7
3 Children, the youngest 3–5	8.28	8.28	100	2.04	2.45	75.2
3 Children, the youngest 6–12	7.45	7.50	98.8	1.26	2.13	64.9
Total	*6.48*	*6.52*	*99.0*	*1.56*	*2.25*	*80.3*

Data source: Italian Time Use Survey 2003 (own calculation)

Table 9.3 Average daily hours dedicated to paid work by family typologies and sex. Average calculated on the whole sample, and only on doers and percentage doers, on any given day

	Women			Men		
	Average time on the whole sample	Average time only on doers	% doers	Average time on the whole sample	Average time only on doers	% doers
Childless	3.18	7.11	46	5.29	8.18	66.1
1 Child, 0–2	1.55	5.55	32.6	6.28	8.19	77.9
1 Child, 3–5	2.01	5.37	35.9	6.16	8.33	73.3
1 Child, 6–12	3.06	6.36	47.0	6.08	8.07	75.6
2 Children, the youngest 0–2	1.35	6.00	26.4	6.01	8.15	72.9
2 Children, the youngest 3–5	2.13	6.08	36.2	6.24	8.27	75.8
2 Children, the youngest 6–12	2.07	5.57	35.5	5.55	8.02	73.7
3 Children, the youngest 0–2	1.11	5.09	22.9	6.34	8.23	78.4
3 Children, the youngest 3–5	1.39	5.39	29.1	6.03	7.55	76.5
3 Children, the youngest 6–12	1.41	6.09	27.3	5.55	8.00	73.9
Total	*2.20*	*6.22*	*36.8*	*6.01*	*8.14*	*73.1*

Data source: Italian Time Use Survey 2003 (own calculation)

Regardless of family typology, virtually all women perform an activity of unpaid work, while amongst men, the participation is not universal: one man out of five does not perform any domestic or care activities, and the proportion is even higher for men having three children, if the youngest is over three (Table 9.2). On the whole, even considering only 'doers', men devote themselves to unpaid work about a third of the time of women: about 2.5 h per day, as against 7 (Table 9.2).

As for paid work, only slightly more than a third of the women performed a labour market activity on the day of the interview versus about two-thirds of men (Table 9.3). Working men spent more than 8 h in related paid work activity on an average weekday, working women about 2 h less. Differences shrink to 1 h only amongst the childless. Amongst women, labour supply decreases with the number of children but tends to increase with the age of the youngest. For men, the profile is flatter, but in this case, the time devoted to work increases slightly when there are children (Table 9.3). In a previous comparative study, we showed that this behaviour of fathers is observed only in Italy, as in France, Sweden, and the USA, the opposite is true: fathers work less than childless men (Anxo et al. 2011) see also par. 9.2.

In the following paragraphs, we check if the differences in time use patterns according to different family typologies still hold when we control for other possible confounders.

9.5 An Explorative Analysis of Time Use: Models and Variables

We run three separate OLS models for the couple and then, separately, for men and women: in the first, the dependent variable is the time that couples dedicate to childcare, the second is run on paid work, and the third on total work (paid and unpaid). The rationale is first to assess the time cost of children for the couple and subsequently for each parent, according to our typologies (see Table 9.1), net of the effect of other control variables.

Amongst these, we include the following:

- The age of each partner, in three broad classes (25–34, 35–44, and 45–54 years).
- The mix of partners' education, in seven categories: (1) both partners have high education (degree or over), (2) both partners have medium education (secondary school certificate), (3) both partners have low education (less than a secondary school certificate), (4) man with high and woman with low education, (5) man with intermediate and woman with low education, (6) man with intermediate and woman with high education, and (7) man with low and woman with high education.
- Dummies describing the couple's labour supply: (1) both partners work full-time, (2) man works full-time and woman part-time, (3) man works full-time, and woman is a housewife (male breadwinner couple), and (4) man does not work full-time (a residual category). Of course, these last dummies will be excluded in the regression on total work.

- Dummies for the self-evaluation of the economic resources of the household (household income is unfortunately not asked in this survey). Economic resources are estimated to be (1) fine, (2) adequate, or (3) scarce.
- Dummies for the households that outsource part of care activity and domestic tasks: we merge them into the same category because only 5% of the couples declare that they rely on paid aid for these specific activities.
- Three dummies for the days of the week: (1) weekday, (2) Saturday, and (3) Sunday.
- Dummies for the region (North, Centre, South).

When we run our regressions separately on men and women, we consider the level of education of each partner separately and not in combination. In addition, we include the number of daily hours of paid work of each partner (but, again, not in the regression on total work).

We present our findings in two ways. The parameters are given in the Appendix Tables 9.4, 9.5, 9.6 and 9.7, together with their standard errors and *p*-values. We also present figures, which show how the predicted values (number of daily hours of work) evolve with the number of children, by family typology, net of other confounders. The reference couple is childless; the partners are both poorly educated, work full-time, report adequate economic resources, and do not outsource domestic and care tasks. They live in the north of Italy and were interviewed on a weekday.

9.6 Model Findings: The Time Cost of Children for the Couple

In Italy, when a first child is born, parents spend a considerable amount of time on childcare, other things being equal: more than 4 h a day (Fig. 9.1). When the only child grows up and goes to school, his/her (time) cost declines but is still more than 1 h and a half a day. The number of children matters much less than the age of the youngest: the profile of time use is almost flat when the number of children increases. In short, substantial economies of scale are possible with child-care because adults can care for more children simultaneously, and, occasionally, they can have elder children look after the young ones.

A partially different way of reading these findings is that children who grow up in a larger family receive less (separate) attention from their parents in a sort of 'dilution effect' (Craig 2007). It is not clear if and how this may affect the 'quality of children': the impact is potentially negative, but there may instead be positive consequences deriving from the early socialisation process with brothers and sisters.

The picture changes when we consider total unpaid work including domestic activities, childcare, and care of other household members (Fig. 9.1). Childless couples spend a remarkable quantity of time performing unpaid work: more than 5.5 h a day, which increases to more than 9.5 after the birth of a baby. This effort declines somewhat as the baby ages, down to slightly <7.5 h when he/she reaches

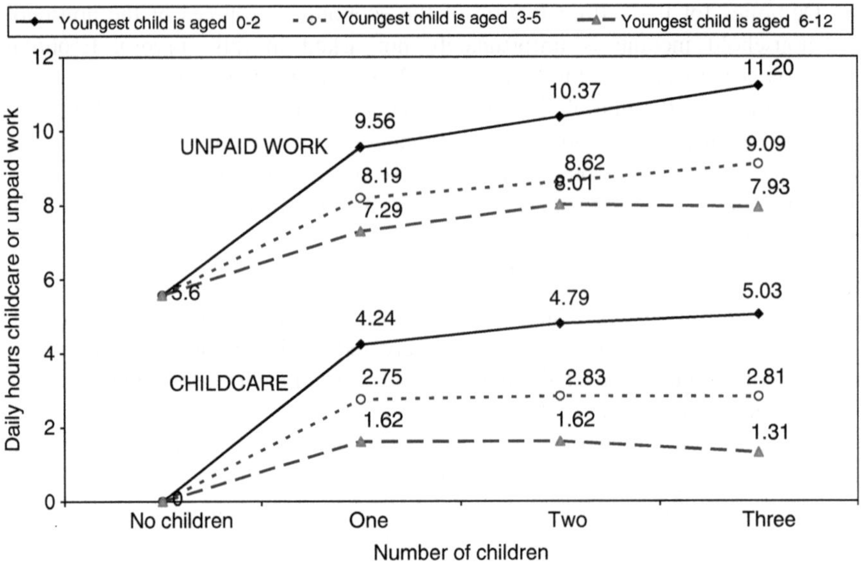

Fig. 9.1 Daily hours of childcare and unpaid work performed by the couple according to the number of children and age of the youngest child, net of other confounders (Italy, 2003) (Data source: Italian Time Use Survey 2003 (own calculation))

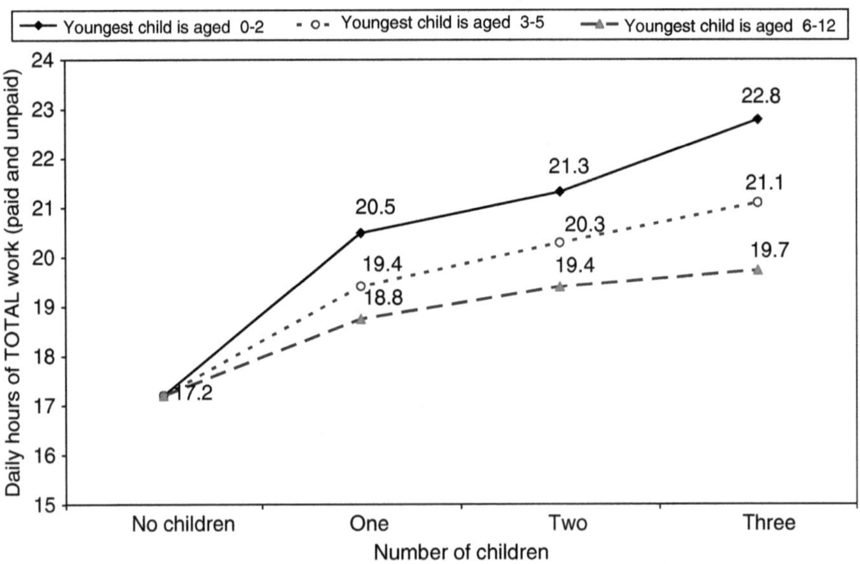

Fig. 9.2 Daily hours of total work (paid and unpaid) performed by the couple according to number of children and age of the youngest child, net of other confounders (Italy, 2003) (Data source: Italian Time Use Survey 2003 (own calculation))

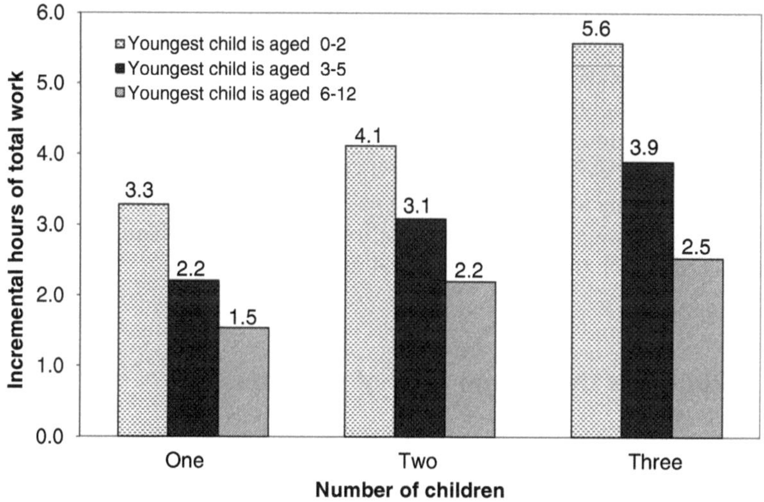

Fig. 9.3 Daily additional hours of total work (paid and unpaid) performed by the couple for the marginal child, by rank and age of the youngest child, net of other confounders (Italy, 2003) (Data source: Italian Time Use Survey 2003 (own calculation))

school age. With more children, unpaid work increases: less than proportionally but non-negligibly with the only exception of those family with three children whose the youngest in school age (Fig. 9.1).

If we consider total (paid and unpaid) work, we see that parents with an only child of preschool age work 20.5 h per day, and the time increases with the number of children close to 23 h, but again less than proportionally (Fig. 9.2). The same holds also for parents whose youngest child is in some older age group but at a lower level: for instance, from 19.4 h a week when there is only a toddler to 21 when there are three children and the youngest is a toddler (Fig. 9.2). When the youngest child is in school age, the profile by number of children is similar, but shifted at lower level of daily workload, ranging from 18.8 to 19.7 h (Fig. 9.2).

The net variation in time use for parents, as opposed to the childless couple, is summarised in Fig. 9.3. Couples take time from other activities (personal care or sleep for instance) in order to cope with their children, but the time cost of children on the whole decreases substantially with age, independently of their number. Not surprisingly, changes are more evident for parents who have a baby at home since they work 3.3 extra hours a day if the child is alone, up to more than 5 if he/she has two siblings. Time costs decrease with the age of the child, and school-age children are remarkably less time intensive; however, they still cost 1.5–2.5 h a day, depending on the number of (older) siblings they have.

The direct cost of children (childcare time) does not seem to be influenced by parental age, once we control for education (Table 9.4 in Appendix). Education is associated with an increase in childcare time – even if the time of more educated parents is a more expensive input for child-rearing – and the magnitude of this effect is larger when men have a high level of education. The effect of the variable is not significant on the unpaid and total work because it plays differently on various components of time use by gender (see following paragraph). Time dedicated by the couple to childcare and unpaid work is at a minimum when both partners work full-time, while in all the other employment combinations, it increases. There is no significant association between the subjective perception of adequacy of economic resources and time use. Nor does using paid external aids have any impact on child costs. Couples living in the south of Italy dedicate less time to childcare and unpaid work than those resident in the north, but it is in the centre where the total cost of children is higher on the whole (Table 9.4 in Appendix).

9.7 Who Pays the (Time) Cost of Children?

Let us now evaluate how child costs are distributed between mothers and fathers. Mothers of an infant spend between 3 h (if the child is an only child) to almost 4 h (if the child is the youngest in a family with three children) in childcare per day (Fig. 9.4a). If the youngest is a school-age child, costs are lower: around 1.3 h. Men are substantially less involved, slightly more than half as much (Fig. 9.4b). When they have only one infant, 64% of the total household active childcare is performed by mothers, but their burden reaches 67% for larger families. When children grow old, gender roles are less imbalanced, but women still perform up to 60% of the total care.

Women's time dedicated to unpaid work exceeds 6 h a day even without children and rises to 8–10 h a day for the largest family with at least one child under 3 (Fig. 9.4a). Conversely, men's time devoted to unpaid work is relatively flat, at 4 or 5 h a day, even in the most demanding families (Fig. 9.4b). The gender imbalance in the distribution of unpaid work is evident even amongst childless couples – where men perform only 3.5 h of domestic tasks while women more than 6 – but worsens when children, especially infants, are present. Comparing Fig. 9.4a, b, we notice that fathers substitute domestic tasks with childcare when they have young children; this holds also for women but to a lesser extent, as they typically reduce their labour market supply (see Fig. 9.5). For unpaid work, the gender imbalances are at their peak: in no case do women perform <64% of the household production.

Gender differences decline when we consider total household production (Fig. 9.5): the total workload of childless men and women is virtually the same, but in the transition to parenthood, women increase their total work more than men. This is particularly true amongst mothers of older children in larger families, whose share of the workload exceeds 52% (68% of the unpaid work). It is surprising that gender differences are almost the same regardless of the age and the number of children since for children under 3 they would be partly justified by biological reasons (e.g. breastfeeding).

In Fig. 9.6, we show the additional daily hours of total work performed by women and men with children, by number of children and age of the youngest: this is what we define as the incremental time cost of children. The incremental cost of

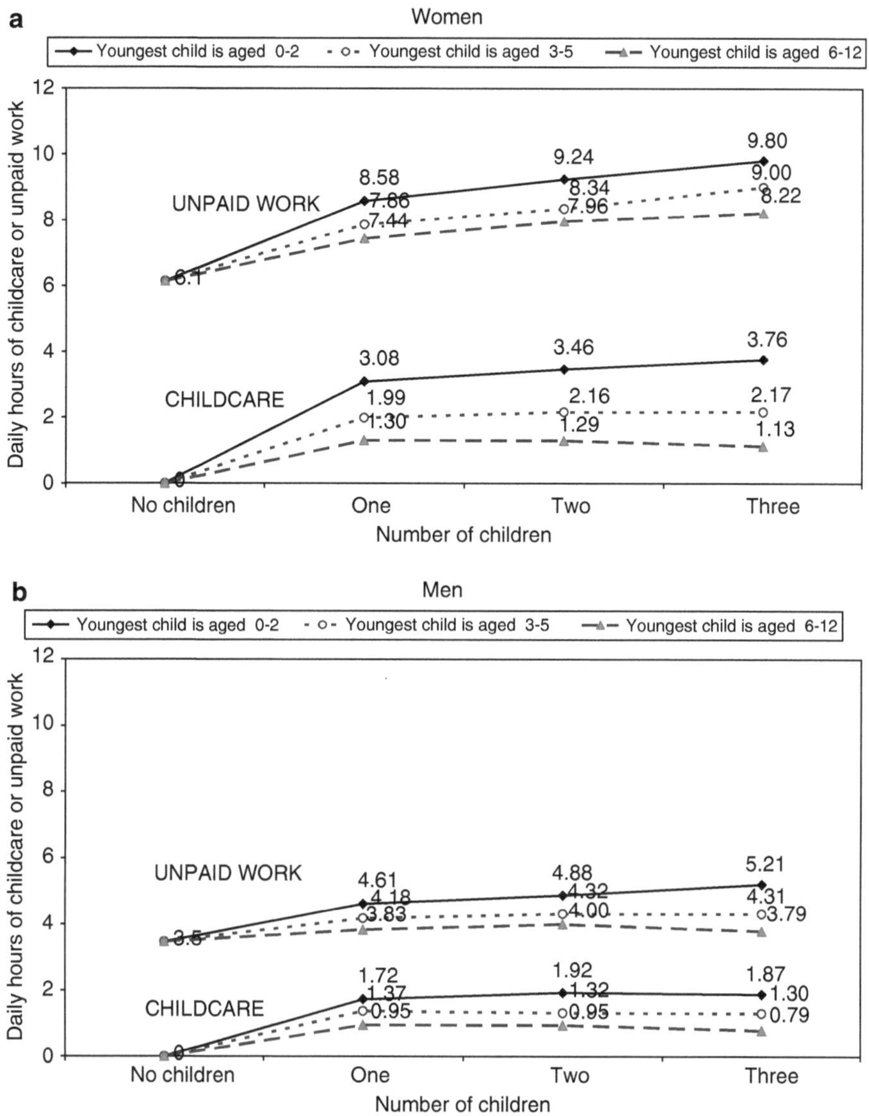

Fig. 9.4 Daily hours of childcare and unpaid work performed by women (**a**) and by men (**b**) according to the number of children and the age of the youngest child, net of other confounders (Italy, 2003) (Data source: Italian Time Use Survey 2003 (own calculation))

children is always higher for women. For instance, mothers of one child under three reduce their self-care and leisure time by 2 h a day, while fathers reduce it by little more than 1 (Fig. 9.6). If there are three children, and one is an infant, mothers have to renounce to more than 3 h a day, while men give up <2.4. The costs of children shrink considerably for both men and women when children reach school age, but

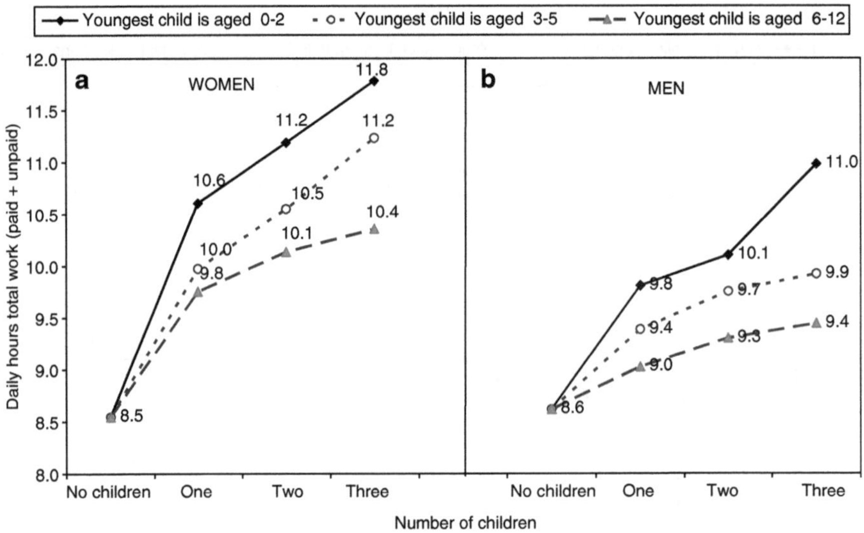

Fig. 9.5 Daily hours of total work performed by women (**a**) and men (**b**) according to the number of children and the age of the youngest child, net of other confounders (Italy, 2003) (Data source: Italian Time Use Survey 2003 (own calculation))

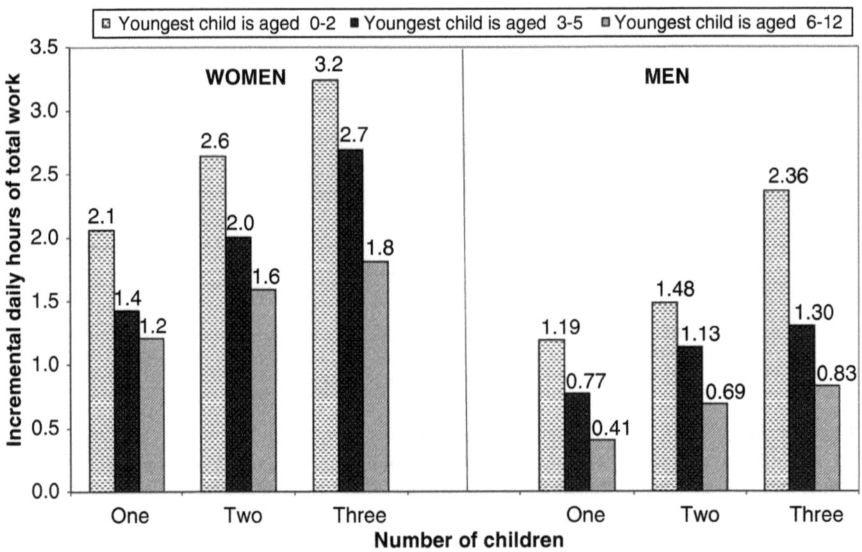

Fig. 9.6 Incremental time cost of children with respect to childless women or men, net of other confounders (2003) (Data source: Italian Time Use Survey 2003 (own calculation))

they still remain substantial for mothers, between 1 and 2 h for those having three children, while for men, they are always <1 h (Fig. 9.6).

However, the gender role set seems to be less unequal as the number of children grows: for instance, for the first infant, women pay more than 63% of the incremental cost of children, while for three children (the youngest under three), they pay 58%. Selection may have a part here, if fertility is higher amongst the most egalitarian couples in Italy (see, for instance, Mencarini and Tanturri 2004; Mills et al. 2008). Conversely, the proportion of incremental child cost paid by women increases as the age of the youngest increases: three-quarters of the cost of one child in school age is paid by mothers. In this case, we may wonder whether men activate themselves only in case of extreme need, that is, when children are babies.

Let us now look at the other covariates. Although not every coefficient is statistically different from zero, time dedicated to childcare declines with age for both partners (Table 9.5 in Appendix), while time for unpaid work increases with age (Table 9.6 in Appendix): it is sensible to argue that younger parents substitute domestic activities with childcare. The total cost of children paid by women increases with age, while for men, no significant effect is found (Table 9.7 in Appendix). Higher education is linked to a stronger investment of both parents in childcare (Table 9.5 in Appendix). More educated women are less committed in domestic tasks, while the opposite is true for more educated men, confirming previous findings in literature (Table 9.6 in Appendix) (see, for instance, Bianchi et al. 2000; Coltrane 2000; Presser 2003; Sayer et al. 2004). The total cost of children is reduced for more educated women, while for men no statistically significant association is found (Table 9.7 in Appendix). It is interesting to notice that mothers' time for childcare and for unpaid work is inversely linked to their commitment in the labour market while directly linked to their partners' working hours. The opposite is observed for fathers. This means that – apart from social and gender norms – each partner adapts time use according to their own and their partner's needs. Both men and women living in the south are less committed in childcare. Conversely, southern women dedicate more time to unpaid work and so to domestic work, while the opposite is true for southern men, other things being equal. In the south of Italy, therefore, gender roles are imbalanced and shaped according to more traditional values. The total cost of children is higher for women resident in the south – in spite of their lower time dedicated to childcare and to their lower labour market commitment – while it is reduced for fathers living in the south, with respect to that of their northern peers (Table 9.7 in Appendix).

9.8 Discussion

This chapter investigates how Italian couples' time use varies, qualitatively and quantitatively, when they have children and how it changes according to the number of children and their age. The idea is that the presence of a child impacts deeply on the use of time, causing an important contraction of time for self-care and leisure time. This is what we define as the marginal time cost of children.

The analysis was carried out using the most recent round of data from the Italian Time Use Survey (2002–2003). Time budgets represent a unique source of information, but they are not perfect. First, they do not provide longitudinal but only cross-sectional data, and the interpretation of our results requires special caution. Selection, for instance, can bias our findings. Imagine that those who prefer large families spend more time doing housework even before having children: the arrival of a child does not alter their use of time very much, but in a cross-sectional observation we are implicitly assuming that, without children, they would have used their time like those who are childless. Second, the cost of children can be underestimated, as we do not have any good quality data on the concurrent (or secondary) activity (see for instance Folbre et al. 2005; Craig and Bittman 2008). Parents – especially mothers – frequently mind their children while attending to another task, reported as the main activity, e.g. ironing and looking after children. With the new survey carried out in 2009, it will be possible to compute the cost of children and take secondary activities into account. Finally, a reflection should be devoted to the 'meaning' of the cost of children, which in this term might appear only as a burden for parents. In developed societies, indeed, the benefits of having children are mainly psychological, and parents usually consider spending time with them as a benefit rather than a cost.

Despite their limitations, model results seem to corroborate the hypothesis that Italian children are particularly time intensive. Ceteris paribus, in Italy, a child under 3 requires from parents more than 3 h of additional work per day, compared to the childless reference couple. This means an equal reduction in self-care and leisure time. Unfortunately, our models do not allow us to say whether this is linked more to cultural reasons or structural constraints, such as the lack of alternative services for outsourcing either some care or domestic tasks. It is not very easy to compare our results with previous findings in other countries, as the age interval for parents are different (as the average age at parenthood differs substantially across countries), and age brackets chosen for the age of the children are not the same (in the Italian case, they are designed according to the main steps into the school system). But even more important, in the Australian study, Craig and Bittman (2008) also include childcare as a secondary activity and include in childcare (*passive childcare*) the part of leisure time that parents spend with their children (e.g. going to the swimming pool with children is not considered parents' pure leisure time). In that case, childcare time is obviously much larger than in Italy (for an infant under two, more than 10 h a day), and the total cost of children is necessarily bigger: for one child under 2, it is more than 7 h. A tentative comparative work with France (where secondary activities are also not included in the analysis) reveals that an infant child costs its parents less in France than in Italy, that is, more than an hour and a half less (Tanturri et al. 2011).

In Italy, the time cost increases with the number of children but less than proportionally: substantial economies of scale are possible in this respect. Similar – or even larger – economies of scale are also found in Australia and in France, where in some cases even the average cost – and not only the marginal – of each child seems to decrease as the family enlarges. The time cost decreases substantially as the age of the youngest grows in Italy, as in the other two countries. In all countries, it is also found that the effect of children's age outweighs that of the number of children in the family (Craig and Bittman 2008; Tanturri et al. 2011). The very high cost of an infant may depend on the lack (or inaccessibility) of crèches for infant care. Mandatory school, in fact, reduces the cost of older children very substantially in all countries.

In Italy, the increase in time dedicated to childcare and unpaid work associated with a further child is always higher for women than it is for men. In the same way, parenthood affects daily workload (total work) more seriously for women than for men, in both absolute and relative terms. In other words, it is confirmed that parenthood implies a deterioration of gender equity in Italy, similarly to what is found in other countries such as Australia and France (Craig and Bittman 2008; Tanturri et al. 2011). Gender gaps are smaller in France (but because French women work less at home and not because men work more there) and larger in Australia (where including secondary activities increases mothers' workload much more). In Italy, the imbalance in the proportion of the cost paid by men and women is less pronounced when children are young and for larger families.

Family and care policies could reduce Italian women's workload by giving extensive institutional support for very young children (as in France, for instance). The big issue is that these sorts of policies are very expensive and in an aged society – as the Italian one – could be seen as unfavourable by the majority of public opinion, as they could divert public funds either from elderly care or from their pensions to the younger generations. In other countries (such as in the Scandinavian countries), targeted gender policies have contributed to rebalancing gender inequalities in this domain by promoting the involvement of fathers in order to reduce the fraction of child costs paid by mothers, and thus such policies have sustained fertility (Olah 2011). Similar actions would be extremely beneficial also for Italy. In fact, in the north of Italy where gender roles are less traditional, women are more educated, and the time costs of children are lower for women, a fertility recovery has been recently observed.

Acknowledgements I gratefully acknowledge financial support from the Italian MIUR/PRIN 2007 (Research Project: 'The cost of children. Estimates, connections with the low Italian fertility, policy implications, and determination of a fair child support payment when parents divorce'), from the GALILEO Programme (Research project on: Le coût de l'enfant en temps sur le cycle de vie en France et en Italie), and from MIUR/PRIN 2009 (Research Project: 'A new childbearing and childrearing regime?').

Appendix

Table 9.4 OLS regression results for couples. Dep. variable: time devoted to childcare, unpaid work, and total work. Coefficients, standard error, and *p*-values

	Childcare			Unpaid work			Total work		
Variables	Coefficient	S.E.	Pr > |t|	Coefficient	S.E.	Pr > |t|	Coefficient	S.E.	Pr > |t|
Intercept	−0.068	0.1	0.5013	5.566	0.21	<.0001	17.206	0.25	<.0001
Couple typology (childless)									
1 Child, 0–2	4.308	0.11	<.0001	3.989	0.22	<.0001	3.287	0.27	<.0001
1 Child, 3–5	2.818	0.12	<.0001	2.626	0.24	<.0001	2.208	0.3	<.0001
1 Child, 6–12	1.685	0.11	<.0001	1.719	0.23	<.0001	1.548	0.28	<.0001
2 Children, the youngest 0–2	4.861	0.11	<.0001	4.801	0.23	<.0001	4.117	0.28	<.0001
2 Children, the youngest 3–5	2.903	0.11	<.0001	3.056	0.23	<.0001	3.087	0.28	<.0001
2 Children, the youngest 6–12	1.688	0.09	<.0001	2.445	0.19	<.0001	2.196	0.23	<.0001
3 Children, the youngest 0–2	5.100	0.17	<.0001	5.629	0.35	<.0001	5.579	0.43	<.0001
3 Children, the youngest 3–5	2.878	0.17	<.0001	3.526	0.34	<.0001	3.895	0.42	<.0001
3 Children, the youngest 6–12	1.380	0.14	<.0001	2.368	0.28	<.0001	2.530	0.34	<.0001
Women age (35–44)									
F age 25–34	0.086	0.08	0.2551	−0.269	0.16	0.082	−0.191	0.19	0.321
F age 45–54	−0.07	0.11	0.5236	0.555	0.22	0.013	0.354	0.28	0.202
Men age (35–44)									
M age 25–34	−0.066	0.08	0.425	−0.326	0.17	0.055	−0.197	0.21	0.351
M age 45–54	−0.19	0.08	0.022	0.192	0.17	0.255	−0.022	0.21	0.918
Education level (both low education)									
Both high education	0.53	0.13	<.0001	−0.201	0.27	0.457	−0.594	0.33	0.075
Both medium	0.413	0.08	<.0001	0.09	0.16	0.569	−0.147	0.19	0.445
M high, F lower	0.753	0.13	<.0001	0.37	0.25	0.146	0	0.32	0.999
M medium, F high	0.483	0.14	0.0003	0.037	0.28	0.893	−0.878	0.34	0.01
M medium, F low	0.313	0.1	0.002	0.176	0.21	0.392	−0.415	0.26	0.105
M low, F higher	0.224	0.09	0.0082	0.082	0.17	0.634	0.054	0.21	0.798
Labour supply (both full-time)									
M full-time, F part-time	0.163	0.08	0.051	0.374	0.17	0.028	–	–	–
M full-time, F housewife	0.254	0.07	0.0002	1.79	0.14	<.0001	–	–	–
M no full-time	0.268	0.12	0.0231	1.73	0.24	<.0001	–	–	–
Economic resources (adequate)									
Economic resources – fine	−0.061	0.17	0.7158	−0.124	0.34	0.718	−0.195	0.43	0.648
Economic resources – scarce	0.07	0.07	0.324	0.158	0.14	0.274	−0.405	0.18	0.022
External aids (no)	0.012	0.13	0.9261	−0.415	0.26	0.111	−0.082	0.32	0.798
Day of the week (weekday)									
Sunday	−0.338	0.07	<.0001	−0.967	0.14	<.0001	−9.849	0.17	<.0001
Saturday	−0.258	0.07	<.0001	1.695	0.13	<.0001	−3.577	0.17	<.0001

(continued)

Table 9.4 (continued)

	Childcare			Unpaid work			Total work		
Variables	Coefficient	S.E.	Pr > |t|	Coefficient	S.E.	Pr > |t|	Coefficient	S.E.	Pr > |t|
Geographical area (north)									
Centre	−0.021	0.08	0.7843	−0.139	0.16	0.386	0.431	0.2	0.03
South	−0.211	0.06	0.001	−0.396	0.13	0.003	−0.174	0.16	0.27
R-quadr corr	0.438			0.2315			0.450		
N	4,827			4,827			4,827		

Data source: Italian Time Use Survey 2003 (own calculation)
Reference category in parenthesis

Table 9.5 OLS regression results for men and women. Dep. variable: time devoted to childcare. Coefficients, standard error, and *p*-values

	Women			Men		
Variables	Coefficient	S.E.	Pr > |t|	Coefficient	S.E.	Pr > |t|
Intercept	0.260	0.08	0.0008	0.294	0.06	<.0001
Couple typology (childless)						
1 Child, 0–2	2.824	0.08	<.0001	1.427	0.06	<.0001
1 Child, 3–5	1.727	0.08	<.0001	1.080	0.06	<.0001
1 Child, 6–12	1.040	0.08	<.0001	0.657	0.06	<.0001
2 Children, the youngest 0–2	3.201	0.08	<.0001	1.626	0.06	<.0001
2 Children, the youngest 3–5	1.902	0.08	<.0001	1.023	0.06	<.0001
2 Children, the youngest 6–12	1.034	0.06	<.0001	0.653	0.05	<.0001
3 Children, the youngest 0–2	3.496	0.12	<.0001	1.580	0.09	<.0001
3 Children, the youngest 3–5	1.906	0.12	<.0001	1.010	0.09	<.0001
3 Children, the youngest 6–12	0.868	0.09	<.0001	0.495	0.07	<.0001
Age (35–44)						
Age 25–34	0.113	0.05	0.014	−0.007	0.04	0.855
Age 45–54	−0.118	0.07	0.0797	−0.079	0.04	0.042
Education (low)						
High education	0.287	0.07	<.0001	0.320	0.05	<.0001
Medium education	0.142	0.04	0.0007	0.149	0.03	<.0001
Economic resources (adequate)						
Economic resources – fine	0.055	0.12	0.6417	−0.143	0.09	0.116
Economic resources – scarce	0.028	0.05	0.5616	0.017	0.04	0.643
External aids (no)	0.034	0.09	0.7031	−0.036	0.07	0.594
Day of the week (weekday)						
Sunday	−0.496	0.06	<.0001	−0.237	0.05	<.0001
Saturday	−0.372	0.05	<.0001	−0.127	0.04	0.001
Working hours						
M working hours	0.052	0.01	<.0001	−0.079	0	<.0001
F working hours	−0.123	0.01	<.0001	0.037	0.01	<.0001
Geographical area (north)						
Centre	0.006	0.06	0.9145	0.005	0.04	0.906
South	−0.095	0.04	0.0292	−0.104	0.03	0.002
R-quadr corr	0.460			0.247		

Data source: Italian Time Use Survey 2003 (own calculation)
Reference category in parenthesis

Table 9.6 OLS regression results for men and women. Dep. variable: time devoted to unpaid work. Coefficients, standard error, and *p*-values

	Women			Men		
Variables	Coefficient	S.E.	Pr > |t|	Coefficient	S.E.	Pr > |t|
Intercept	6.144	0.14	<.0001	3.472	0.11	<.0001
Couple typology (childless)						
1 Child, 0–2	2.437	0.13	<.0001	1.143	0.11	<.0001
1 Child, 3–5	1.717	0.15	<.0001	0.709	0.12	<.0001
1 Child, 6–12	1.295	0.14	<.0001	0.360	0.11	0.002
2 Children, the youngest 0–2	3.094	0.14	<.0001	1.404	0.12	<.0001
2 Children, the youngest 3–5	2.200	0.14	<.0001	0.844	0.12	<.0001
2 Children, the youngest 6–12	1.819	0.11	<.0001	0.530	0.09	<.0001
3 Children, the youngest 0–2	3.66	0.21	<.0001	1.738	0.18	<.0001
3 Children, the youngest 3–5	2.858	0.20	<.0001	0.841	0.17	<.0001
3 Children, the youngest 6–12	2.073	0.17	<.0001	0.322	0.14	0.02
Age (35–44)						
Age 25–34	−0.242	0.08	0.0029	−0.144	0.08	0.06
Age 45–54	0.442	0.12	0.0002	0.192	0.07	0.01
Education (low)						
High education	−0.422	0.12	0.0003	0.203	0.10	0.038
Medium education	−0.266	0.07	0.0003	0.115	0.06	0.067
Economic resources (adequate)						
Economic resources – fine	−0.046	0.21	0.8235	−0.295	0.18	0.091
Economic resources – scarce	0.207	0.09	0.0157	−0.087	0.07	0.228
External aids (no)	−0.394	0.16	0.0113	−0.135	0.13	0.302
Day of the week (weekday)						
Sunday	−2.319	0.10	<.0001	−1.284	0.09	<.0001
Saturday	−0.132	0.09	0.1397	0.236	0.08	0.002
Working hours						
M working hours	0.134	0.01	<.0001	−0.329	0.01	<.0001
F working hours	−0.612	0.01	<.0001	0.075	0.01	<.0001
Geographical area (north)						
Centre	0.194	0.10	0.0453	−0.083	0.08	0.309
South	0.352	0.08	<.0001	−0.534	0.06	<.0001
R-quadr corr	0.502			0.314		

Data source: Italian Time Use Survey 2003 (own calculation)
Reference category in parenthesis

Table 9.7 OLS regression results for men and women. Dep. variable: time devoted to total work. Coefficients, standard error, and *p*-values

	Women			Men		
Variables	Coefficient	S.E.	Pr > |t|	Coefficient	S.E.	Pr > |t|
Intercept	8.544	0.13	<.0001	8.615	0.14	<.0001
Couple typology (childless)						
1 Child, 0–2	2.059	0.15	<.0001	1.191	0.17	<.0001
1 Child, 3–5	1.426	0.17	<.0001	0.771	0.19	<.0001
1 Child, 6–12	1.208	0.15	<.0001	0.407	0.18	0.0216

(continued)

Table 9.7 (continued)

	Women			Men		
Variables	Coefficient	S.E.	Pr > |t|	Coefficient	S.E.	Pr > |t|
2 Children, the youngest 0–2	2.642	0.15	<.0001	1.484	0.18	<.0001
2 Children, the youngest 3–5	2.004	0.16	<.0001	1.134	0.18	<.0001
2 Children, the youngest 6–12	1.588	0.13	<.0001	0.685	0.14	<.0001
3 Children, the youngest 0–2	3.235	0.24	<.0001	2.364	0.27	<.0001
3 Children, the youngest 3–5	2.688	0.23	<.0001	1.303	0.27	<.0001
3 Children, the youngest 6–12	1.811	0.19	<.0001	0.827	0.22	0.0001
Age (35–44)						
Age 25–34	−0.240	0.09	0.009	0.066	0.12	0.5832
Age 45–54	0.351	0.14	0.009	−0.086	0.12	0.4576
Education (low)						
High education	−0.310	0.13	0.017	0.043	0.15	0.7802
Medium education	−0.150	0.08	0.075	−0.074	0.10	0.4522
Economic resources (adequate)						
Economic resources – fine	−0.100	0.24	0.672	−0.156	0.27	0.5659
Economic resources – scarce	0.019	0.10	0.845	−0.395	0.11	0.0004
External aids (no)	−0.206	0.18	0.242	0.002	0.20	0.9915
Day of the week (weekday)						
Sunday	−4.177	0.09	<.0001	−5.699	0.11	<.0001
Saturday	−1.239	0.09	<.0001	−2.375	0.11	<.0001
Geographical area (north)						
Centre	0.285	0.11	0.01	0.137	0.13	0.2797
South	0.201	0.09	0.02	−0.381	0.10	0.0001
R-quadr corr	0.361			0.383		

Data source: Italian Time Use Survey 2003 (own calculation)
Reference category in parenthesis

References

Anxo, D., Mencarini, L., Pailhé, A., Solaz, A., Tanturri, M. L., & Flood, L. (2011). Gender differences in time use over the life course in France, Italy, Sweden, and the United States. *Feminist Economics, 17*(3), 159–195.

Bianchi, S., Milkie, M., Sayer, L., & Robinson, J. (2000). Is anyone doing the housework? Trends in the gender division of household labor. *Social Forces, 79*, 191–228.

Coltrane, S. (2000). Research on household labor: Modeling and measuring the social embeddedness of routine family work. *Journal of Marriage and the Family, 62*, 1208–1233.

Coltrane, S., & Adams, M. (2008). *Gender and families*. Lanham: Rowman & Littlefield.

Cooke, L. P. (2003). *The South revisited: The division of labour and family outcomes in Italy and Spain* (IRISS Working Paper Series, No. 2003–12). Luxembourg: CEPS/Instead.

Craig, L. (2007). *Contemporary motherhood. The impact of children on adult time*. Aldershot: Ashgate.

Craig, L., & Bittman, M. (2008). The incremental time costs of children: An analysis of children's impact on adult time in Australia. *Feminist Economics, 14*(2), 57–85.

Craig, L., & Mullan, K. (2010). Parenthood, gender and work-family time in the United States, Australia, Italy, France and Denmark. *Journal of Marriage and the Family, 72*, 1344–1361.

Crompton, R. (2006). *Employment and the family. The reconfiguration of work and family life in contemporary societies*. Cambridge: Cambridge University Press.

Dalla Zuanna, G. (2001). The banquet of Aeolus: A familistic interpretation of Italy's lowest low fertility. *Demographic Research, 4*, 133–161.

Dalla Zuanna, G., & Micheli, G. (2004). *Strong family, familism and lowest-low fertility*. Dordrecht: Kluwer Academic Press.

De Santis, G. (2004). The monetary cost of children. Theory and empirical estimates for Italy. *Genus, 60*(1), 161–183.

De Santis, G., & Livi Bacci, M. (2001, June 23–28). *Reflections on the economics of the fertility decline in Europe*. Presented at the Euresco conference on the second demographic transition in Europe, Bad Herrenalb.

Del Boca, D. (1997). Rigidità del mercato e costo dei figli. *Polis, 11*(1), 51–65.

Del Boca, D. (2003). *Low fertility and labour market participation of Italian women: Evidence and interpretations* (OECD Labour Market and Social Policy Occasional Paper, No. 61). Paris: OECD.

Del Boca, D., Pasqua, S., & Pronzato, C. (2005). Employment and fertility in Italy, France and the UK. *Labour, 19*(4), 51–77.

Di Pino, A. (2004). On the economic estimation of the time devoted to household chores and childcare in Italy. *Genus, 60*(1), 139–160.

Folbre, N. Y., Finnoff, J., Fuligni, K., & Sidle, A. (2005). By what measure? Family time devoted to children in the United States. *Demography, 42*(2), 373–390.

Gauthier, A., Smeeding, T. M., & Furstenberg, F. (2004). Do we invest less time in children? Trends in parental time in selected industrialised countries since 1960s. *Population and Development Review, 30*(4), 647–671.

ISTAT. (2005). *L'uso del tempo, anni 2002–2003*. Rome: Istituto Nazionale di Statistica.

ISTAT. (2007). Essere madri in Italia. *Statistiche in breve, Famiglia e società*. Rome: National Istituto of Statistica.

ISTAT. (2011). *Rapporto annuale. La situazione del paese nel 2010*. Rome: Istituto Nazionale di Statistica.

Kohler, H. P., Billari, F., & Ortega, J. A. (2002). The emergence of lowest low fertility in Europe during the 1990s. *Population and Development Review, 28*(4), 641–680.

Livi Bacci, M. (2001). Too few children and too much family. *Daedalus, 130*(3), 139–156.

McDonald, P. (2000a). Gender equity in theories of fertility transition. *Population and Development Review, 26*(3), 427–439.

McDonald, P. (2000b). Gender equity, social institutions and the future of fertility. *Journal of Population Research, 17*(1), 1–16.

Mencarini, L., & Tanturri, M. L. (2004). Time use, family role-set and childbearing among Italian working women. *Genus, 60*(1), 111–137.

Mills, M., Mencarini, L., Tanturri, M. L., & Begall, K. (2008). Gender equity and fertility intentions in Italy and the Netherlands. *Demographic Research, 18*(1), 1–26.

OECD. (2001). *Doing better for families*. Paris: OECD.

Ogg, J., & Renaut, S. (2006). The support of parents in old age by those born during 1945–1954: A European perspective. *Aging and Society, 26*, 723–743.

Olah, L. (2011). Should governments in Europe be more aggressive in pushing for gender equality to raise fertility? The second YES. *Demographic research special collection, "Rostock debate on demographic change," 24*(9), 217–224.

Presser, H. (2003). *Working in a 24/7 economy: Challenges for American families*. New York: Russell Sage.

Reher, D. S. (1998). Family ties in Western Europe: Persistent contrasts. *Population and Development Review, 24*(2), 203–234.

Salvini, S. (2004). La bonaccia delle Antille. *Genus, 60*(1), 19–38.

Santini, A. (1995). *Continuità e discontinuità nel comportamento riproduttivo delle donne italiane del dopoguerra: Tendenze generali della fecondità delle coorti nelle ripartizioni tra il 1952 e 1991* (Working Paper No. 53). Florence: Department of Statistics "G. Parenti".

Sayer, L. C., Bianchi, S. M., & Robinson, J. P. (2004). Are parents investing less in children? Trends in mothers' and fathers' time with children. *The American Journal of Sociology, 110*(1), 1–43.

Tanturri, M. L., Paihlé, A., & Solaz, A. (2011, February 2–4). *Are children more costly in terms of time for the Italian parents than for the French ones?* Paper presented at Giornate di Studio della Popolazione, Ancona.

About the Authors

Valeria Bordone is a researcher at the Vienna University of Economics and Business (WU) – Research Institute Human Capital and Development, Wittgenstein Centre for Demography and Global Human Capital (IIASA, VID, WU).

Pier-André Bouchard-St-Amant is a Ph.D. student in economics from Queen's University and a collaborator to the Research Chair in Taxation and Public Finance (CFFP) of the Université de Sherbooke.

Patrick Charbonneau is an associate with the Department of Demography at the Université de Montréal and a Graduate Research Assistant.

Amélie Cossette is a Graduate Student at the Université de Montréal.

Gustavo De Santis is Professor of Demography at the Department of Statistics, University of Florence. He is President of the Scientific Council of the INED (Paris, France) and Chair of the IUSSP Scientific Panel on the Impacts of Population Ageing.

Yann Décarie is a Ph.D. student at the Institut National de la Recherche Scientifique (INRS) in Montreal, Quebec, and a Graduate Research Assistant.

Pierre Fortin is Professor Emeritus of Economics at the Université du Québec à Montreal (UQAM). He is a Fellow of the Royal Society of Canada, a member of the Board of Directors of the Canadian Institute for Advanced Research and Research Fellow of the CD Howe Institute.

Fernando Gil-Alonso is a Ramón y Cajal programme researcher, funded by the Spanish Ministry of Science and Innovation and the European Social Fund, and a member of the University of Barcelona's research group in Population, Territory and Citizenship (Grup de Recerca en Població, Territori i Ciutadania).

Luc Godbout is Professor at the Faculty of Business Administration from the Université de Sherbrooke, Senior Fellow in Public Finance at the Research Chair in Taxation and Public Finance (CFFP) and researcher at the Research Center on Aging.

G. De Santis (ed.), *The Family, the Market or the State?: Intergenerational Support Under Pressure in Ageing Societies*, International Studies in Population 10,
DOI 10.1007/978-94-007-4339-7, © Springer Science+Business Media Dordrecht. 2012

Janice A. Keefe is Professor of Family Studies and Gerontology at Mount Saint Vincent University, Canada. She holds a Canada Research Chair in Ageing and Caregiving Policy and is Director of the Nova Scotia Centre on Aging.

Jinkook Lee is Senior Economist at RAND Corporation and Professor at Pardee RAND Graduate School.

Jacques Légaré is Professor Emeritus of Demography at the Université de Montréal and Fellow of the Royal Society of Canada.

Taizo Motonishi is Professor of Economic Policy at the Faculty of Economics, Kansai University.

Drystan Phillips is research programmer at RAND Corporation.

Suzie St-Cerny is researcher at the Research Chair in Taxation and Public Finance (CFFP) of the Université de Sherbooke.

Maria Letizia Tanturri is Researcher in Demography at the University of Padova (Italy).

Index

G. De Santis (ed.), *The Family, the Market or the State?: Intergenerational Support Under Pressure in Ageing Societies*, International Studies in Population 10,
DOI 10.1007/978-94-007-4339-7,

MIX
Papier aus verantwortungsvollen Quellen
Paper from responsible sources
FSC® C105338

FSC
www.fsc.org

If you have any concerns about our products,
you can contact us on
ProductSafety@springernature.com

In case Publisher is established outside the EU,
the EU authorized representative is:
Springer Nature Customer Service Center GmbH
Europaplatz 3, 69115 Heidelberg, Germany

Printed by Libri Plureos GmbH
in Hamburg, Germany